Inclusive Instruction for Students with Emotional and Behavioral Disorders

Inclusive Instruction for Students with Emotional and Behavioral Disorders

Pulling Back the Curtain

John William McKenna Ph.D.
and
Reesha Adamson Ph.D.

LEXINGTON BOOKS
Lanham • Boulder • New York • London

Published by Lexington Books
An imprint of The Rowman & Littlefield Publishing Group, Inc.
4501 Forbes Boulevard, Suite 200, Lanham, Maryland 20706
www.rowman.com

6 Tinworth Street, London SE11 5AL, United Kingdom

British Library Cataloguing in Publication Information Available

Library of Congress Cataloging-in-Publication Data

Names: McKenna, John William, 1963- editor. | Adamson, Reesha Maylene, editor.
Title: Inclusive instruction and students with emotional and behavioral disorders : pulling back the curtain / edited by John William McKenna and Reesha Adamson.
Description: Lanham : Lexington Books, 2020. | Includes bibliographical references and index. | Summary: "This book is essential reading for stakeholders invested in inclusive instruction for students with emotional disturbance (ED). Research and policy-based recommendations are provided, as are resources for school-based practitioners and parents/guardians alike"—Provided by publisher.
Identifiers: LCCN 2020031585 (print) | LCCN 2020031586 (ebook) | ISBN 9781498596428 (Cloth : acid-free paper) | ISBN 9781498596435 (ePub)
Subjects: LCSH: Inclusive education. | Special education. | Mentally ill children—Education. | Mainstreaming in education.
Classification: LCC LC1200 .I5455 2020 (print) | LCC LC1200 (ebook) | DDC 371.9/046—dc23
LC record available at https://lccn.loc.gov/2020031585
LC ebook record available at https://lccn.loc.gov/2020031586

Contents

1 Introduction 1

2 Free Appropriate Public Education: The Foundation of Special Education 5

3 Practices for Improving Academic Achievement: Lessons Learned and Limitations of Intervention Research 17

4 Explicit Vocabulary Instruction in the Inclusive Classroom 31

5 Use of Graphic Organizers to Improve Academic Content Acquisition 41

6 Writing Strategies for Elementary Age Students with Emotional Disturbance, by Robai Werunga 49

7 Inclusive Mathematics Practices for Students with Emotional Disturbance, by Jessica Nelson 63

8 Differentiation of Instruction for Students with Emotional Disturbance 73

9 Using Technology to Support Inclusive Instruction 83

10 Daily Progress Reports and Behavioral Contracts to Support Inclusive Education 93

11 Function-Based Thinking to Support Inclusive Instruction 109

12 Trauma-Informed Support: Considerations for Students with Emotional Disturbance Who Have Experienced Trauma, by Felicity Post 117

13 False Promise of Learning Styles-Based Instruction, by John William McKenna, Reesha Adamson, and Eliza Bobek   131

14 Progress Monitoring in the Inclusive Classroom   139

15 Collaboration in Inclusive Instruction   151

16 Abandoning Readiness, by Maria Kolbe, Inclusion Facilitator 167

17 Closing Commentary   181

References   185

Index   205

About the Authors   213

About the Contributors   215

Chapter 1

Introduction

How public education can best serve students with disabilities has long had the attention of various stakeholders (see Fuchs and Fuchs, 1994; Kauffman, 1993). Concerns regarding the manner in which students with disabilities are served are warranted, as they are a protected class of student: federal policy mandates that students with disabilities receive a free appropriate public education (FAPE). Furthermore, students with disabilities are to be provided FAPE in the least restrictive environment (LRE). This means that these students are to be educated in the same educational settings (e.g., public general education classrooms) as their peers who do not have disabilities to the maximum extent that is appropriate. This need to achieve FAPE and LRE mandates represents a significant challenge for educators, as they must base student placement decisions on the services and supports that they require and the degree to which they benefit from them (McKenna and Brigham, 2019).

When serving students with disabilities, districts increasingly rely on placement in general education classrooms or inclusive instruction. Potential benefits of inclusive instruction include improved access to the general education curriculum, more frequent opportunities to socialize with their peers who do not have a disability, and improved access to models of prosocial behavior. Some research also suggests that students with disabilities who are educated in general education classrooms perform better in school and have more positive outcomes after leaving K-12 education. However, research has not established that placement in general education caused these improved outcomes, as it is possible that students who are educated in more specialized settings have different and more pervasive needs than those students who are educated in general education classrooms. Schools may also rely on inclusive instruction due to the quality of instruction and services in what are considered "segregated" educational settings and the outcomes that are associated with their use (see Bettini, Cumming, Merrill, Brunsting, and Liaupsin, 2017; Obiakor, Harris, Mutua, Rotatori, and Algozzine, 2012). However, concerns have also been expressed regarding the degree to which students with disabilities benefit from general education (see Fuchs, Fuchs, McMaster, and Lemons, 2018), as indicated by their continued underperformance in school and poor transition outcomes. Inclusive instruction involves meeting the needs of diverse student populations in a typical general education classroom, which may consist of students who have various levels of proficiency in the prerequisite skills and knowledge that is necessary to access instruction, and who may also require different types of instructional methods that must be implemented with sufficient quality and consistency to make progress in school (Kauffman and Badar, 2016).

Stakeholders have also expressed concerns regarding how schools operationalize inclusive instruction for students who receive special education services for emotional disturbance (ED; Brigham, Ahn, Stride, and McKenna, 2016). ED is,

> a condition exhibiting one or more of the following characteristics over a long period of time and to a marked degree that adversely affects a child's educational performance:
>
> A. An inability to learn that cannot be explained by intellectual, sensory, or health factors.
> B. An inability to build or maintain satisfactory interpersonal relationships with peers and teachers.
> C. Inappropriate types of behavior or feelings under normal circumstances.
> D. A general pervasive mood of unhappiness or depression.
> E. A tendency to develop physical symptoms or fears associated with personal or school problems.
>
> (ii) Emotional Disturbance includes schizophrenia. The term does not apply to children who are socially maladjusted, unless it is determined that they have an emotional disturbance under paragraph (c)(4)(i) of this section. (IDEIA, 2004; Section 300.8 Child with a disability)

Despite the unwavering efforts of school-based practitioners and their parents/guardians, students with ED continue to underperform in school, experience high rates of dropout and disciplinary exclusion, and be inadequately prepared to enter adult life after K-12 schooling (Brigham, McKenna, and Brigham, 2019; U.S. Department of Education, 2018). In fact, observation research has documented some of the challenges experienced by practitioners when attempting to provide inclusive instruction to this student population (McKenna, Adamson, and Solis, 2019). Challenges associated with inclusive instruction include, but are not limited to, a lack of knowledge and expertise to teach students with specialized needs, difficulties adapting instructional methods and materials, insufficient time for collaboration, and insufficient resources and supports to leverage during instruction (Fuchs et al., 2018; Kauffman and Badar, 2016; McKenna, Adamson, et al., 2019; Solis, Vaughn, Swanson, and McCulley, 2003). In fact, we think it is likely that the reader of this book is one of the many practitioners or parents/guardians who have a vested interest in ensuring that teachers have sufficient skills to educate students with specialized needs and that practitioners and students teach and learn in conditions that promote their success.

The purpose of this book is to (1) provide an overview of the legal mandates associated with inclusive instruction for students with ED, (2) discuss common challenges and potential roadblocks to inclusive instruction and effective collaboration, (3) and make recommendations for instructional practice, behavioral support, and monitoring of student response to inclusive instruction. We support our contentions with research evidence, our experiences as teacher educators and professional development providers, and our previous experiences as school-based practitioners serving students with ED. In an effort to provide a comprehensive discussion of inclusive instruction for students with ED, we supplement our perspectives with additional chapters written by other professionals with substantial expertise in serving this student population in general education settings.

Throughout this book, we emphasize the need for schools to employ research-based practices to improve student outcomes, the need to engage in collaboration and discussion to continually refine and evaluate school practice, and the legal mandate to consider the full continuum of placement options when serving students with disabilities. Inclusion is not, and cannot be, a one-size-fits-all approach (Brigham et al., 2016; Kauffman and Badar, 2016). Educational placement, by law, is decided on a student-by-student basis. However, every minute that a student with a disability is educated outside of a general education classroom must be justified (e.g., it has to serve an important purpose and benefit students). Schools will only realize the potential effectiveness of inclusive instruction through ongoing collaboration and carefully matching student strengths and areas of need with practitioner use of instructional and behavioral supports that results in objective data demonstrating student progress toward meaningful academic, behavioral, and social goals. With this in mind, some students with ED are best served in a "dedicated" classroom or school setting. By dedicated, we mean a classroom or school setting that is staffed with professionals with highly specialized skill set, who employ specialized curriculums and interventions that are based on research. There is substantial research on effective academic and behavioral interventions for students with ED who are educated in dedicated educational settings (see Gage, Lewis, and Stichter, 2012; Garwood, 2018; Hodge, Riccomini, Buford, and Herbst, 2006; Losinski, Cuenca-Carlino, Zablocki, and Teagarden, 2014). In regards to inclusive instruction, practitioners must supplement the research that is available with their professional judgment, the values and goals of the Individualized Education Program (IEP) team, and progress-monitoring data to make informed decisions about how to serve them (McKenna, Garwood, and Parenti, in press). Due to the absence of a substantial body of intervention research, IEP teams must also use professional recommendations to inform how they operationalize inclusive instruction for students with ED (McKenna, Newton, and Bergman, 2019).

We welcome feedback from our readers. Please do not hesitate to e-mail us your comments, questions, and suggestions for future revisions and extensions. We look forward to hearing about your successes as well as the challenges you experience. We look forward to hearing from policymakers, school-based practitioners, parents/guardians, and of course, those who are most important: the students.

Chapter 2

Free Appropriate Public Education
The Foundation of Special Education

The Individuals with Disabilities Education Improvement Act (IDEIA, 2004) mandates that districts provide students with disabilities a free appropriate public education (FAPE). However, there has been substantial debate regarding how FAPE has been operationalized and the degree of benefit that should be conferred to students with disabilities. The characteristics of an "appropriate" education have been central to this debate, with the amount or degree of educational benefit that is consistent with an appropriate education, a point of contention and disagreement. This debate has since been considered by the Supreme Court of the United States (SCOTUS), which provided some clarification and confirmed important rights and responsibilities associated with special education services. In this chapter, we report on recent developments regarding the provision of FAPE for students with disabilities. We then discuss the primary role of specialized services and supports and selection of the least restrictive environment (LRE) as a secondary consideration in the pursuit of FAPE. We believe this discussion is essential due to the tendency (1) to educate students with disabilities in general education classrooms to the maximum extent "possible" rather than the maximum extent that is "appropriate," (2) to incorrectly assume that the needs of all students with disabilities can be met or are best met in general education settings, or (3) to view placement in general education as an intended outcome of special education rather than actual progress in academic, social, and behavioral skills (see Anastasiou and Kauffman, 2012; Brigham, Ahn, Stride, and McKenna, 2016; Kauffman, Landrum, Mock, Sayeski, and Sayeski, 2005).

ᵥ F. V. DOUGLAS COUNTY SCHOOL DISTRICT

ᵣew *F. v. Douglas County School District*, a child diagnosed with ᴊism and attention deficit hyperactivity disorder (ADHD) made minimal academic and behavioral progress in response to the Individualized Education Program (IEP) provided by the district. The child's parents rejected the IEP that was proposed for the following year (e.g., fifth grade), believing that it did not account for their child's regressive behavior and more pervasive educational and behavioral needs, as indicated by his poor and declining performance in fourth grade. In fact, supports proposed in the IEP for fifth grade were similar to those in the IEP for fourth grade. The parents believed that their child's behavior adversely affected his ability to access the general education curriculum and that their child needed different services. Pointing to the inadequacies of the proposed IEP, the parents contended that the district did not complete a behavioral assessment and then use this information to create a behavioral intervention plan (BIP) that addressed their child's behavioral needs. The parents also contended that the district provided progress reports that were inappropriate because they contained summary statements of their child's performance and statements regarding whether or not their child was on target to achieve his IEP goals. According to the parents' perspective, the absence of appropriate progress reports adversely affected their ability to fully participate as IEP team members. In response to their concerns, the parents placed their child in a private school for students with autism, where their child's regressive behavior not only subsided but effective academic and behavioral progress was made. The parents then attempted to obtain reimbursement for the private school tuition, based on their belief that the district did not provide their son FAPE. In turn, the district believed they had complied with federal special education mandates and so were not responsible for providing compensation.

IMPLICATIONS OF THE SUPREME COURT'S DECISION

In a unanimous decision, the Supreme Court ruled that "some benefit" cannot be defined as some amount of benefit greater than none. Previously, this level of benefit was referred to as "merely more than de minimis." This standard for FAPE was previously upheld by the Tenth Circuit Court and was the standard that the public school district argued they were required to meet. Prior to the Supreme Court's ruling, IEPs only needed to provide minimal or a trivial amount of educational benefit (Yell and Bateman, 2017). However, although the Supreme Court struck down the notion that an IEP only needed to provide "merely more than de minimis" benefit, the Court did not specify an amount that special education services should provide.

At this time, there is no single operational definition for an appropriate education (Prince, Yell, and Katsiyannis, 2018; Yell and Bateman, 2017). This is because the provision of FAPE must be considered on a case-by-case basis. IEPs do not need to provide services that are considered ideal but must be based on services and supports that provide opportunities for "academic and functional advancement" (U.S. Department of Education, 2017; p. 6). As stated by Prince and colleagues (2018), "The purpose of an IEP is to set a plan for advancement in a student's academic and functional abilities" (p. 323).

A key consideration when planning IEPs is that they should be "reasonably calculated to enable a child to make progress in light of the child's circumstances" (U.S. Department of Education, 2017; p. 1). When operationalizing this mandate, IEP teams must consider the following information: parent/ guardian perspectives, professional expertise and judgment, previous student progress in areas that are adversely affected by their disability, the student's potential for development, previous supports and instruction and student response to this programming, student performance in relation to grade-level expectations, and the impact of student behavior on school outcomes (U.S. Department of Education, 2017). Again, this is an individualized decision that is discussed and determined during the IEP meeting, a process in which parent/guardian involvement is mandated. Considering regulations related to transition planning and transition services, the perspectives, interests, and preferences of students with disabilities should also be included in these discussions no later than fourteen years of age. However, it is recommended that students with disabilities are included much earlier (Brigham, McKenna, and Brigham, 2019).

The Supreme Court also mandated that a student's IEP must be "appropriately ambitious" (U.S. Department of Education, 2017; p. 5). Again, what is considered "appropriately ambitious" for a given student is an individualized decision made by the IEP team, which would include parents/guardians, school-based professionals, and students with disabilities who are of age. However, the Supreme Court did state "advancement from grade to grade is appropriately ambitious for most children in the regular classroom" (e.g., students educated in general education settings; U.S. Department of Education, 2017; p. 7). When developing the IEP, the general education curriculum and state standards serve as a guide for decision-making, with the selected specialized services and supports and instruction providing access and opportunities to achieve appropriately ambitious goals. Furthermore, the Supreme Court stated that the IEP must include behavioral goals, objectives, and services when challenging behavior adversely affects the student's learning or the learning of other students (U.S. Department of Education, 2017). Behavioral supports, when necessary, should be based on positive behavior strategies and interventions, which have a substantial research base supporting their effectiveness (Flannery, Fenning, Kato, and McIntosh, 2014; Gage, Lewis, and Stichter, 2012; McKenna, Flower, and Adamson, 2016). However, the Supreme Court did not mandate the use of research-based practices (Prince et al., 2018), but use of research-based practices is consistent with federal general education and special education policy (see McKenna, Solis, Brigham, and Adamson, 2018). School teams are also more likely to meet requirements related to FAPE when the IEP is based on such practices (Prince et al., 2018). Furthermore, schools are only mandated to "consider" the use of positive behavior supports when challenging behavior affects teaching and learning, which is a somewhat nebulous if not lower standard than if schools were required to provide function-based interventions in these instances to promote the achievement of FAPE mandates (see Yell, 2019).

IEP teams must also determine the manner in which student progress will be assessed (Prince et al., 2018). This includes a consideration of what skills and competencies to assess, the person or persons responsible for conducting the assessment, and how often performance is assessed. When a student is not making expected progress, the IEP team must consider the degree to which the IEP is appropriate for the student, in consideration of this insufficient progress (U.S. Department of Education, 2017). In regards to discussions regarding the adequacy of the IEP, the IEP team may meet at any time during the school year, such as prior to mandated annual reviews. Although school districts are responsible for determining when these meetings should occur, parents and guardians are well within their rights to request them as they believe necessary (U.S. Department of Education, 2017). This right to request a team meeting highlights the necessity of keeping parents/guardians informed regarding their child's response to IEP services and the degree to which the student is on target for achieving their annual goals. The expectations regarding progress monitoring and sharing this data with parents/guardians are central to their active and ongoing involvement in the IEP process and FAPE mandates.

DETERMINING LRE

Selecting a student's LRE or educational placement is secondary to decisions regarding "what" (e.g., services) to provide a student and "why" (e.g., how the disability adversely affects performance, use of research-based practices to improve performance; see Cook, Landrum, Tankersley, and Kauffman, 2003;

Kauffman and Bader, 2016). However, in school practice, conversations regarding "where" to provide services can take precedence when developing a student's IEP (see Brigham et al., 2016; Brigham, McKenna, Lavin, Brigham, and Zurawski, 2018; Kauffman and Bader, 2016). Discussions regarding student placement must occur after discussions related to parent/ guardian and student vision, parent/guardian and student concerns, current levels of performance, the manner in which a student's disability adversely affects school performance, specialized services, supports, and instruction a student requires, and contingencies for assessing student response to the IEP. Much like the other aspects of an IEP, student placement is an individualized decision (U.S. Department of Education, 2017). Take, for example, the IEP template used by schools in Massachusetts. This template provides not only a structure for the actual written IEP but the conversations that should occur when developing this document during the IEP meeting. If you look at this template, you will see how the section in the document related to student placement appears toward the end of the template and appears after these previously mentioned and essential aspects of the IEP (e.g., current levels of performance, goals and objectives, specialized services and supports). With this in mind, placement in general education classrooms is not an appropriate LRE for all students with disabilities due to the size of the gap between the academic, social, and behavioral demands encountered in this setting and a student's current level of performance, the manner in which a disability adversely affects school progress, and the level of specialization and expertise some students require to profit from school (see Fuchs, Fuchs, McMaster, and Lemons, 2018; Kauffman and Hallahan, 1996; Lemons, Vaughn, Wexler, Kearns, and Sinclair, 2018; McKenna et al., 2018).

In its guidance document on the *Endrew F.* Supreme Court decision, the U.S. Department of Education (2017) noted that general education might not be the LRE for every student who receives special education services. This acknowledgment that general education may not be an appropriate LRE for all students with disabilities is also supported by the final decision in the *Endrew F.* case: Upon receiving guidance from the Supreme Court, the lower court adjusted their previous ruling and awarded the parents tuition reimbursement. In this case, the parents believed that the school district was unable to meet the specialized needs of their child and elected to enroll him in a substantially separate school, based on the belief that this substantially separate school would be able to deliver the necessary specialized supports their child required to obtain FAPE. In fact, IDEA Part B regulations mandate that all districts must ensure that the full continuum of alternative placement options is available to students with disabilities. Considering the Supreme Court's guidance and the subsequent reconsideration of the case by the lower court, the *Endrew F.* case is confirmation of the necessity to consider the full continuum of placement options, based on the assumption that alternative placements can provide a higher degree of specialization to students who require more intensive supports and a greater degree of curricular and instructional modifications. Considering the continued poor school performance of students with disabilities (see Fuchs et al., 2018), there are likely many students with disabilities in our country who do not have their needs met by general education instruction, regardless of whether or not this instruction is appropriately differentiated, explicit and systematic, and supported by tiered systems of academic and behavioral support.

IMPLICATIONS FOR STUDENTS WITH EMOTIONAL DISTURBANCE

During the 2014 to 2015 school year, 5.7 percent of students receiving special education services did so under the Emotional Disturbance (ED) disability category (U.S. Department of Education, 2017). Of these students receiving special education services for ED, 47.1 percent spent 80 percent or more of the school day in general education classrooms. Another 17.4 percent of these students spent between 40 percent and 79 percent of the school day in these settings. This means that a substantial number of students with ED nationally receive a significant amount of instruction in general education classrooms (and perhaps this is the reason why you are continuing to read our little book!). This tendency to determine the general education classroom as a student's LRE may in part be due to concerns regarding the effectiveness and appropriateness of more restrictive or substantially separate educational settings (see Obiakor, Harris, Mutua, Rotatori, and Algozzine, 2012). However, terms such as "restrictive" and "substantially separate" are poor if not inappropriate descriptors for classrooms, programs, and schools that provide highly specialized instruction and supports to students that require them. A more accurate name for these types of settings is "dedicated settings": the professionals employed in these settings are dedicated to meeting the highly specialized needs of their students. Furthermore, research suggests that inclusive instruction is incredibly complex and requires substantial resources and professional expertise (Shin, Lee, and McKenna, 2016; Solis, Vaughn, Swanson, and McCulley, 2012). Outcome data also suggests that many students with disabilities are likely underserved in general education classrooms (e.g., see data for students with disabilities from the National Assessment of Educational Progress, our "Nation's Report Card"). Furthermore, there is limited academic intervention research to inform school practice (see McKenna et al., 2018; chapter 3 provides a more in-depth discussion of this issue). These findings and data highlight the need for IEP teams to engage in informed discussions that are based on the student's individualized pattern of strengths and areas of need.

Placement in general education does not ensure that students with ED will receive the specialized services and supports and access to the general education curriculum that is necessary for success in this setting (Kauffman and Bader, 2016; Solis et al., 2012). The gap between the academic performance of general education peers and students with ED grows over time (Gage et al., 2017), which may cause students with ED to experience high levels of stress in general education classrooms. As a result, IEP teams must make certain that school-based practitioners have the necessary resources, supports, and expertise to maximize the potential effectiveness of inclusive instruction. The effectiveness of inclusive instruction must be based on the degree to which students make academic, social, and behavioral progress rather than the percentage of time a student is educated in a general education classroom. The adequacy of an IEP is determined by the degree that the student benefits from it, and not the settings in which they are educated or the amount of time they spend in them. Tangible outcomes that promote current and future success in school, community, work, and interpersonal relationships are the primary goal.

GUIDING QUESTIONS TO INFORM
DECISION-MAKING

Before moving on to the next chapter, we offer IEP teams the following guiding questions to facilitate targeted discussions on the operationalization and the relative effectiveness of inclusive instruction for students with ED. We do not profess this list to be all-"inclusive" or all-encompassing. In fact, we believe that these types of discussions are best informed by the questions generated by those who actively participate in a student's IEP meeting and that these discussions are to be framed by a parent/guardian's vision statement and the student's interests, hopes, and dreams. We offer the following questions with supporting rationales as a broad set of considerations framed by the rights and responsibilities associated with federal special education law as well as practical and ethical considerations:

1. What do the parent/guardian and student hope to achieve over the course of the school year? What prerequisite skills and competencies need to be developed to achieve these goals? What specialized services, supports, and instruction are necessary to achieve these goals?
   Rationale: IEPs are framed by the vision statement. Skills and competencies require proficiency in specific prerequisite skills. It is important

to identify these prerequisite skills and consider how the IEP will provide the student opportunities to develop them. This may require instruction that targets knowledge and skills in standards from previous grades.

2. What student strengths can be leveraged to promote student access to general education instruction? What student strengths can be leveraged to promote access to the peer relationships and social activities that occur in the general education classroom? How can we leverage them?

   Rationale: All students have strengths, although in at least some instances it may difficult to identify them, particularly when the student is experiencing academic, social, and/or behavioral difficulties in school. In these instances, conversations regarding student deficits or "problems" may dominate IEP-related discussions. Strength-based approaches can be used to improve areas in need of development as well as to improve student engagement and motivation.

3. What skills are necessary for the student to access the academic and social activities in general education? Is the student's current level of performance in these necessary skills sufficiently proficient and consistent for the student to benefit from placement in general education? What skills need to be taught for the student to profit from inclusive instruction? What are the most effective methods for teaching these skills?

   Rationale: It is important to consider a student's current level of performance within the context of the expectations/demands (e.g., academic, behavioral, social) placed upon them in general education settings. The gap between student's current level of performance and class demands may be too great for the student, based on the degree of specialization, modifications, and supports that the student requires.

4. When present in a general education classroom, what percentage of instructional time is the student engaged in class activities? What percentage of time is the student off task during general education instruction?

   Rationale: Students must be on task/engaged in positive behavior to benefit from inclusive instruction. Physical placement in a classroom does not confer benefit.

5. In a typical school day, what percentage of general education instruction does the student miss due to challenging/off-task behavior? What percentage of general education instruction does the student miss due to time spent outside of the classroom for things such as planned breaks, earned free time or activities, and other forms of positive reinforcement?

   Rationale: Similar to above. Also, school teams must strategically consider what students are missing when they are outside of the general education classroom. For example, students with ED benefit from instruction that is explicit such as modeling and clear explanations (McKenna, Adamson, and Solis, 2019). Is the student missing this type of instruction when outside of the classroom? If so, then the student is less likely to achieve success in the general education classroom.

6. Do general education teachers have sufficient expertise and experience working with students with ED? What supports do general education teachers need to meet a student's individual academic and behavioral needs? What contingencies are available to provide teachers relevant professional development and coaching with performance feedback?

   Rationale: Teachers have areas in need for development, just like students. Inclusive instruction requires a "village" to work best. Professionals with expertise in inclusive instruction and research-based instructional methods are part of this village. Investing in teacher success promotes student success.

8. What sources of supplementary intervention and support (e.g., tiered systems of academic and/or behavioral support) are available that can address areas of student need or student skill deficits?

   Rationale: General education instruction on its own cannot meet the needs of all students. Tiered systems of academic and behavioral support are necessary for students who require more intensive instruction or opportunities to develop different types of skills or prerequisite skills. Students with ED often require and benefit intensive academic and behavioral intervention (Maggin, Wehby, Farmer, and Brooks, 2016).

9. What contingencies are in place so that teachers and related service providers have ongoing conversations regarding student performance, student needs, and effective support methods? What contingencies are in place so that parents/guardians and the student can participate in these conversations?

   Rationale: Inclusive instruction takes a "village." If professionals are not talking together, then they are not working together. Ongoing discussion and collaboration is essential to student success, particularly for students with ED because they tend to be "moving targets" (e.g., they have changing needs, episodic behavior, and difficulties adapting to the school environment).

10. Do teachers that provide co-taught instruction have frequent and consistent opportunities to co-plan instruction and to debrief instruction?

    Rationale: Similar to above. Co-teaching is incredibly complicated. Teachers who teach with one another need consistent time to plan and debrief instruction to maximize the potential effectiveness of co-taught instruction. Co-teachers need time to discuss challenges and develop methods for addressing them as well as to acknowledge (if not celebrate) their successes.

11. What contingencies are in place to assess student behavioral and academic progress? Is assessment based on measures that are valid and reliable?

    Rationale: Progress-monitoring data is necessary to determine the degree to which students are making progress in response to the instruction and services that are provided. Assessments should be technically adequate so that classroom decisions are based on accurate and relevant data.

12. Is assessment occurring frequently enough to inform discussions regarding student's current levels of performance, rate of progress, and educational programming? Is this data used to inform collaborative discussions and school decision-making? How is this data used to inform collaborative discussions and school decision-making? Is this data shared and discussed with parents/guardians?

    Rationale: Similar to above. It is not the data schools collect. It is the conversations that schools/IEP teams have about the data and the decisions they make based on data.

13. Are there additional areas of student performance that are not covered by current assessment practices? How can this information be used to inform decision-making? How can this information be collected so that it can inform decision-making?

    Rationale: Student needs (and strengths) change over time. It is important for assessment practices to align with changes in student performance and changes in student needs.

14. What contingencies are in place so that student difficulties or challenges become an opportunity for student growth? What contingencies are in place so that student difficulties or challenges become an opportunity for teacher professional development and growth?

    Rationale: Challenges and struggles are an opportunity for learning and growth, for both school-based professionals and students. Student difficulties signal student needs as well as teacher needs.

15. Are all aspects of the IEP being implemented as conceived and intended? If not, what supports and changes are necessary to make certain that all aspects are implemented as conceived and intended?

    Rationale: A disconnect between services and supports as written in the IEP and how (and what) they are actually delivered is possible. Just because something is written into an IEP does not mean that the student receives it or that the support is implemented with sufficient frequency, consistency, and quality. It is important to emphasize and assess fidelity of implementation, as insufficient progress can be due to a student needing different services or due to poor implementation of services that are appropriate (see McKenna and Parenti, 2017).

16. Does the IEP as currently conceived appropriately address current student needs and future goals? What amendments are necessary so the IEP accounts for current student needs and future goals?

Rationale: Student needs (and strengths) change over time. IEPs and the services within them need to align with current student needs so that they may benefit from school. IEP teams may need to confer prior to the next annual review to make informed adjustments that target changing needs and strengths.

Chapter 3

Practices for Improving Academic Achievement

Lessons Learned and Limitations of Intervention Research

Instruction in general education classrooms emphasizes academic content and skills due to a reliance on curriculums based on college and career readiness standards (Ciullo, Ortiz, Al Otaiba, and Lane, 2016). This focus on academics represents a significant challenge for students receiving special education services for Emotional Disturbance (ED) who are educated in inclusive classrooms. For example, students with ED may display a range of problem behaviors that adversely affect academic achievement (Kauffman and Landrum, 2017). In response to this challenge, school teams may emphasize interventions and supports that address problem behaviors, making academic performance and remediating these types of deficits less of a priority (Nelson, Benner, and Boharty, 2014). Compounding this issue, teachers may have difficulty adapting instruction effectively (Kauffman, 2015; Neisyn, 2009), employ strategies that result in students receiving less instruction overall (Brigham, Ahn, Stride, and McKenna, 2016; McKenna, Adamson, and Solis, 2019), or have difficulty implementing practices with sufficient quality due to competing demands on their time and expertise (McKenna, Flower, Falcomata, and Adamson, 2017). However, schools are responsible for providing all students ample opportunities to profit from school.

Schools must provide instruction, services, and supports designed to meet both the behavioral and academic needs of students receiving special education services for ED (Brigham, McKenna, Lavin, Brigham, and Zurawski, 2018; Gage, Adamson, MacSuga-Gage, and Lewis, 2017). This holds true for those students with ED who are educated in inclusive educational settings (Brigham et al., 2016), particularly when one considers the recent Supreme Court decision in the *Endrew F. v. Douglas County School District* case. According to the Supreme Court, students with disabilities must be provided an Individualized Education Program (IEP) that is designed to confer meaningful benefit, based on the student's individual situation (Yell and Bateman, 2017). Prior to this ruling, districts could potentially be held to the "de minimis" standard for a free appropriate public education (FAPE), depending on the geographic location of the district (e.g., the interpretation of FAPE varied from state to state). In its ruling, the Supreme Court struck down this lower standard of what constitutes FAPE, stating this was inconsistent with the intentions of federal special education law. In regards to students with disabilities who are educated in general education classrooms, it is now possible to interpret FAPE in the following manner: IEP services should confer sufficient benefit for students to pass classes that are based on grade-level content (Yell and Bateman, 2017). This increased expectation for FAPE represents a significant challenge for school districts, who may have previously focused their efforts on limiting problem behaviors rather than developing behavioral, social, and academic skills in concert (see Brigham et al., 2016). When providing opportunities for skill development, it is necessary to use methods with empirical evidence of effectiveness.

Federal legislation mandates use of research-based practices for instructional situations in which they exist (see Every Student Succeeds Act [ESSA], 2015; Individuals with Disabilities Education Improvement Act [IDEIA], 2004). Research-based practices are those with empirical research that demonstrate their effectiveness (Cook, Cook, and Collins, 2016). Evidence-based practice (EBP), a commonly used concept in education that is related to research-based practice, refers to practices that have been validated as effective according to a specific set of research standards or quality indicators. In an essence, an EBP is a research-based practice that met a specific set of criteria for being deemed an EBP, with this criterion typically based on an accumulation of studies using rigorous research designs (e.g., permitting some degree of causal inference between the use of a practice or intervention and changes in student performance). Research-based and EBPs are very different from "best practices," which tend to be practices that lack an empirical basis and are based on a personal professional recommendation.

In addition to specific practices, EBP may also refer to a decision-making framework or process: school-based practitioners (e.g., teachers, instructional coaches, social workers, school psychologists, administrators) consider research evidence in concert with their values, expertise, knowledge of their students, and student goals to make informed instructional decisions (Cook et al., 2016). This notion of EBP as a framework coupled with the increased expectation for FAPE has implications for inclusive instruction for students with ED: Practitioners must consider the available research on practices for improving academic achievement in concert with their values, professional expertise, and the vision and goals stated in the IEP to meet these increased expectations for FAPE. Decision-making regarding inclusive instruction cannot be driven by values, professional judgment, and goals alone.

SYSTEMATIC REVIEWS

Systematic literature reviews are commonly performed to identify EBPs and areas for future research that are necessary to inform school practice (see Epstein, Atkins, Cullinan, Kutash, and Weaver, 2008; Flower, McKenna, and Upreti, 2016). Literature reviews may identify a pool of research studies in a specific area and then evaluate this body of research according to an established set of research quality indicators, which tend to be created by expert research panels (e.g., What Works Clearinghouse Procedures Manual 4.0, U.S. Department of Education, 2017; Council for Exceptional Children: Standards for Evidence-Based Practice in Special Education, 2014). Upon completion of this process, researchers make recommendations for school practice based on those studies with sufficient rigor (e.g., studies that permit some degree of causal inference between the use of a practice and changes in student performance). By drawing conclusions from only well-designed studies, researchers seek to ensure the accuracy and trustworthiness of their recommendations for school practice. One such effort to identify effective practices by applying quality indicators to a pool of studies is salient to inclusive instruction of students with ED.

McKenna, Solis, Brigham, and Adamson (2019) reviewed intervention studies focusing on the academic achievement of students with ED who were taught in general education classrooms. The researchers completed a synthesis of published syntheses (e.g., a review of systematic reviews) to identify intervention studies in which at least one student with ED was provided an instructional practice or intervention in a general education classroom and had their academic performance assessed. Each identified intervention study was evaluated according to the What Works Clearinghouse Standards (WWC; U.S. Department of Education, 2017), a set of research quality indicators that are commonly used in special education. Although this set of quality indicators is quite rigorous (e.g., thought to have a challenging criterion for EBPs), it is commonly used by the federal government when awarding grant money in education and special education. Examples of federal competitions that award points based on the degree to which proposals meet WWC standard for research evidence include the Promise Neighborhoods grant competition and the Full Service Community Schools grant program. Thus, this systematic review of academic-focused intervention studies is an excellent source of information on the lessons learned and limitations of intervention research, which practitioners should consider along with their professional expertise, values, and IEP goals and vision statements when determining how best to operationalize inclusive instruction for students with ED.

In this chapter, we provide an overview of the intervention studies identified and analyzed in this systematic review. We then report major findings from this synthesis of syntheses. Next, we provide a summary of each intervention study. Lastly, we make recommendations for planning inclusive instruction for students with ED, in consideration of study findings, limitations, and related research.

SYNTHESIS OF SYNTHESES

A synthesis of syntheses was performed to identify intervention studies in which at least one student receiving special education services for ED or its equivalent (e.g., clinical diagnosis consistent with ED) was taught in a general education classroom and had their academic performance assessed. First, a multistep search was performed to identify systematic reviews focusing on the academic performance of students with ED that were published between the years 2004 and 2017. 2004 was used as the search start date because the least restrictive environment (LRE) requirement for students with disabilities was reauthorized at this time. This search identified seventeen systematic reviews. Intervention studies included in the seventeen reviews were then analyzed to identify those studies that met selection criteria. Upon completion of this process, a total of eight intervention studies were identified, with the majority of studies included in the reviews representing tier 2 or tier 3 interventions or interventions conducted in dedicated school settings (e.g., self-contained classrooms, resource room, specialized schools, etc.).

CORPUS OF STUDIES

Six intervention studies were conducted with students in the secondary grades (Bell et al., 1990; Maheady et al., 1987; Maheady et al., 1988; Mastropieri et al., 1998; Mastropieri et al., 2006; Prater et al., 1992) and two with students in the elementary grades (Rafferty, 2012; Wehby et al., 2005). Of the eight intervention studies, only four disaggregated outcomes for students with ED (Bell, Young, Blair, and Nelson, 1990; Prater, Hogan, and Miller, 1992; Rafferty, 2012; Wehby et al., 2005). Meaning, four studies reported data on the specific outcomes of students with ED. The remaining four studies reported academic outcomes for students in aggregate, which prevents researchers and practitioners from drawing conclusions regarding the degree to which interventions were effective at improving the academic performance of students with ED. In these studies, we know how well students did on average or collectively, but we do not know the degree to which students with ED benefited (or not). Of the four studies that reported specific outcomes for students with ED, none employed a research design that met WWC design standards with or without reservations. According to research quality indicator coding, each study was rated as not meeting standards. As a result, causal inferences cannot be made by these studies regarding the use of interventions and changes in student academic performance. In sum, findings from the synthesis of syntheses suggest that few studies overall have investigated the effects of interventions on the academic performance of students with ED who are educated in general education classrooms. Findings from this pool of studies must also be viewed with caution due to a tendency to not report outcomes specifically for students with ED and a reliance on research designs that lack sufficient rigor (e.g., designs that do not meet WWC standards; designs that do not permit causal inferences). Table 3.1 provides descriptive information for each intervention study. In the following section, we provide a summary of each intervention study that met selection criteria for the synthesis of syntheses.

SUMMARY OF INTERVENTION STUDIES

Bell et al. (1990) investigated the effects of classwide peer tutoring on the academic performance of six fifteen-year-old students with emotional disturbance (ED) educated in two general education history classes. Five of the students with ED received instruction in a district program for students with ED, and one student with ED received instruction in a resource room setting. In addition to the six students with ED, one student with a learning disability (LD) and fifty-two general education students participated in this study. A classroom teacher provided the peer tutoring intervention with a paraprofessional or another teacher, both of whom were assigned to the school's program for students with ED. Initially, students were assigned to one of two teams, with the teacher using previous social studies test scores to balance each team in regards to academic performance. Student partners were then created within each team by pairing high-performing students with low-performing students. During the intervention session, students first read a chapter and then completed study sheets in groups and individually. Classwide peer tutoring sessions then occurred before and after teacher lecture. During peer tutoring sessions, students served both as a tutor and a tutee for equal amounts of time (e.g., ten minutes in each role). Each pair of students were given a set of fact flash cards that was based on information from

Table 3.1 Studies Investigating Effects of Interventions on Academic Achievement

Authors	Participants	Intervention	Duration	Results	Social Validity
Bell, Young, Blair, and Nelson (1990)	6 BD 5 M and 1 F Mean age 15.16 years	Classwide peer tutoring Pairings set each week based on test performance from previous week Each student served as tutor and tutee for 10 minutes Points awarded for following procedures and correct answers on tests	3 20-minute tutoring sessions per week 4 to 6 weeks	Students with BD improved test scores by 1 to 3 grades	Perceived effective by students Students would continue to participate in peer tutoring Students desired use in other subject areas
Maheady, Sacca, and Harper (1987)	28 LD or BD 9th and 10th grade	Classwide student tutoring teams Teachers given fewer students and special education consultation prior to intervention Students assigned to groups of 3 to 5 Students awarded points for correct responses and following procedures	2 30-minute tutoring sessions per week 6 to 7 weeks	Improved mathematics performance	Students had positive perceptions of tutoring General education teachers expressed difficulty selecting content and skills for worksheets and quizzes Preparation was time-consuming
Maheady, Sacca, and Harper (1988)	14 LD or BD 7 M and 7 F Mean age 16.6 years All 10th grade	Classwide peer tutoring Teachers given fewer students and special education consultation prior to intervention	2 30-minute sessions per week 3 3 20 minute sessions per week for 2 weeks 12 to 16 weeks	Improved weekly test scores Decrease in # of students failing tests Students with disabilities made greater gains	Teachers had positive perceptions of peer tutoring and student outcomes
Mastropieri et al. (1998)	1 ED M 4th grade	Inquiry-based/activity-based instruction Accommodations Materials were considered "optimal" for accommodating students Student with ED was paired with one student when other students worked in small groups	3 days per week 7 weeks in duration	Students with disabilities in intervention condition made greater academic gains than nondisabled students in comparison condition	Students in intervention condition had more positive perceptions of science More students in intervention condition reported science as their favorite class

Study	Participants	Intervention	Frequency/Duration	Results	Perceptions
Mastropieri et al. (2006)	7 EBD 8th grade	Inquiry-based instruction, differentiated instruction, and peer tutoring 3 levels of materials were developed to support differentiation Students with EBD worked on lowest-level materials first Activities could be completed multiple times to promote student learning Students worked in groups of 2 or 3	Daily 12 weeks in duration	Intervention students made greater test gains Intervention students had better high stakes test scores	Student perceptions varied Students had more positive perceptions of game-based activities Teachers perceived materials helpful Teachers perceived materials beneficial for students with disabilities Teachers expressed difficulties providing intervention due to pressures to prepare students for high stakes tests
Prater, Hogan, and Miller (1992)	1 BD 14 years old 9th grade	Self-monitoring	Initially self-monitoring for 30-minute intervals for 4 days in resource room Duration varied by class setting	Improved performance on mathematics tests and on-task behavior	Teachers had positive perceptions of the intervention
Rafferty (2012)	4 ED 2 M and 2 F Mean age 7.8 years 2nd grade	*Time Warp Plus* and self-monitoring School-wide positive behavior supports	7 or 11 sessions over 3 weeks	Improved reading fluency Improved on-task behavior during small and whole group reading instruction	On-task behavior approached that of peers
Wehby, Lane, and Falk (2005)	1 ED; M; 5.96 years old; K	Scott Foresman Reading program and PATR	Foresman: 75 minutes 4 days per week PATR: 20 minutes 3 to 4 times per week for 9 weeks	Improved reading performance	Teachers believed intervention was effective and would recommend it to other teachers Did not perceive intervention as effective on problem behavior

Note. BD = behavior disorder, M = male, F = female, LD = learning disability, ED = emotional disturbance, PATR = Phonological Awareness Training for Reading, EBD = emotional and behavioral disorders; **K = Kindergarten**.

a class study sheet. Tutors would state a fact and then ask a question that was designed to prompt tutee recall of the fact. Tutors gave behavior specific praise to tutees for correct responses. For incorrect responses, tutors restated the fact and then restated the question. According to the researchers, the peer tutoring intervention was effective at improving the test performance of students with ED. However, this study employed a single case design that did not meet WWC standards, preventing causal inferences to be made between the use of peer tutoring and changes in academic performance.

Maheady et al. (1987) investigated the effects of classwide student tutoring teams on the mathematics performance of twenty-eight students with LD or ED in grades nine and ten. Sixty-three general education students also participated in this study. As part of typical school practice, teachers were assigned smaller classes and provided special education consultation services to better support students with disabilities in general education classrooms. Students with disabilities also received daily resource room support for two class periods. For ninth graders, mathematics content was based on a textbook called *General Math* (Shaw, Wheatley, Kane, and Schaefer, 1980). Instruction in tenth grade classrooms was based on teacher selected materials, which emphasized applied problems in various areas of mathematics. During the intervention phase, students were assigned to groups of three to five for peer tutoring, with students strategically grouped to provide a balance between high and low performers. Teachers first taught new content and skills for one to two periods using lecture and modeling. Students then participated in two thirty-minute peer tutoring sessions. During tutoring, students were given worksheets and directed to support one another on the task. Students were also given a deck of cards, with each card having a number that corresponded to a worksheet question. One student served as tutor, who selected a card and read the question. All other members of the team completed the problem and were awarded points for correct responses. In the event of an error, students were directed to correctly complete the problem three times and then earned points. Students then switched roles and selected a new problem using the card deck. In the event teams completed all worksheet problems prior to the end of class, teams worked through the worksheet again. In addition to correct responses and completing the error correction procedure, students earned points for cooperation, awarding points correctly, and providing error correction appropriately. In this study, the researchers reported improved mathematics performance for students with disabilities. However, the researchers did not disaggregate data for students with ED, preventing conclusions regarding the degree to which the intervention benefited this student population.

Maheady et al. (1988) investigated the effects of a classwide peer tutoring intervention on the academic performance of fourteen tenth grade students receiving special education services for ED or LD. Thirty-six general education students also participated in this study. As part of typical school practice, participating teachers were assigned smaller classes in an effort to better support students with disabilities in general education (e.g., fifteen to twenty students per class, with three to six being students with disabilities). The school also provided these teachers ongoing special education consultation services. During intervention, teachers led students through lecture- and discussion-based activities for one to two periods. Students then participated in thirty-minute tutoring sessions for two to three periods. During each session, students served as tutor and tutee. Prior to tutoring, students were randomly assigned to one of two teams, with each team competing to obtain the greatest number of points. Tutors read questions to tutees, who wrote and stated the correct answer. Points were earned for correct responses. Tutors stated correct answers when given an incorrect response and then tutees wrote the correct answer three times. Tutors earned points for error correction. In this study, the researchers report improved weekly test scores and grades. However, results for students with ED were not disaggregated, preventing conclusions regarding the degree to which the intervention was effective for these students.

Mastropieri et al. (1998) investigated the effects of activity-based science instruction with three fourth grade general education classrooms. One classroom, which included five students with disabilities, received the intervention condition, which also included instructional accommodations. Of the five students with disabilities who received intervention, one student received special education services for emotional disturbance. Intervention content, materials, and activities were based on the *Science of Technology for Children* (STC; 1992), which was selected by the researchers because its design was considered advantageous to inclusion. Perceived strengths of this curriculum included a focus on prerequisite skills and concepts, student progress monitoring, integration of technology, and hands on activities. Students in two classrooms received typical textbook-based instruction, which served as a comparison condition. In this study, students with disabilities made academic gains that exceeded those of students without disabilities in the textbook condition. Students in the intervention condition also had more positive perceptions of science. However, this study did not specifically report outcomes for the student with the emotional disturbance.

Mastropieri et al. (2006) investigated the effects of peer tutoring, differentiated instruction, and hands on activities on the science achievement of students in eighth graders in inclusive classrooms. A total of 213 students participated from 13 classes. Forty-four students had a disability, seven of which had ED. For the intervention condition, three sets of differentiated materials were created with each set representing a different level of difficulty/ providing a different level of support. Students were assigned to partners or groups of three, with low-achieving students assigned to work with higher-performing students. Low-performing students initially worked with the materials that had the lowest level of difficulty/highest level of support, and then progressed to more challenging material upon mastery. In this study, students in the intervention condition outperformed control group students on science posttests and on the state's high stakes assessment. However, results for students with ED were not disaggregated.

Prater et al. (1992) investigated the effects of a self-monitoring intervention on the mathematics performance and on-task behavior of a ninth grader receiving special education services for ED. In this study, the intervention was provided in multiple classroom settings: general education mathematics class, general education English Language Arts class, and a resource room class. When in the resource room, the student completed assignments from his general education classes. During the time of the study, resource room support consisted of spelling practice. In regards to the self-monitoring intervention, it was initially provided in the resource room setting and then introduced in the general education classes. The student was also provided explicit instruction in examples and non-examples of on-task behavior. The student was taught how to use a self-monitoring sheet with visuals and how to respond to an audio prompt to self-assess on-task behavior. Audio prompts were faded over time. A poster also served as a visual prompt. According to the researchers, the intervention was effective at improving mathematics test scores and on-task behavior. However, this study also used a design that did not meet WWC design standards for single case research.

Rafferty (2012) investigated the effects of a self-monitoring intervention with four students with ED ranging in age from seven years eight months to eight years two months. The self-monitoring intervention was provided during reading instruction, which was based on *Time Warp Plus* (2006). The self-monitoring intervention was based on the mnemonic SLANT (Ellis, 1991), which stands for the following: (S) Sit up; (L) Look at the speaker; (A) Answer the questions; (N) Note key information; (T) Track the talker. Students were provided a vibrating timer set for two-minute time intervals, which served as a prompt for students to self-assess if they were on task. *Time Warp Plus* (2006) consisted of partner reading, graphing of words read correctly, whole group instruction, and small group stations. In this study, the researchers report improvements in on-task behavior and reading fluency. However, this study used a design that did not meet WWC standards for single case studies. As a result, a causal inference between the intervention and changes in student performance cannot be made.

Wehby et al. (2005) investigated the effects of multicomponent intervention on the reading performance of one kindergartner receiving special education services for ED. Two kindergartners receiving services for Other

Health Impairment (OHI) and one receiving services for speech and language impairment (SLI) also participated. All students received support in a self-contained classroom for students with disabilities who performed emotional and behavioral challenges. The reading intervention consisted of the Scott Foresman Reading program (Foresman, 2000) and the Phonological Awareness Training for Reading program (PATR; Torgeseon and Bryant, 1994). In this study, the reading intervention was provided by school staff and research assistants. Specifically, a general education teacher, a special education teacher, a teacher for students who are English Language Learners (ELL), and a special education aide and two research assistants provided the intervention to one class of twenty-six students, twenty-two of which did not have a disability. Instruction with Scott Foresman consisted of whole and small group activities, including chorale reading, sight word practice, and instruction in parts of speech. Instruction in PATR consisted of reading, spelling, rhyming, sound segmenting, and blending activities. Although student response to intervention varied, overall the intervention was effective at improving reading performance. However, this study employed a design that did not meet WWC standards, which prevents causal inferences.

RECOMMENDATIONS FOR INCLUSIVE INSTRUCTION

In the following section, we make four recommendations for improving the academic performance of students with ED in inclusive settings. These recommendations are based on findings from the synthesis of syntheses, trends across intervention studies, and related literature. Recommendations include multidisciplinary collaboration, reasonable workloads and classroom support, tiered systems of academic support, and ongoing academic progress monitoring.

Multidisciplinary Collaboration

General education teachers possess content knowledge but may lack sufficient training and expertise to support students with disabilities (Conderman and Hedin, 2015). Considering the challenge of providing effective instruction to students with ED as well as the limitations of intervention research with an academic focus (see McKenna et al., 2019), multidisciplinary collaboration is essential to improve achievement. In the absence of plentiful high-quality intervention research with disaggregated outcomes for students with ED, school-based professionals must largely rely on professional expertise, values, and the goals and vision IEP teams have for students when planning inclusive instruction. Professionals such as special education teachers, school psychologists, paraprofessionals, and school administrators can provide valuable information and assist with making key decisions when planning inclusive instruction. However, sufficient and consistent time is essential to collaboration as it is necessary to discuss: student strengths and areas for development, changing interests and preferences, prerequisite skills necessary for academic success, student competency in prerequisite skills, strategies for explicitly teaching prerequisite skills, scheduling time for explicit instruction in prerequisite skills, and adaptations to ameliorate potential barriers to academic success. The importance of collaboration for co-planning and decision-making holds true whether professionals provide consultation services, co-taught instruction, or another form of direct service (Idol, 2006; Magiera and Zigmond, 2005; Solis, Vaughn, Swanson, and McCulley, 2012; Weiss and Lloyd, 2002). Collaboration is also critical in instances in which students with ED receive multiple services from different providers such as when accessing multitiered systems of support and/or services within the full continuum of placements (e.g., partial inclusion, school within a school model, resource room support, inclusion facilitator support). In the absence of collaborative planning, teachers may fail to select appropriate instructional practices and adaptations (Murawski and Lochner, 2011) or students may receive services and supports that lack cohesion. If professionals are not talking together, then they are not working together. Considering the importance of using available time in the most productive manner, we suggest using a formal and consistent structure for collaborative planning meetings. One such example is Team Implemented Problem Solving (TIPS; Newton, Todd, Algonzzine, Horner, and Algozzinne, 2009; go to the following URL for more information: https://www.pbis.org/training/tips).

Reasonable Workloads and Ongoing Support

School administrators must consider teacher workloads when planning inclusive instruction. In two intervention studies (Maheady et al., 1987; Maheady et al., 1988), general education teachers were provided comparatively smaller class sizes so that they could more effectively employ inclusive instructional practices. Smaller class sizes may permit teachers to provide more frequent feedback, individualized attention, and support to students with ED. It should also be noted that teachers in both studies were provided ongoing special education consultation services as part of typical school practice. Ongoing consultation is one way to improve the ability of general education teachers to provide the specialized supports and instruction that are necessary for students with ED to potentially benefit from inclusive instruction. However, consultation services on its own may be insufficient, as special educators have knowledge and skills in specialized practices and supports that are likely to benefit students with ED, and general educators may struggle to use these methods in the absence of direct services from a special educator (McKenna et al., 2019; McKenna, Newton, and Bergman, 2019).

The study by Wehby et al. (2005) serves as another example of the types of classroom supports that may be necessary to support academic instruction in inclusive settings. In this study, a general education teacher, a special education teacher, a teacher for students who are ELL, and a special education aide assisted with the implementation of a multicomponent reading intervention. Considering the importance of literacy skills to school and post-school success (see Ciullo et al., 2016), an "all-hands-on-deck" approach to literacy instruction is reasonable but may not be feasible. Yet this study does highlight the necessity of ongoing collaboration and strategic decision-making when planning inclusive instruction, in consideration of finite school resources.

Students in Bell et al. (1990) received support in the school's program for students with ED and a resource room. In other intervention studies, students with ED received support in other settings within the full continuum of placement options (e.g., their LRE was not full inclusion). Students with ED received resource room instruction (Bell et al., 1990; Maheady et al., 1987; Prater et al., 1992) or support in self-contained classrooms (Wehby et al., 2005). In consideration of this finding, we recommend that schools continue to leverage the full continuum of service options to support the inclusive instruction of students with ED. Schools are also reminded that a consideration of the full continuum of service options is a legal mandate (Kauffman and Bader, 2016). These studies provide examples of how some schools struck a balance between general education instruction and time spent receiving specialized instruction and supports in another educational setting, and how time in these other educational settings were used to support skill development.

Tiered Systems of Academic Support

The special education community has long expressed concerns regarding a reliance on general education instruction (adapted or otherwise) to improve the school performance of students with disabilities (Fuchs et al., 2015; Kauffman and Bader, 2016; Vaughn, Denton, and Fletcher, 2010). In fact, there is little empirical research documenting the effects of accommodations on academic achievement (Fuchs et al., 2015). Students with learning difficulties require more time engaged in academic instruction and instruction in smaller groups. In addition, students with learning difficulties need opportunities to develop the prerequisite skills and competencies that are necessary for success with grade-level content. This type of instruction can be provided within a tiered system of academic support. In fact, many intervention studies included in the syntheses analyzed in the syntheses (e.g., McKenna et al., 2019) could be considered tier 2 or tier 3 interventions. In sum, "Neither *location* nor *exposure* is synonymous with *access*" (Fuchs et al., 2015; p. 154). Leveraging tiered systems of academic support may be one way to improve student access to general education instruction. Please see the National Center on Intensive Intervention for more information on tiered systems of academic and behavioral support: https://intensiveinterv ention.org.

Ongoing Progress Monitoring

When providing inclusive instruction, school teams must use data to determine the degree to which students are benefiting from instruction. Placement or time spent in general education cannot and should not be used as a criterion for the success of inclusive practice. Data on academic performance should be used as evidence for the effectiveness of inclusive instruction (Fuchs et al., 2015; McLeskey, Waldron, and Redd, 2014). Progress monitoring should also be used to design specialized supports and instruction, inform decisions regarding resource allocation, and identify teacher training needs (Fuchs et al., 2015; McLeskey et al., 2014). The National Center on Intensive Intervention website has additional information on academic and behavioral progress monitoring, as does Chapter 14 in this book.

CLOSING THOUGHTS

The movement toward inclusive education and inclusive schools has benefited many students with disabilities. However, this has created a number of complex challenges for administrators, teachers, students with disabilities, and their parents/guardians. Education that is truly inclusive provides beneficial opportunities to students with disabilities, and provides teachers with the necessary training, support, and materials to accomplish this goal. Most importantly, students benefit from these efforts, as indicated by objective performance data rather than summary statements, subjective information, or time spent in the general education classroom. When considering the effectiveness of inclusive instruction for students with ED, schools must consider the degree to which students make academic progress and the degree to which this progress is sufficient for FAPE mandates. The absence of research-based practices for improving the academic performance of students with ED who are educated in general education classrooms highlights the critical need for ongoing collaboration by multidisciplinary teams, progress monitoring, and data-based discussions and adjustments to service delivery.

Chapter 4

Explicit Vocabulary Instruction in the Inclusive Classroom

Although students can learn the meaning of new words through frequent and wide reading, students with emotional disturbance (ED) may spend less time engaged in reading, thus limiting their opportunities to learn new words in this manner. Limited vocabulary knowledge can then place students with ED at a significant disadvantage, particularly when they receive instruction in general education classrooms. For example, vocabulary knowledge is essential to comprehending grade-level texts and to success in content area classes (Ahmed et al., 2016; Roberts, Torgesen, Boardman, and Scammacca, 2008; Vaughn et al., 2009). Explicit and sustained (e.g., ongoing and occurring over time, multiple opportunities to learn and use new words in a meaningful context) vocabulary instruction is thus necessary for student success in inclusive classrooms (Brownell, Sindelar, Kiely, and Danielson, 2010). However, teachers assigned to inclusive classrooms may employ ineffective methods (Ford-Connors and Panatore, 2015; Jayanthi et al., 2018; Kennedy, Rodgers, Romig, Lloyd, and Brownell, 2017) such as "teaching by mentioning," dictionary work, copying definitions, and writing sentences with the target word. In fact, observation research suggests that teachers may infrequently provide vocabulary instruction to students with ED, and may use ineffective methods when doing so (McKenna, Adamson, and Solis, 2019). When providing vocabulary instruction, it is recommended that teachers use a variety of methods with research supporting their effectiveness. In this chapter, we discuss key considerations for selecting words for instruction and research-based methods for improving the vocabulary knowledge of students with ED.

PREPARATION FOR VOCABULARY INSTRUCTION

Selecting Words. It can be difficult for teachers to select words for instruction because there are so many that could potentially be taught (Archer and Hughes, 2011). As a result, selecting words involves the use of professional judgment to prioritize words to spend instructional time on. Teachers should select words that are central to comprehension of the material they will teach and those that students will later use in some meaningful way (e.g., reading, writing, and/or speaking/discussion; Archer and Hughes, 2011). For example, teachers can select words that are essential to understanding the text to be read and that will be helpful to students in another school context (e.g., when reading another text, when receiving instruction in another class). Some educators refer to these types of words as tier 2 vocabulary (see Jayanthi et al., 2018). "Accumulate" and "misfortune" are examples of tier 2 words: students are more likely to encounter these words when reading then when speaking with their peers.

Teachers should also select words that are central to the comprehension of instructed concepts, skills, and texts but are more specific to the content area (e.g., science, social studies/civics education, mathematics, English Language Arts). These words are commonly referred to as tier 3 vocabulary: For example, the word "civilization" is central to the content standards for history and social sciences in Massachusetts. Teaching the meaning of civilization may also help students learn the meaning of the word "civil," another term that students are likely to encounter in the social sciences. The word "colony" is also central to understanding social studies and history content in Massachusetts. Spending class time on the word "colony" will help students better understand the term "colonization." Although colony is a word that students may infrequently encounter in other curriculum areas, teachers should provide instruction in this word when it is central to success with grade-level content such as when teaching relevant topics in social studies and history.

Additional guidance. Domino and Taylor (2009) make additional recommendations for thinking strategically about selecting words to explicitly teach. They recommend considering the context in which words appear in the text (e.g., narrative, expository) students will read. Prior to assigning students a passage or chapter to read, teachers should review/read the text for key vocabulary and identify the context in which they appear in the reading. Words that appear in a "misdirective" or a "nondirective" context should be considered for instruction. Misdirective is a context that may cause the reader to misinterpret a word's meaning. Nondirective refers to a context that does not provide sufficient information for the reader to accurately interpret a word's meaning. Words that appear in a context that promotes understanding are not selected for instruction. Of course, words selected for instruction should be essential to comprehension, are either unknown or are words that students have limited experience with, and are essential to success in future activities (e.g., reading comprehension, authentic writing tasks, class discussions). It has also been recommended that teachers focus on providing instruction on five high utility words at a time so that struggling students do not become overwhelmed by the number of new words targeted for instruction (Mason, Reid, and Hagaman, 2012). Finding a balance between providing high-quality opportunities to learn the meaning of new words while simultaneously not overwhelming students with ED with excessive task demands is challenging. However, the more opportunities students have to develop vocabulary knowledge, the greater their ability to improve their background knowledge and reading comprehension skills, which are essential to success in inclusive classrooms.

Allocating Time for Instruction. It is recommended that teachers schedule consistent and frequent opportunities for students to engage in vocabulary instruction. For students to learn the meaning of new words, they need multiple opportunities to work with them. Instruction can occur before reading (e.g., to develop background knowledge), during reading (e.g., to discuss the target word in context), and after reading (e.g., review and extension activities). This need for frequent, meaningful opportunities to engage with vocabulary words is particularly salient for students with ED, who may have less-developed vocabulary knowledge and limited relevant background knowledge due to their academic and behavioral difficulties. With these factors in mind, teachers should select three to five words each week for instruction (Archer and Hughes, 2011), being mindful to periodically provide opportunities for review of previously instructed terms. As a result, instruction involves explicitly introducing new terms and then following up with various extension activities so students can continue to develop, refine, and extend their knowledge.

Creating Student-Friendly Definitions. The use of student-friendly definitions is central to explicit and effective vocabulary instruction (Archer and Hughes, 2011; Beck and McKeown, 2007). Student-friendly definitions are accurate and include only words that students know and are able to understand (Archer and Hughes, 2011). This is important because students are unlikely to learn a new word if the definition includes words that are unknown or confusing to them. It is thus essential that the definition is something that the students can understand and make sense of. The focus of vocabulary instruction should be on the definition of the target word and not words within its definition. It should be noted that definitions contained in dictionaries are typically not student-friendly. Consider the word "merchant." According to the online version of the Merriam-Webster dictionary, a merchant is "a buyer and seller of commodities for profit." For students to understand this definition, students must know the meaning of "commodities" and "profit." In this example, at least some students may need additional instruction in the meaning of both words to develop an understanding of the target word (e.g., merchant). This complicates the learning process by adding additional layers of difficulty to the task (e.g., students need to learn the meaning of additional new words in order to learn the meaning of the target vocabulary word). It should also be noted that dictionary definitions may be written using complex syntax (e.g., the sequence in which individual words are arranged in a sentence), thus also providing an additional challenge to students who are attempting to learn a new word. With this in mind, teachers should be mindful of syntax when creating student-friendly definitions.

To facilitate student understanding of new words, teachers should create student-friendly definitions when preparing activities for vocabulary instruction. According to Dimino and Taylor (2009), student-friendly definitions contain specific information about the meaning of the word and are derived from words that students are already very familiar with (e.g., words they use when speaking and writing). Definitions should also be written using a syntax that is easily understood by students. Let's consider the previous example: "merchant." A more student-friendly definition would be, "a person who buys and sells products to make money." In instances in which the target word has multiple meanings, instruction should focus on the definition that is most salient to success in the current curriculum or academic task. As students gain an understanding of the target word, teachers can provide additional instruction in these additional meaning (e.g., extend the initial meaning and initial student understanding).

Introducing a New Word

Teachers should present a visual, written representation of the whole word, pronounce it to students, and then tell students why it is important to learn it (e.g., you will see it when you read the next section; knowing this word will help you understand and/or know more about XYZ). Teachers should then visually present the word to students in syllable form (e.g., the word broken up into syllables), pointing to or highlighting each syllable (e.g., in bold lettering) as they pronounce it. The idea is to draw students' attention to each syllable as you pronounce it, so that the visual of the word part/syllable and the verbal pronunciation are presented simultaneously to students. This type of explicit instruction may help students accurately decode the word when they encounter it when reading. Also, if students cannot pronounce the word, they will have difficulty learning its meaning and using it in a meaningful way (e.g., reading, discussion, writing). Teachers should also repeat this procedure in future lessons (e.g., use repetition) so that students are better able to remember how to pronounce and decode/recognize the target word during reading. Teachers should then read aloud the student-friendly definition and underline the key words within the definition that can help students remember its meaning. Students are then provided a visual representation of the vocabulary word and a brief, explicit explanation on how the visual relates to the vocabulary words (e.g., an explanation of how the visual is an accurate representation of example of the target word). Teachers can point out specific aspects of the visual and make the explicit connections to the meaning of the word (e.g., link aspects of the visual to aspects of the definition).

Provide Examples and Non-examples

Once students are given the student-friendly definition, teachers should provide students with examples of the word (Dimino and Taylor, 2009). Initial examples should fit the context in which the word will be encountered during academic activities (Archer and Hughes, 2011). Examples that are not salient to this context should also be provided to help students generalize the meaning of the word to other situations. Examples can be a physical example of the term (e.g., an action, an object), additional visuals that accurately represent the term (e.g., charts, diagrams, pictures), or a clear verbal explanation (Archer and Hughes, 2011). However, when using concrete and/or visual examples, teachers should also provide an explicit verbal explanation to support student understanding. Teachers can also use examples from the student's personal experiences and then connect them to the intended context (e.g., the context in which students are about to encounter the word). This may be particularly critical for students with ED, who may have limited background knowledge and who may be averse to learning unfamiliar concepts or skills.

For example, consider the word "alternative." This is a high utility word because it frequently appears in academic texts, as indicated by its inclusion in the Academic Word List (AWL) by Coxhead (2000) and the Academic Vocabulary List (AVL) by Gardner and Davies (2013). To promote student understanding and engagement, teachers could point out a recent situation in which students had an opportunity to make a choice. The teacher can then explain how making a choice is similar to choosing an alternative.

Non-examples of the instructed word should also be provided because they help students clarify and refine their understanding (Biemiller, 2001). Non-examples help students understand instances in which a word's meaning is not applicable and are particularly important when the word is complex or difficult to understand. One strategy for creating non-examples is to remove one important characteristic from the definition and use this as the non-example. Students can then attempt to discern between the two (an example and a non-example) and provide an explanation as to why the example is in fact an example (e.g., how does this fit with the target word's definition?) and why the non-example is in fact a non-example (e.g., how does this conflict with the target word's definition? What key characteristic or characteristics are missing?). In addition to promoting academic engagement during vocabulary instruction (e.g., discussion), this is an effective way to informally assess student understanding. Having students create their own examples and non-examples and providing an explanation of how it is representative of an example or non-example is another effective way to actively engage students with ED during vocabulary instruction, informally assess student understanding, and to identify students or aspects in need of reteaching. This is also a potential method for providing opportunities for students to discuss the meaning of target vocabulary with a partner or in a small group (e.g., students can discuss their examples and non-examples, or critique each other's examples and non-examples). Another way to assess student understanding is to have them create lists of synonyms or antonyms and have them provide an explanation as to how the meanings are similar or different from the instructed word. Another way to use examples and non-examples during instruction is to give students the word and its definition and a list of examples and non-examples. Students then use aspects of the definition to explain how items from the list are an example or non-example of the target word. The list can include short scenarios, pictures, synonyms, or antonyms, as well as examples and non-examples from their own experiences.

Graphic Organizers

Graphic organizers such as a concept map can be used to introduce a new vocabulary word, activate relevant background knowledge that is necessary to learn the meaning of a new word, and to extend and refine student understanding of a word (Ruetebuch, Ciullo, and Vaughn, 2013). Educators may find graphic organizers particularly useful when initially introducing a word to students because it provides an easy structure for teachers and students with ED to follow. Figure 4.1 is an example of a graphic organizer that teachers can use when introducing words. This graphic organizer includes the target word and a student-friendly definition, examples and non-examples, synonyms and antonyms, and an example sentence with the target word used in an appropriate context.

When using graphic organizers in an inclusive classroom, it is important for teachers to model how to complete the graphic organizer using an explicit talk aloud while entering the correct information in the correct location. As teachers guide students through a discussion of information salient to target word and the graphic organizer, they should write the information into a copy of the graphic organizer so that students in the classroom easily see it. Teachers

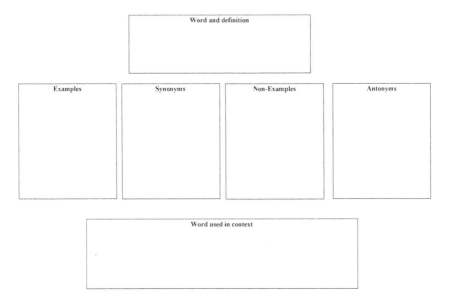

Figure 4.1   Vocabulary Graphic Organizer.

should use a "lead" and "follow" format of instruction (e.g., teachers model completing a part of the graphic organizer, then student complete that part of the graphic organizer; see Carnine, Silbert, Kame'enui, Slocum, and Travers [2017] for more information on how this method of direct instruction can support student learning). When students "follow," teachers should use active supervision to identify students who are off task or who need additional time entering information and provide behavior-specific praise (e.g., nice job taking accurate notes!). As students become more familiar with completing the graphic organizer, teachers should provide opportunities for students to complete them on previously instructed vocabulary and concepts in small groups, with a partner, and independently. Once completed, the graphic organizer can serve as a study guide or as a tool for supporting discussion and writing. Teachers should provide students behavior specific praise for attending to modeling, following directions, maintaining effort, correcting their mistakes, and asking clarifying questions. Student effort, error correction, and active participation during vocabulary instruction can also be reinforced through the use of token economies and other contingencies for providing reinforcement.

Focus on the Meaning of Word Parts

The next step in introducing the word is to teach the meaningful parts of the word. Morphemes are the smallest unit of meaning within a word. When students are provided instruction in morphemes, they are better able to learn and retain the meaning of instructed words and to generalize this knowledge to learn new ones (Reed, 2008). Instruction in morphemes involves breaking a vocabulary word into its meaningful parts and teaching the meaning of the individual parts. Let's consider the word "prehistoric." This word can be broken down into the prefix "pre," which means before, and the base word "historic" (e.g., a word that can have a prefix or suffix added to it), which means historical importance or being famous. Instruction in prefixes, and being mindful of the need to use student-friendly definitions, may be particularly useful to struggling readers such as students with ED. Prefixes appear at the beginning of the word, so an understanding of prefixes may also help students with word identification and with determining the meaning of unknown words that have not been explicitly taught. Prefixes also tend to have the same meaning regardless of how they are used, making them a potentially useful tool for students to leverage. Instruction in the meaningful parts of words should also include suffixes (e.g., identification of them in the target word and their meaning). Let's consider the word "courageously." This word includes the base word "courageous," which means brave. It also includes the suffix "ly," which means having the characteristics or the qualities of.

Although morphological instruction is effective, it is recommended that it be used in concert with other research-based instructional practices for vocabulary (Reed, 2008) and for this instruction to occur over time to maximize the effectiveness of this method (Swanson, Vaughn, and Wexler, 2017). Teachers can also provide instruction in Greek and Latin roots during content area vocabulary instruction as students encounter them in the curriculum. After teaching the meaning of the individual parts of the word, teachers should provide students with the student-friendly definition. Students should not be asked to look up the definitions of words because this is an ineffective instructional method and thus a waste of valuable instructional time. Teachers only have a finite amount of time with their students, and this time can be maximized when they use practices that are research-based.

Continued Instruction

In order to learn and to be able to use new vocabulary in meaningful ways (e.g., writing, speaking, comprehending the text they read), students must have multiple, meaningful exposures or opportunities to work with the word (Graves, 2006; Stahl and Fairbanks, 1986). With this in mind, vocabulary instruction must be ongoing and occur over time. Once a word has been introduced to students (e.g., initial instruction), students must have opportunities to work with it to promote deep understanding and retention. Memorizing definitions, copying definitions, and using target words in a sentence are not considered meaningful opportunities to work with vocabulary because they do not require students to (1) convey their understanding of the word, (2) create something new using the word, or (3) provide evidence that the word is used in a correct context.

Teaching vocabulary words before and after reading provides students multiple exposures to target words (Swanson et al., 2017). Providing vocabulary instruction before and after reading provides students opportunities to review instructed words, which is an essential component of vocabulary instruction (Archer and Hughes, 2011). Continued instruction can consist of reading, writing, and discussion-based activities. For example, students can be provided focus questions to guide discussion of a vocabulary word within the context of the content of instruction (Swanson et al., 2017). Focus questions can be used as a writing prompt (e.g., quick write), peer-to-peer discussion, small group discussion, or whole group discussion. However, it is recommended that teachers use peer and/or small group discussion prior to whole group discussion to promote student engagement and success during whole group discussion. In essence, peer and small group discussion can help students with ED refine their understanding of the target word or their response to the focus question, which may promote more active participation during whole group discussion. In essence, peer and small group can be used to develop confidence and readiness for whole group activities/discussion.

CLOSING THOUGHTS

Vocabulary instruction that activates prior knowledge and includes contingencies for explicit modeling and explanation, guided practice, and independent practice is essential (Archer and Hughes, 2011; Dimino and Taylor, 2009), particularly for students who may have limited background knowledge and are resistant readers such as students with ED. Students need multiple exposures and opportunities to use new terms to truly master them. This proves particularly true for students who engage in challenging behaviors such as students with ED, as they may engage in passive or off-task behavior during instruction, thus limiting their ability to access instruction. Practitioners are encouraged to use positive behavior supports including providing reinforcement for effort and academic task completion to improve student engagement, as well as providing clear expectations for what students are required to do during instruction.

Chapter 5

Use of Graphic Organizers to Improve Academic Content Acquisition

Social and academic growth follows a parallel pathway that requires teachers to consider development of both components in concert to promote student success. Creating systems that can support students to take on the commonly daunting task of an academic challenge *and* limit the occurrence of task avoidance is a struggle for many educators. Teachers of students within inclusive settings must identify, create, and implement the academic supports that individual students need to reach their academic goals but do so in a manner that prevents students from becoming dependent on adults for success. The curricular format for setting students up for success and independence must be systematic and provide students multiple opportunities to practice during the many stages of learning within a classroom.

For students with and at-risk for emotional disturbance (ED) the process of completing an academic task can be daunting. Many cognitive processes must take place to accomplish just task initiation, let alone, complete a project. It is critical that teachers and instructional support staff are trained to support these cognitive processes and help students develop proficiency and independence. Classrooms can move beyond just behavioral supports for success by providing the academic supports that are needed. Many students with ED are at minimum two grade levels behind their academic peers (Nelson et. al, 2004). This gap between their performance levels and that of their peers can create instructional and programming dilemmas for Individualized Education Plan (IEP) teams. More students are spending time with their general education peers for instruction, so effective supports are needed to ensure that the cognitive tasks required for academic success can become second nature to students. For inclusion to be effective, students with ED have to be provided opportunities to develop their academic skills in addition to behavioral and social skills.

Overall, the development of cognitive strategies for student success requires careful instructional planning and support. Planning must be carefully designed to scaffold for each individual learner and provide the cognitive structures required to increase performance, decrease any self-defeating barriers, and enhance the likelihood that skills can be fluent, generalized, and performed more independently in the future. This goal can be overwhelming and seem insurmountable, but in the following pages we will outline this process for you and help you understand how to easily embed this curricular design within your classroom.

PRINCIPLES OF GRAPHIC ORGANIZER STRATEGY INSTRUCTION

One tool for improving student's cognitive processes required to excel at academic performance is through the use of a graphic organizer. For example, writing is critical to student success and is considered by many as foundational to academic success. In fact, writing is one of the most common ways for students to demonstrate what they know. However, writing is incredibly complex and requires students to develop a plan, compose a draft (e.g., execute the plan), evaluate their work, and then effectively revise—with the latter stages sometimes requiring multiple iterations and revisions. The benefits of using a strategy to assist with this foundational process can be summarized by highlighting the three key outcomes that come from strategy instruction aligned with content (Santangelo, Harris, and Graham, 2008). First, the concept of using a graphic organizer for strategy instruction is designed to simplify complex processes into tangible actions using a step-by-step format for completion. Second, the list of items required to create a course of action described through graphic organizer instruction gives students insight into the stages that they have completed and what is left to be done. Finally, the use of a graphic organizer also takes abstract mental operations and gives them a concrete format for processing and completion.

Designing Content Acquisition through Graphic Organizers

A key component to success is that students are able to access the curriculum within inclusive environments. Truly inclusive classrooms provide opportunities for students to increase their active engagement during academic instruction and access the curriculum that is being taught. To this end, graphic organizers is a strategy that can be generalized across academic content areas and is sufficiently flexible to adapt to meet the individualized needs of students. A common graphic organizer used within multiple settings is the use of a Venn diagram. This type of graphic organizer helps students to organize and visualize similarities and differences between two or more concepts. This graphic organizer could be used across disciplines. The design of these graphic organizer strategies (e.g., Venn diagram) can assist students across multiple executive functioning domains, allow them to take abstract concepts, and make them more tangible. The process of understanding how to support the effective use of graphic organizers must come back to the key outcomes that they are attempting to achieve through their use. To make this concept more tangible, let us compare the design of a graphic organizer to the job of an architect and the design of a tall skyscraper building.

Structure

For an architect the design of a building rests on having a solid foundation and a structure that can withstand natural elements and Mother Nature. In this analogy, the is a student's background knowledge. Independent use of graphic organizers requires students to be explicitly taught how it will assist them to achieve an end goal and the processes associated with their use. Beyond just basic instruction and a student's individual schema, it is also critical to focus on the background knowledge that a student has related to the academic content and even the use of graphic organizers themselves. Choosing which graphic organizer is taught to assist students in the completion of a task allows the adult to individualize the organizer to ensure that completion of the task becomes within the student's independency level. This means that the teacher must have a general idea of the student's abilities to help discern what type of graphic organizer is going to be needed. An example may be that for a writing task, some advanced students are able to create an outline and only include key words to help them structure their task to completion. However, for other students the task of creating key words may require a level of skill and independence that students do not presently have, so the graphic organizer may include larger concepts and key words and have students rewrite those concepts in their own language. These two tasks help students to achieve the same goal but be differentiated based on what supports the student needs to complete a task independently. Creating a graphic organizer, which can meet this spectrum of student's needs (e.g., differentiated materials, in this instance, a differentiated graphic organizer), allows students of significant varying abilities to access the content and build a structure for success that is at their own individual level and threshold for independence.

The foundation of being taught how to utilize a graphic organizer is critical for student use. However, structure and organization of a graphic organizer will allow for success throughout the task, not just at initiation. In our skyscraper analogy we will compare our graphic organizer to steel beams. Steel beams provide a frame for each floor within a building and ensure the occupants safety even at extreme heights. This parallels the importance of structure within our graphic organizers as we move through the academic task. Graphic organizers are built so that each concept builds off of the next to get to the final product. Having a solid structure where each layer allows for students to connect to the next provides a format to success.

Organization

The format and design of graphic organizers may vary by nature; however, the goal of these tools is to take a complex design and end product and create a format for reaching that end which allows students to visually see the end goal and layout. With sufficient explicit modeling and guided practice in the use of specific graphic organizers and how they are used to complete specific academic tasks, students are able to see in a small space the tasks and organization required to complete a much larger project. Graphic organizers must be created with organization in mind. The format must be designed in such a way that students can take content and expand beyond the organizer, adding additional details and supporting information to achieve an extended version of the organizer that approximates the end product. Again, teacher modeling and opportunities for guided practice are necessary to promote student success and eventual independence with this task. Consider comparing organization to the specific design of floors within our skyscraper. Each floor must be designed for occupant movement and ease for navigation of the building. In our graphic organizer this same construct must be completed. Design within each level of the organizer must be considered and formatted so that each level is able to help the individual accomplish their goal, but it must also include the concept of movement. It needs to allow for an ease of navigation and a format that can help the student to get ideas and concepts within a succinct manner and get their plan out in an efficient manner. The organization of a graphic organizer should be designed so that they are a tool that will help students to organize what others may be able to do in their head on paper or technology for a permanent product to refer to as they complete the task.

Collaboration

Almost every skyscraper that you enter has some fashion of a lobby and also common space within the different floors. This idea of common space allows for collaboration for students with their peers and also with their teacher at inception and also for each level. Students are able to connect with other students and have meaningful dialogue at each step along the way. This allows them to share ideas and their own thoughts about the level. They are also able to collaborate with the classroom teacher or another support staff. Classroom staff are able to visually see what students have typically conceptualized within their heads. This provides an opportunity to talk through ideas, refine them, and expand on areas that may not have sufficient clarity. These types of collaborative discussions provide assistance to students in a manner which does not require specific one-on-one attention throughout the activity but does allow for targeted check-ins and an outline of where a student has come from within a task and where they plan on going. This collaboration between a teacher and a student typically initiates with the teacher modeling the completion of a graphic organizer and modeling when to use specific types of graphic organizers for tasks. Teachers are then able to follow up with guided practice of using graphic organizer and slowly build in more opportunities for students to practice independently.

Building Academic Momentum

Once a foundation and structure are created in a building the actual construction of the walls and interior can seem to be a much quicker task. This is the same with using graphic organizers within the classroom. The design of the graphic organizer allows for the classroom teacher to provide students with a level of independence through visual guidance with targeted check-ins and monitoring. Teachers can accomplish this by giving students tasks to begin with that they know students can accomplish. An example may be that a teacher stops by a student's desk and asks them about the first step within the graphic organizer and what they are thinking they may put down. The teacher may have the student orally describe their plan. This way the teacher can build their confidence in knowing that their ideas are correct before they begin writing down their response. In doing this type of check-in it gives students an opportunity to achieve success with minimal support and creates a culture where students are given tools for achievement and confidence to rise to the targeted goal. It also provides a sense of security for students who may be more hesitant to take academic risks and put their thoughts and ideas out there where they may have experienced failure within the past. Graphic organizers allow for a format that students can become accustomed to build their fluency toward academic competency and creates an internal schema where they can learn how to break down these complex processes into something more tangible. It is not at all uncommon for students to still use components of the graphic organization structure well after the tool has been removed. In essence, we, as educators, have helped build a pathway within the student's brain to get to our end goal.

Considerations for Implementation

Graphic organizers are most often used when students are trying to achieve a larger and seemingly more complex task. They are also used when students are going to be expected to complete a similar structure or format multiple times or as a basis for varying degrees of skills. The most common areas of use of graphic organizers are within writing content areas (Mastropieri and Scruggs, 2014). However, there is much research within reading, math, and even behavior (Bak and Asaro-Sadler, 2013; Burke, Boon, Hatton, and Bowman-Perrott, 2015; Hauth, Mastropieri, Scruggs, and Regan, 2013; McDaniel and Flower, 2015). Using graphic organizers across time allows students to build fluency with the strategy format and to develop a sense of understanding and organization that can hopefully be generalized to similar tasks with the eventual removal of the graphic organizer.

Self-Regulatory Strategies

Teaching students self-regulatory strategies to improve and enhance the learning process at times needs to go beyond just the tool of a graphic organizer and expand to a framework which focuses on explicit instruction, modeling, and guided practice to address student behavioral strengths and challenges in addition to their academic task (Bak and Asaro-Saddler, 2013). The use of Self-Regulated Strategy Development (SRSD, Harris and Graham, 1999) is probably the commonly researched strategy for improving student behaviors through cognitive and affective processes in collaboration. This strategy has been researched at all age levels of students and within multiple classroom and instructional contexts. SRSD takes the concept of something like the graphic organizer and gives the teacher and student a mode of collaboration on the process to ensure that students are engaging in higher-level skills. This is typically considered a strategy to be used in the writing context and incorporates six instructional students to improve a student's writing: developing background knowledge, discussing the strategy, modeling the strategy components, memorizing the steps of the strategy and any accompanying mnemonic devices, supporting the students' acquisition of the strategy, and independent practice performance. These processes allow for such specific self-regulation as goal setting, self-reinforcement, and self-monitoring—and evaluation.

IEP Considerations

The use of graphic organizers can be a powerful tool for students' success, but it is also something that should be carefully considered and even added as a specific component with the IEP for students that will be frequently accessing curriculum and the academic expectations of inclusive environments. There are multiple ways in which the structure of support of graphic organizers can become a part of a student's IEP. One way is to reference within the students' present level their success with a graphic organizer structure. However, this may not ensure that this strategy is being utilized consistently and across environments. Graphic organizers can be directly included as an accommodation for students where specific environments are outlined to ensure access and availability. In addition, for students who still may need more support to develop a solid foundation for graphic organizer use, it may be appropriate to create a goal to address the independent use of graphic organizers to support the learning of academic content. Regardless of the level of support that a student requires in their educational plan, it is critical that all adults understand the components of graphic organizer design and how to assist students to develop independence. The use of graphic organizers does not change the content or expectation of performance for students but simply gives them a concrete visual format for organization of a larger more abstract task.

Examples of Graphic Organizers

Graphic organizers can be found throughout the educational community and vary from Venn diagrams to concept maps, to simple acronyms to support learning. It can also be a self-created model that is simply sketched in tandem with thinking out loud, with or without teacher support. This website contains multiple graphic organizers which can be reproduced and used: https://www .edrawsoft.com/share-graphic-organizer.php.

When thinking about structuring and using graphic organizers you should think about what is the most effective way to arrange this information. How many groupings and then within those groups are there multiple subcomponents? If there are multiple grouping and subcomponents, then you should directly consider how to break those down and visually represent. If students are comparing or contrasting a Venn diagram is useful. If students are matching concepts to one another then a concept map may be useful. Ultimately, you will need to preplan and decide which format of graphic organizer is best suited to the task you would like students to accomplish.

CLOSING THOUGHTS

Overall, graphic organizers can support the learning of academic content. Providing an appropriate level of support is critical when considering how to provide tandem academic and behavioral support to students with emotional and behavioral issues within inclusive environments. The goal of any successful classroom is to meet student's needs and to create a level of rigor and competency that can successfully prepare students for academic settings and other academic obstacles. Having graphic organizers embedded within the curriculum allows classroom teachers to support individual students and provides a framework for inclusion.

Chapter 6

Writing Strategies for Elementary Age Students with Emotional Disturbance

By Robai Werunga

Possessing strong writing skills has countless benefits that include positive overall school outcomes; students who are taught (and master) these skills from an early age generally experience academic success across the curriculum and are less likely to struggle in overall literacy and communication (The National Early Literacy Panel; NELP, 2008). Specifically, writing has been found to improve (a) reading (Graham and Herbert, 2011), (b) writing outcomes for all students (Graham, and Perin, 2007; Rogers, and Graham, 2008), and (c) increase on-task behavior (Mason, Kubina, Valasa, and Cramer, 2010; Jacobson, and Reid, 2010). This means that, now, more than ever, students need to be proficient writers to be successful in school and in their post-school pursuits (Graham, 2013; Graham and Herbert, 2011; Harris, Graham, and Adkins, 2015; Trilling et al., 2009).

Historically, teachers have struggled with engaging students in meaningful writing instruction in general education settings (Cutler and Graham, 2008; Graham, McKeown, Kiuhara, and Harris, 2012; Graham, Capizzi, Harris, Herbert, and Morphy, 2014; Gillespie, Graham, Kiuhara, and Hebert, 2014). One reason for the challenges faced by teachers when it comes to writing instruction is government policies that have prioritized reading, math, and STEM-related subjects at the expense of writing (Graham 2016; Graham, Harris, and Santangelo, 2015; Magrath et al., 2003). As a consequence, teachers are not adequately prepared and supported to teach writing (Gillespie, Graham, Kiuhara, and Hebert, 2014; Graham, Capizzi, Harris, Hebert, and Morphy, 2014; Graham, Harris, Mason, Fink-Chorzempa, Moran, and Saddler, 2008).

For students with emotional disturbance (ED), evidence suggests that many struggle academically in most areas, including writing (Sutherland, Lewis-Palmer, Stichter, and Morgan, 2008). For these students, providing

49

academic support in this area is critical, considering that there is a correlation between academic performance and social behaviors (Arnold et al., 1999). For example, students who repeatedly experience failure academically have been found to be prone to violent and socially unacceptable behavior (Choi, 2007; Miles and Stipek, 2006). Conversely, there is evidence to suggest students' behaviors are likely to improve once they start to experience academic success (Arnold et al., 1999; Lane, 2007). This may suggest that even for those students who have been identified as ED, providing opportunities for academic success in all areas, including writing, may help improve their social skills (Werunga, 2018).

The fact that many students with ED have academic challenges that include writing, coupled with the preceding evidence of teachers struggling with effective writing instruction, presents a challenge for teachers working with this group of students in the inclusive setting. A lack of structure and effective writing strategies can result in negative learning outcomes for the entire class as well as students with ED. Therefore, as the number of students with ED receiving services in inclusive increases (Cook, Rao, and Collins, 2017), it is imperative that teachers working with these students adopt strategies that promote overall writing achievement while reducing problem behavior.

Graham (2013) emphasizes the importance of teaching students what he refers to as "foundational writing skills" particularly in the early grades. These skills, that include handwriting, spelling, vocabulary development, sentence construction, writing process, writing strategies, genre knowledge, must be taught explicitly (e.g., modeling, guided practice with immediate teacher feedback, independent practice) and systematically for students to master them. Students who do not receive instruction in these critical skills in the elementary grades are at a great risk of failing to meet established grade standards in later grades. In addition, in the absence of timely and appropriate interventions, these students are likely to continue displaying incompetence beyond the classroom, which in turn could impact their ability to secure and maintain employment; 90 percent of white-collar jobs and 80 percent of blue-collar jobs require skilled writing (National Commission on Writing, 2006). These risks intensified for students with disabilities, including those identified with ED.

Graham (2013) provided several recommended practices that have been found to be effective for teaching foundational skills. In the following section, a summary of these practices is provided followed with examples of how elementary school teachers can tap into these practices to ensure the writing success of students with ED in the inclusion classroom. Table 6.1 provides a summary of these practices.

Table 6.1   Recommended Writing Practices

Provide ample time for writing;
Increase students' knowledge about writing;
Foster students' interest, enjoyment, and motivation to write;
Explicitly teach writing skills as well as writing processes and strategies;
Use frequent assessment to inform instruction; and
Make use of technological writing tools.

Source: Graham, S. (2013). It all starts here: Fixing our national writing crises from the foundation.

PROVIDE AMPLE TIME FOR WRITING

Teachers must provide students with lots of opportunities to practice and apply writing skills, for them to be successful at writing (Graham, 2013). One way teachers can ensure that their students get multiple opportunities to engage in writing is through writing across the curriculum while exposing students in various forms of writing (Graham, 2013).

Writing across the curriculum. What this means is that teachers become intentional in incorporating writing opportunities when teaching other subjects there is growing evidence to point to the collateral benefits of engaging students in writing across the curriculum (Graham and Hebert, 2011; Klein, Hug, and Biltfell, 2018; Rivard, 1994). In mathematics, for example, writing has the potential not only to help students make sense of mathematical concepts but also to help teachers gain deeper insights into students' thinking and understanding of these concepts (Countryman, 1992). Such strategies like using freewriting, learning logs, journals, letters, autobiographies, and research papers in mathematics have been found to result in positive outcomes (Countryman, 1992). Although often recommended for use for students in grades six to twelve (Chong, 1993), these strategies can also be successfully utilized to benefit students in early grades including those with ED who receive support in the general education classroom. For example, after teaching (e.g., modeling) second grade students addition with regrouping strategies, writing can be incorporated during guided and/or independent practice, whereby the student is asked to explain the steps he/she used in solving the problem. Here, instead of giving students several problems to solve, the teacher could assign only one or two problems then ask the students to describe how they came up with the answer(s). For a student with ED, writing tasks can be a source of anxiety and frustration and may cause students to perform inappropriate behaviors. Therefore, to alleviate any possible behavioral issues during this activity, a teacher should explain task expectations in advance and make it clear to the student with ED that he/she will only be completing X number of problems. In addition, the teacher should provide choice. For example, the teacher can say to the student with ED, "If you include the required writing, you can complete only two problems, but if you do not then you will have to complete five problems." Figure 6.1 illustrates how teachers can complete this.

Another way in which teachers can promote writing across curriculum is employing the exit ticket strategy (Harrison, 2004). Exit tickets are generally used at the end of a lesson, or class session. Exit tickets, when used in the context of writing, are effective because they are designed to not only require the student to recap the essential elements of a lesson but also allow the students to communicate succinctly using organized writing strategies (Harrison, 2004). For example, at the end of a math lesson, the teacher can dedicate three to five minutes to have students summarize what they learned and give them a guideline on what to include in the summary. The guideline can also serve as a rubric for assessing the student's writing. For this strategy to be effective teachers must first teach students how to write a summary using genre-specific strategies. To support students with ED, the teacher can

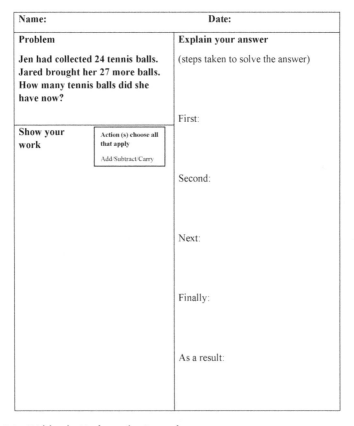

Figure 6.1   Writing in Mathematics Example.

Math Exit Ticket

Instructions: In your own words, summarize what you learned in today's lesson. Make sure to include a topic sentence, at least 3 supporting details, and a conclusion	
Plan (Graphic Organizer)	Write
Topic Sentence:	
Detail 1:	
Detail 2:	
Detail 3:	
Conclusion:	

Figure 6.2   Example Math Exit Ticket.

provide a graphic organizer; graphic organizers are visual cues and provide structure for completing the task; this is very critical for students with ED who tend to thrive in structured environments (Cartledge and Johnson, 1996) (see a sample exit ticket guide given in figure 6.2).

Involve Students in Various Forms of Writing

Students in the elementary schools are typically exposed to four basic types of writing. These include narrative writing, descriptive writing, expository writing, and persuasive/opinion writing (Morin, 2019) (see Table 6.2 for a description of each type of writing, with examples of activities that go along with it). Considering the issue of time constraints (discussed previously), teachers may find it hard to involve students in the aforementioned forms of writing. Once again, writing across curriculum can be instrumental in helping teachers accomplish this. For example, referring to the mathematics example, the writing activity infused in the guided and/independent practice can be presented as a descriptive or expository piece. Teachers can spend a few minutes at the beginning of the guided or independent practice to quickly go over the expectations for the explanation component of the practice task. In addition, teachers could turn this narrative into a review activity; at the end of the unit, students could write a letter to their parents or a pen pal narrating to them how to they learned how to solve addition problems with regrouping. Furthermore, this same activity could be turned into a persuasive/opinion piece, whereby the students are asked to justify to the teacher and classmates why their answer for a given problem is the right answer and another student's answer is not correct. To support students with ED in the inclusive classroom, once again offering options for the students may go a long way to alleviate potential problematic behaviors and ensure success in assigned tasks. For example, the teacher can provide the options on how to complete the task; students can complete the task in pairs or in small groups or individually. In addition, for students with ED who struggle to produce texts, teachers could allow other alternative forms of representing their understanding. A good example that has been found effective with students at-risk of ED (Pierson and Glaeser, 2005) is the use of comic strips. Providing students with comic strip templates allows the freedom to express their understanding of what has been learned and retained. Providing this choice can be both fun (K12Reader) and motivating (Curriculum Corner, 2017) for the reluctant and/or struggling writers (Table 6.2).

Increase Students' Knowledge about Writing

Children demonstrate an ability to express themselves as early as preschool years (Burke, 2007). Most of this expression is done verbally. However, if not appropriately managed, students' verbal expressions can result into classroom management issues; excessively talkative students and tattletales have been known to be a source of frustration for many teachers in the early grades including those working with students with ED and some teachers react by dismissing the target students (Kersey and Masterson, 2010). For students with ED, dismissing their concerns as tattling may lead to negative consequences that include escalation of problem behaviors. Instead, teachers can capitalize on this by exposing their students to the idea of expressing themselves in writing. One way that teachers can do this is by teaching the message principle—the notion that what is said verbally can be written down (Freeman, 1998). In practice, this principle should be applied as a classroom management tool as early as kindergarten, particularly for students who talk excessively. To begin the teacher can start small. For example, at the beginning of a thirty-minute whole group math lesson, the teacher can give each student two to three sticky notes. Next, the teacher instructs all students that

Table 6.2 Types of Writing

Genre	Description
Narrative writing	Tells a story. Most commonly used in personal essays (e.g., "What I Did to Celebrate the Holidays"). It can also be used for fictional stories, plays, or even a plot summary of a story read or intends to write. Typically written in the first person and is organized sequentially, with a beginning, middle, and end.
Descriptive writing	Used to create a vivid picture. It gives clear and concise description of an object, thing, places, experiences, persons, and situation/event. The students use sensory information to enable readers to use their five senses to understand the topic of the essay. It focuses on one subject and uses specific detail to describe it.
Expository writing	Involves to-the-point and factual writing. It includes definitions, instructions, directions, and other basic comparisons and clarifications. It does not include descriptive detail and opinion. Expository writing is a crucial skill for students to acquire as it is required in higher grades and many careers beyond school.
Persuasive/Opinion writing	This writing that is used to convince the reader of a particular point of view or issue. Also called an argumentative writing because it argues for or against a point of view or a position and then to support that opinion in a way that convinces the reader to see it the same way. Persuasive writing typically contains a position, reasons for the position, and supporting details.

Source: Adapted from Morin (2019).

for the next thirty minutes there should be no sidebar conversations or any form of talking unless directed by the teacher. The teacher then can instruct students to use the sticky notes and write down any pressing thing that they want to share during this thirty-minute period. At the end of the thirty minutes, the teacher can either ask students to share some of the things written or collect the sticky notes from the students and make a "consultation appointment" with each student during seatwork or individual practice to review what is written on their sticky notes. This simple exercise can be the basis for more writing activities that can be infused seamlessly into daily classroom activities, and involve all students.

Foster Students' Interest, Enjoyment, and Motivation to Write

Student motivation to write has often been listed as one of the main factors that contribute to poor writing outcomes for many students including those with ED (Ennis, Harris, Lane, and Mason, 2014). Compounding this issue, many students with ED struggle with responding positively to feedback due to poor self-image (Gresham, 1995). In addition, when writing is a struggle, many tend to engage in task avoidance, which manifests as problematic behaviors (Ennis, Jolivette and Boden, 2013). For these students, writing activities that do not single them out as struggling writers may be advantageous. An example of this type of activity is interactive writing (Burton, Johnson and Furgerson, 1996). Interactive writing is a collaborative teaching/learning strategy in which teacher and students jointly compose and write texts with students as novice writers and the teacher as the expert writer (Mackenzie, 2015). The inherent features of the interactive writing (i.e., structure, inter-active conversation, teacher and peer collaboration, and explicit instruction; Fitzgerald and Amendum 2007) have the potential to foster student's interest as well as motivation to write. To support students with ED while engaging in interactive writing, teachers can tie group contingencies, to task completion. An example of this would be a class celebration for a milestone completed in the writing process or sharing and discussing written products completed as a group. This way, the student with ED receives recognition for their efforts without having to single them out.

Explicitly Teach Writing Skills as Well as Writing Processes and Strategies

Apart from giving tasks and assignments that require some form of written responses, teachers in inclusive classrooms, and those working with students with ED in particular, should dedicate time and space to explicitly teach the writing process (e.g., modeling, guided practice with immediate feedback, followed by opportunities for independent practice). This involves strate-gies for composing specific genres. This must include the use of visual cues, graphic organizers as well as modeling of the writing. In addition, providing grade-appropriate written models (i.e., anchor texts) for every genre is ben-eficial for students. For students with ED, having anchor texts and graphic organizers is particularly useful in the inclusive setting; they provide struc-ture and self-regulation (Harris and Graham, 2016), an important skill that students with ED often struggle with (Cook, Rao, and Collins, 2017). One practice that has been found to be particularly effective with students with ED is Self-Regulated Strategy Development (SRSD; Harris and Graham, 1992). SRSD is a well-established valid instructional model used to teach a variety of writing strategies to all students across grade levels. A very handy resource for elementary school teachers working with students with ED in inclusive classroom is *Powerful Writing Strategies for all Students* by Harris, Graham, Mason, and Friedlander (2008). In this book, the authors provide clear, easy to follow, strategies for genre-specific instruction using SRSD.

Use Frequent Assessment to Inform Instruction

Assessment is one of the critical components of effective instruction (Spinelli, 2011). When it comes to writing, Behizadeh and Pang (2016) identified three formats by which students can be assessed: (a) indirect psychometric which is aligned with multiple-choice tests, (b) direct psychometric which is aligned with traditional "direct writing assessment" or on-demand essay assessments, and (c) direct sociocultural which is aligned with portfolio assessment. Of the three, Behizadeh and Pang recommend direct sociocultural assessment as a formative assessment tool for teachers. This form of assessment elicits the use of portfolios to assess students' writing over a period of time and has often been hailed as best practice in supporting rigorous literacy learning (Behizadeh and Pang, 2016). Thus, adopting this approach to student assessment would be beneficial for elementary grade students, including those with ED. For students with ED in particular, portfolios can serve as organizational tools. This provides structure, which is essential for their success (Cartledge and Johnson, 1995). In practice, the approach involves teachers setting up each student with a writing portfolio in the form of a binder (0.5–1 inch), at the beginning of the year, and designate it as a one-stop destination for all and any writing activities completed by a student in the course of the year. This can include writing completed across content area, copies of written products completed in groups, or as a class, and written products completed during specific assigned writing blocks. The binders can be personalized and divided into several sections based on genres and/or subject. It should also include all feedback from peers and the teacher. Each student should be allowed to organize his or her own binder based on their preferences with guidance from the teacher. Doing so creates a sense of ownership; ownership leads to responsibility which may in turn lead to commitment to writing. In addition, with a portfolio, students are able to see the quality of their writing over a period of time. This can be motivating in and of itself.

In regard to grading written work for struggling writers with ED, it is important to provide feedback that encourages and motivates them to keep striving to improve their writing; How teachers respond to these students' efforts in writing sets the tone for the trajectory of their progress. When grading individual written products try these strategies: (a) Place a symbol at specific parts of students' responses to alert the student that the section needs some attention. For example, if a student forgets to place a punctuation mark at the end of a sentence, place a check mark at the spot where the punctuation is supposed to be; (b) include general comments at the end of the essay, making sure to start with something positive. For instance, if punctuation is a recurring issue, first start by recognizing the student's neat handwriting or "great penmanship." Then refer the student to the check marks in their response and clearly state the "purpose of the checks" and encourage them to revisit their writing and correct the errors; (c) address common errors together. For example, if most of students have persistent punctuation errors, design a simple mini-lesson to address the issue rather than write it on individual papers. This way all students get to hear the information at the same time and are provided instructions to address the common error and/or misconception; (d) utilize a rubric in all grading. This could be task-specific, when engaging students in writing across the curriculum. This helps pinpoint exactly what the student needs help with or where the student needs more of a challenge; rubrics provide a quick and more efficient way to evaluate student progress in writing; (e) incorporate student reflection in grading. Student reflection can be a powerful assessment tool that teachers can utilize to inform their instruction. For students with ED, reflection offers an opportunity to voice their frustrations about the given task and can be a way to channel their emotions. One way to encourage students to do this is using a rating scale (see Figure 6.3 for an example rating scale for lower elementary grade students). Reflection is also an opportunity for students to comment on their effort and task persistence, and how they contribute to positive changes in writing performance.

Using the above strategies could be beneficial in two ways. First, an "X" mark in place of proofreads or line edits will make the feedback less daunting and easier to understand for the student. Second, it allows the students the opportunity to try and figure out the issues/problems brought to their attention on their own, thus promoting reflection. More importantly, it reduces the time spend by the teacher on providing extensive feedback for each individual student. This time can be allocated to more meaningful writing engagements within the class.

Make Use of Technological Writing Tools

As technology becomes more accessible in schools, teachers have the ability to tap into powerful and flexible writing tools that can have a significant impact on the writing process and on the social context for writing in the schools (MacArthur, 1998). For students who struggle with composing due to issues related to fine motor skills, such tools as keyboarding and "dictate to scribe" are useful (MacArthur, 1996). Speech to text technologies can also assist with motor difficulties or deficient keyboarding skills. Beyond keyboarding and typing,

Checking my writing

NAME: _____

My sentences start with a capital letter.		
I put a used correct punctuation.		
I did my best with spelling.		
I used my best handwriting.		
My story makes sense to me.		
Comments		

Figure 6.3   Example Self-evaluation Checklist.

there are other ways in which teachers can engage and motivate their most reluctant writers including students with ED. These include using digital story-telling and comic strips web tools. Digital storytelling allows students to engage in composing and sharing stories with other students around the world under the guidance of the teacher. When utilized effectively, using these approaches can foster engagement and promote student motivation to write. Many of these digital tools are available for free to teachers and easy to navigate. Educator's Technology (2012) provides a list of free web-based technological tools that teachers can utilize to enhance student engagement and improve their students' writing skills. Table 6.3 provides a list of ten common digital resources for writing. (For a comprehensive list, visit the sources provided.)

Table 6.3 Resources

Name	Brief Description	Web Link
30hands Learning	User-friendly iOS app for creating a story by adding a narration to photos. It has excellent video tutorials to help users create a story.	http://30hands.com/
Animaker Class	An excellent site with an educational portal for students to create animated stories.	https://class.animaker.com/
BoomWriter	A site for students to create digital stories/books through a collaborative process. Once a story is completed, it gets published online and an actual book can then be ordered.	https://www.boomwriter.com/
Buncee	A digital canvas for creating digital stories and more. It allows educators to track and monitor student progress and assignments.	https://app.edu.buncee.com/
Comic Life	A popular digital comic iOS app for creating comics. Fun and easy.	https://apps.apple.com/us/app/comic-life/id4325378 82
Digital Films	A site for creating a digital animated story and then embed into a site/blog to share it with others.	http://www.digitalfilms.com/
Imagine Forest	An innovative site where a student can create a digital story or use a story starter for brainstorming that writing process.	https://www.imagineforest.com/
Little Bird Tales	A popular site for digital storytelling that allows students to create their own art and record their voice. Also available as an app.	https://littlebirdtales.com/
Make Beliefs Comix	A site for creating digital comics in a number of different languages as well as lots of educational resources.	https://www.makebeliefscomix.com/
Storybird	A great site with educational portal where students create art-inspired stories and then embed into a site/blog.	https://storybird.com/

CLOSING THOUGHTS

Teachers in the inclusive settings have to contend with the rigorous demands of writing instruction, with many states adopting curriculums based on the common core. With the number of students with ED receiving inclusive instruction on the rise, special and general education teachers serving these students need strategies and skills to meet the needs of all their students. For students with ED who are also struggling writers, teachers must be cognizant of writing tasks and/or demands that may serve as triggers for inappropriate behaviors. Hence, teachers must be proactive in finding alternative and creative ways to engage these students in writing activities to maximize their potential, support their writing and emotional needs, and ensure the overall outcomes for these students and their classmates. This does not require inventing new strategies. Rather, taking the generally vetted practices and modifying them to meet the individual needs off these students will set students up for success in writing, promote positive behavioral outcomes, and help nurture an overall positive classroom environment for all learners. This will require teachers to expand their understanding how to teach writing and the idea of self-expression beyond the traditional concept of writing. As our society becomes increasing digital, teachers working with students with ED in the inclusive classrooms should take advantage of this by utilizing easily accessible digital writing tools to make writing activities engaging, meaningful, and above all less daunting for all students, particularly those with ED.

Chapter 7

Inclusive Mathematics Practices for Students with Emotional Disturbance

By Jessica Nelson

When working with students with emotional disturbance (ED), we find that families, schools, and communities all report incredible challenges with both how to reach these students not only behaviorally but academically. The challenging factors with students with ED are that they display both internalizing as well as externalizing patterns of behavior (Lane, 2007). Identifying the emotions that they may be experiencing on a daily basis can present many challenges for teachers.

According to the National Mathematics Advisory Panel report (2008), students with disabilities were significantly below their nondisabled peers in the area of mathematics. In fact, in 2017, 83 percent of fourth graders with disabilities fell in the basic or below basic categories in mathematics. In that same year, 91 percent of eighth graders with disabilities were at the basic or below basic categories. Years later as we look at this data, these statistics have not changed much since first reported in 2015. To help further prevent students with disabilities from falling through the cracks, the National Council for Teachers of Mathematics has an equity principle, which demands high expectations as well as adequate supports and resources for all students and across all settings (National Council of Teachers of Mathematics, 2000). Students in grades four and eight decreased in mathematics proficiency from 2013 to 2015 (National Assessment of Educational Progress, 2015). Many research studies have been done on academic deficits of students with ED. In comparison to their general education peers, students with ED exhibit substantial academic deficits in the areas of writing, reading, and mathematics (Scruggs and Mastroprieri, 1986, Wagner and Davis, 2006, and Haydon et al., 2011).

When working with students with ED, it is noted that behaviors that are displayed can affect not only behavioral and social advances but academic gains as well (Lane, 2007). With the sometimes-poor attendance that is displayed by students with ED, we also see a common practice of retaining these students or these students dropping out of school altogether (Wagner and Davis, 2006). Common practices that have been noted by researchers focus mainly on drill and practice, counting, and the use of conceptual strategies. While not surprising, the more time that students with ED sat in their seats for independent seatwork time, the higher level of disruptive behavior that was displayed in the classroom (Hayling et al., 2008). Due to the fact that many students with ED have a higher rate of absenteeism, many are not prepared for higher-level math skills due to the fact they are missing prerequisite skills such as basic facts (Schwab, Tucci, and Jolivette, 2013).

Research has supported for many years now that students' poor academic and behavioral functioning can be influenced by not only teacher behavior but classroom context as well (Sutherland, Lewis-Palmer, Stichter, and Morgan, 2008). Even with this overwhelming research support, some research is still implying and identifying that teachers of students with ED are still not utilizing evidence-based practices in the classroom (McKenna, Adamson, and Solis, 2019; McKenna and Ciullo, 2016; Wehby et al., 1998).

One major misconception when working with students with ED is that we must control the behaviors before they can learn anything (e.g., the concept of "readiness"). This has caused educators to look past the academic needs of students with ED and focus solely on behavior instead of both academics and behavior (Lane et al., 2002). As educators, we are not only trying to teach but tasked with managing those behaviors while teaching (Colvin, 2001). As teachers, we need to have a multitude of resources and interventions in our toolbox to be able to reach and teach students with ED. The rest of this chapter focuses solely on that. What interventions are proven to be most effective in the area of mathematics for students with ED?

MATHEMATICS STRATEGIES FOR STUDENTS WITH ED IN THE INCLUSIVE CLASSROOM

Self-Regulated Strategy Development (SRSD)

Self-Regulated Strategy Development model (SRSD) was developed by Graham and Harris (1999). A typical SRSD model has six stages: developing background knowledge on the topic of interest, discussing with others, modeling the strategy, memorizing the strategy, supporting your reason, and then performing the strategy independently (Harris and Graham, 1999). This strategy has been used to teach students with disabilities in the areas of reading, math, and writing. Specifically, we will be looking at Self-Regulated Strategy Development for Mathematics (SRSDMATH). This approach developed by

Ennis and Losinski (2018) looks not only how to help students with disabilities with word problems but adds in how to help students in the areas of math calculation, fractions, as well as long division.

The main area that SRSDMATH is focused on currently is fractions. They have developed three main areas: (1) adding and subtracting fractions, (2) reducing fractions, and (3) making improper fractions into mixed numbers. The first strategy is FILMS (Table 7.1).

Table 7.1 FILMS Strategy

F	Find the denominator
I	Identify the multiples
L	Locate the Least common multiple (LCM)
M	Multiply to make new fractions
S	Solve the problem

Source: http://www.srsdmath.com/assets/films-lessons-and-materials.pdf;
Ennis and Losinski (2018).

In the FILMS strategy, students are taught using the SRSD strategy how to add and subtract fractions based on steps that are modeled for the students, through the use of checklists that the students are taught how to use, guided practice, then independent practice so the student is finally performing the strategy on their own. Self-statements as well as a learning contract are also included so that students have buy-in for the strategy and learn to self-monitor.

The second strategy created by Ennis and Losinski (2018) was the strategy CUT (Table 7.2).

Table 7.2 CUTS Strategy

C	Calculate the factors
U	Underline the GCF
T	Time to divide numerator and denominator

Source: http://www.srsdmath.com/assets/cut-lessons-and-materials.pdf; Ennis and Losinski, 2018.

In the CUT strategy, students are taught using the SRSD strategy how to calculate the factors so that students can divide fractions by the greatest common factor. These steps are modeled for the students, through the use of checklists that the students are taught how to use, guided practice, then independent practice so the student is finally performing the strategy on their own. Self-statements as well as a learning contract are also included so that students have buy-in for the strategy and learn to self-monitor.

The final strategy that has been created by Ennis and Losinski for SRSDMATH is the EDIT strategy (Table 7.3).

In the EDIT strategy, students are taught using the SRSD strategy how to convert improper fractions into mixed numbers. These steps are modeled for

Table 7.3 EDIT Strategy

E	Examine whether the numerator is greater than the denominator
D	Divide the numerator by the denominator
I	Insert the quotient as a whole number
T	Turn the remainder into your new numerator

Source: http://www.srsdmath.com/lesson-plans.html; Ennis and Losinski, 2018.

the students, through the use of checklists that the students are taught how to use, guided practice, then independent practice so the student is finally performing the strategy on their own. Self-statements as well as a learning contract are also included so that students have buy-in for the strategy and learn to self-monitor.

Even though SRSD as a reading and writing strategy is well researched, the SRSDMATH is still in its beginning stages. SRSDMATH is continuously working on conducting studies to continue to build support for the use of SRSD in the area of mathematics.

Response Cards

Response cards are one instructional strategy that can be used to engage and encourage active student responding as well as increase the response rates of students with ED. This strategy has been used in a variety of regular education classrooms as well as many special education classrooms (George, 2010). Response cards have also been shown to increase academic achievement when used as an instructional strategy (Haydon, Borders, Embury, and Clarke, 2009).

Response cards can be defined as the use of cards, paper signs, or even whiteboards where students are able to display their responses to questions that have been asked by the teacher during a lesson or small group instruction time (George, 2010). Teachers are able to create response cards ahead of time with options already on the cards in order for the lesson to move more rapidly (i.e., multiple-choice answers, true/false answers, or even words that can be used to answer the questions). When teachers utilize the strategy of response cards, teachers are able to rapidly see in a whole group setting who needs more support/instruction on a topic (e.g., additional modeling, reteaching) and who is ready to move on (Schwab, Tucci, and Jolivette, 2013). Table 7.4 shows an example of a student response card. The student would either cut each of the letters out or could fold the card to display their answer. Another example of a response card would be that you could provide the students with colored paper. For example, handing the students a yellow card, which would be for "true" or "yes" answers, and then provide a different color such as blue, which would be for "false" or "no" answers. In math, a common theme used

Table 7.4   Response Card Example

A	B
C	D

for response cards would be the different mathematical properties. Students would hold up with property they felt was the correct answer to a teacher-guided statement or example.

During a mathematics lesson, you could use the student response cards for many reasons. Some of those reasons would be identifying students who understand the content and those that do not, beginning of your lesson to give students a preview of the lesson and to activate prior knowledge, the end of a lesson as either a review of content or to check for student understanding, and finally response cards can be utilized as a more engaging and fun activity such as a game that reviews content knowledge at the end of a unit lesson.

PALS

Math PALS is a whole class peer-tutoring program that can be used with students in grades K-6. PALS is considered a supplement to your current mathematics curriculum. We know as stated above that teachers now more than ever are faced with the difficulty of handling not only academics in their classroom but also behavior as well. What wasn't spoken to was the fact that teachers are also facing "academic diversity" in their classrooms (Fuchs, Fuchs, Yazdian, and Powell, 2002). With this strategy, teachers are better able to address the needs of all students, including those students with disabilities or the amount of varying skills in their classroom. Students are working on grade-level mathematics skills and are able to practice those mathematics skills with immediate feedback from peers. The mathematics problems are broken down into step-by-step directions for the student to work through. In a classroom, PALS is usually seen as having a higher-achieving student in the area of mathematics paired with a student who is struggling in the area of mathematics. The student who is performing at or above grade level in the area of mathematics can sometimes be referred to as a "coach" or "teacher" and the lower-achieving or performing student can be referred to as the "player" or the "student." The duration of intervention sessions is only thirty to thirty-five minutes and therefore can be used during centers. The teacher creates the pairs. However, pairs should be reassigned on a regular basis so that students have the opportunity to work with all different levels of students.

One study in particular noted that PALS increased both engagement as well as the amount of opportunities to respond for students (Kroeger and Kouche, 2006). Kroeger and Kouche experienced students of all ability levels talking through and working through mathematical problems together.

For the second through sixth grades, PALS Math incorporates two activities in each session. In the first activity, coaching, the stronger student who would be referred to as the coach models a sequence of questions to inspire the weaker student who we refer to as the player to internalize a self-talk approach for solving the part of the mathematics curriculum that the students are working on in class. As the coach models this sequence of questions, the player writes down any answers that they have or can ask follow-up questions to get to the correct answer. The coach uses a set of guiding and clarifying strategies to support the player's understanding and to correct errors. Then once both the students have completed their assigned roles, the curriculum has the students switch roles so that both students have the opportunity to serve as coach and tutee. This also helps so that the same student is not consistently the coach all of the time. After the first activity of coaching, the next approach is a five- to ten-minute practice activity that gives the students time to work on the skill just practiced during coaching, as well as simpler skills at that grade level (What Works Clearinghouse, 2012).

For PALS to be successful for students with ED, teachers must first make sure that they have explicitly trained the students on how to deliver the math PALS strategies. If students are not trained on the material, how to interact with others (e.g., how to give and respond to peer feedback), or are unfamiliar with the lesson, math PALS could potentially be an unsuccessful intervention.

Explicit Systematic Instruction

When students encountered explicit systematic instruction mathematics performance improved. In fact, the National Mathematics Advisory Panel recommends that students with learning problems be given explicit systematic instruction on a consistent basis. Explicit systematic instruction encompasses teaching a specific procedure, idea, or concept in a sequenced manner and one that is highly structured. This strategy has been shown to be effective across all grade levels as well as helping to support students with disabilities (The Iris Center, 2017).

A major piece of explicit systematic instruction involves three components. When using explicit mathematics instruction, the following components must be used in order for students with ED to make academic gains: teacher modeling of the skill, guided practice using the skill, and then academic feedback from the teacher. One of the major components is that teachers must give clear and detailed instructions to students on what skill or concept they will be working on. The teacher will then model the concept or idea through the use of talking out the steps of the problem or using a "think-aloud" strategy. This "think aloud" is used while the teacher is modeling the concept to show the exact steps the students will take to complete the skill or task. Following clear, explicit directions as well as modeling, the teacher will then provide time for guided practice followed by independent practice on the same skill that the teacher has just modeled. Then, the teacher will offer feedback and check for understanding of the skill. Making sure the student is able to generalize and maintain the skill is also a vital component of explicit systematic instruction as well.

Math vocabulary is another area that many students with ED struggle. According to Riccomini, Morano, and Hughes (2017), one way of teaching vocabulary to students in the inclusive classroom is through systematic instruction as well as adapting the curriculum as necessary. When given a word problem, students should begin to look at the problem with three questions in mind: (1) what do I already know about this problem, (2) what do I need to know from this problem such as key words, and (3) how do I solve this problem: What is it asking me to do (Riccomini, Morano, and Hughes, 2017)? For students with ED in the inclusive classroom to understand these questions, teachers must model think alouds for each step so that the student can see and hear how the teacher is walking through the math problem. Once the teacher models it, students are then given the opportunity to become the teacher through collaborative learning. One method suggested by Riccomini, Morano, and Hughes (2017) is to use a think-pair-share activity so students are then given the chance to do a think aloud of a different problem with peers. Once the students have experienced a few models and collaborated with peers, they are then ready to try a problem on their own. They then refer back to those three questions to begin to answer and discuss the vocabulary of the problem and what it is asking them to do.

In a multitude of studies, the use of direct teaching approaches such as explicit systematic instruction has been connected to improved academic gains for students with ED (Gunter, Coutinho, and Cade, 2002; Table 7.5).

Table 7.5   Example of Explicit Mathematics Instruction

Modeling	Guided Practice	Feedback
• Clear and concise words and modeling of what to do and how to do it. Very clear direction. • Think alouds: show students the process of what is going on in your head and how you work out the problem.	• Teacher models how to work through a problem that has been taught. • Step-by-step demonstrations and examples. • Prompts as needed. • Review of skills, both pre-teaching and review as needed.	• Feedback is ongoing. • Feedback is positive and given during the independent practice or right after. • Give corrective feedback as needed.

Source: Adapted from Doabler and Fien (2013).

Ongoing Assessment

For students with ED, it is critical that we are gauging our instruction through the use of assessment. Teachers should be using assessments on their students with ED often to assess not only where they are, but also what they have gained and what they are lacking in terms of mathematical skills. Teachers should be looking at grade-level content but going even further than that to look at the foundational skills students may be lacking as prerequisites (Mulcahy, Krezmien, and Maccini, 2014).

The initial screening should take place at the beginning of the school year to determine what students' strengths and weaknesses are in each area of grade-level content as well as the foundational skills piece. In many schools, we now refer to this as a screening process. This should not just be a beginning of the year multiple-choice test but should also include a diagnostic interview. The purpose of the interview is for the teacher to understand how the student comprehends and works through each math problem. This interview process may give teachers a window into how a student is thinking or approaching specific types of problems by having them talk through their solving process (Mulcahy, Krezmien, and Maccini, 2014).

Once you know where the skills of your students are, then you need to make sure that as you teach new skills and introduce new mathematical topics that you are using frequent progress monitoring to ensure that students are not only understating skills but maintaining the skills as well. Progress monitoring does not just have to be constant tests; you can check student progress through the use of exit tickets, response cards, or again, an informal interview type process. Once we have this data, then we can use this data to drive our instruction. Are we able to move on or does this student need additional modeling, reteaching, and review before moving on?

Resources for Assessment

Progress monitoring is not only a resource for your students with ED; it is made to be used with your entire classroom. Many resources can be found on progress monitoring. The purpose of progress-monitoring assessments is to ensure that your students are responding positively to your instruction (Center on Response to Intervention, 2019). At times, it can be overwhelming to find resources to begin progress monitoring with your students. Many new curriculums are offering progress-monitoring sheets with the curriculum. If you do not have access to a curriculum with progress monitoring, you can still access many free resources from places such as *Intervention Central* or *easy-CBM*. Your district may already have a plan in place for collecting this data though, and that is the place you want to start to determine the best method for your classroom. The Academic Progress Monitoring Tools chart from the National Center on Intensive Intervention is also an excellent resource on progress-monitoring tools, as it is continually updated as new research is conducted in this area.

CLOSING THOUGHTS

In conclusion, students with ED are able to perform well in the area of mathematics when teachers provide instruction that is research-based (e.g., the correct methods, tools, and strategies are provided by teachers). When we use strategies such as SRSD math, explicit systematic instruction, frequent screening and progress monitoring, PALS, and response cards, we are giving our students the tools they need to be successful. If all teachers of students with ED were using these strategies consistently, we would hope to see that the percentage of students with ED who are failing in the area of mathematics would improve, as well as improved mathematics performance in inclusive classrooms.

Chapter 8

Differentiation of Instruction for Students with Emotional Disturbance

When planning and delivering inclusive instruction, educators must consider the content and skills that students learn, the manner in which they will learn it, and how students will demonstrate mastery. Instructional content, methods, and materials must align with students' current levels of academic and behavioral performance so that students have an opportunity to be successful (Tomlinson, 2004). Furthermore, student interests and the mode of learning are additional factors to consider when differentiating instruction. Carefully planned, sequenced, and delivered academic instruction that integrates positive behavior supports is critical to the success of students who receive special education services who are educated in general education classrooms. This proves particularly true for students with Emotional Disturbance (ED), as they may engage in challenging behaviors that disrupt instruction and impede skill and content acquisition (Mitchell, Kern, and Conroy, 2019). Since the majority of students with ED spend a significant amount of time during the school day in general education classrooms (U.S. Department of Education, 2018), it is critical that educators assigned to teach in these settings are able to differentiate instruction to maximize the opportunity to learn.

This balance between instructional and student factors is a dance between the teacher in the classroom and the student. The teacher is an expert in content and curriculum as well as student characteristics, and students should be able to look to that adult to provide necessary guidance and support. In regards to students with ED whose appropriate least restrictive environment (LRE) is general education, students should be able to count on their teachers to provide instruction that is sufficiently adapted and supported so that they can make meaningful progress toward their Individualized Education Program goals and develop increasing levels of competency in the grade-level curriculum. However, it is a concern when students spend significant amounts of time taking a break from the academic and/or social demands of instruction, engaging in challenging behavior, or sitting passively in the classroom. These observable behaviors may indicate inadequate differentiation of instruction, or it may indicate that the student's learning, behavioral, and social needs cannot be addressed through general education instruction even with appropriate differentiation. The idea is for teachers to do the best they can, within the natural limits of the general education classroom; monitor student response to their efforts through the collection of progress monitoring data and student work samples; adjust instruction as needed; and continue to collect data on student response to instruction, documenting the instructional methods that are used, the adjustments that are made, and the degree to which students profit from methods and adjustments.

In addition, students need to be able to advocate for ways in which they would like to learn and explore content (e.g., provide opportunities for students to perform self-determined behaviors). In this manner students are reaching out to explore content and curriculum through the guidance, support, and structure of a trained professional: the teacher. The relationship between teacher and student is similar to that of a coach and players, where a teacher helps to develop students to their full potential, highlighting their strengths and pushing them to the limit of their abilities in a safe environment. In fact, a positive relationship between teacher and student may be particularly critical to academic performance (McKenna, Shin, Solis, Mize, and Pfannenstiel, 2019; Van Loan and Garwood, 2019).

When providing inclusive instruction to students with ED, it is critical that this interchange is seamless and is demonstrated across all potential barriers to learning. By creating a system where teachers are able to reach students where they are at and move them forward, teachers are creating an environment where students feel safe taking risk in their learning, are excited about learning, and are accountable for their progress. When we think of inclusive classrooms, this format is the utopian prototype. Effective inclusive classrooms with differentiated instruction lead to all student's growing in their academic abilities and as a consistent tool for increasing student abilities (Ernest, Thompson, Heckaman, Hull, and Yates, 2011). The construct of differentiated instruction is grounded in cognitive psychology and student achievement (McTighe and Brown, 2005). It is then furthered by principles which support the knowledge and skills in the different content areas, methods for responding to students and their unique characteristics, integrating assessment and instruction, and ongoing monitoring and adjustment of content, methods, and materials (Tomlinson, 1999). However, differentiated classrooms are not just for special education students in special education classrooms. The use of inclusive classrooms can be just as effective if they are designed correctly.

In a study conducted by Kilanowski-Press, Foote, and Rinaldo (2010) special education teachers assigned to general education classrooms were surveyed on their use of inclusive practices. Two models of practice were most commonly used by this sample of special education teachers: co-teaching and the use of volunteers. These two models demonstrate one thing in common; for inclusive settings to be effective and to create this perfect relationship between teacher and student (e.g., for the classroom to be truly "inclusive"), there needs to be more "teachers" to go around and provide support. When specific practices were identified, there was significant variance across individual classrooms. This highlights that there may not be a one-size-fits-all approach to an inclusive classroom. In fact, a recent survey study of the classroom-based practices used by teachers to provide inclusive instruction and support to students with ED noted variability in teachers' use of recommended practices (McKenna, Newton, and Bergman, 2019). This variability in use of instructional practices and supports makes sense, since every student learns differently and will have different strengths which can interchange with each teacher's instructional style and their own unique strengths. However, in our own research (McKenna, Newton, and Bergman, 2019b), special education teachers who provided inclusive instruction and/or support to students with ED reported statistically significant greater knowledge of instructional practices (incorporating student choice into instruction, task sequencing), reinforcement strategies (using a variety of reinforcers, behavior-specific praise, differential reinforcement, token economies, preference assessment), individualized behavioral supports (use of daily behavioral goals, daily report cards, behavior contracts, zones of regulation, feelings charts), and assessment methods (structural analysis, behavior progress monitoring) compared to general education teachers who served this student population. Thus, the presence of a special education teacher may be critical to the potential success of inclusive instruction for students with ED, as it may be unreasonable to expect a general education teacher to have expertise in all of these areas in addition to content area expertise. It also may be incredibly challenging for at least some general education teachers to provide specialized supports and instructional methods while simultaneously meeting the needs of students who do not have disabilities. Thus, providing teachers professional development that targets student needs, coaching to assist with the application of instructed skills to their students, and an appropriate level of resources is critical to differentiation of instruction.

FRAMEWORK FOR DIFFERENTIATION

One framework for differentiation is based off of the REACH mnemonic for supporting a wide variety of students (Rock, Gregg, Ellis, and Gabel, 2008).

Since specific practices that are effective for differentiation vary greatly, understanding these core principles of differentiation can help to support inclusive environments and their effectiveness. The acronym of REACH (see Table 8.1) stands for (R) Reflect on will and skill, (E) Evaluate the curriculum, (A) Analyze the learners, (C) Craft research-based lessons, and (H) Hone in on the data. This strategy has been shown effective across many types of learners and focuses specifically on five components of classroom instruction: teacher, content, learner, instruction, and assessment. As a result, this framework may be helpful when planning and delivering inclusive instruction to students with ED.

When using this strategy in the classroom you must think about yourself as the teacher. You are in fact the decision maker for the classroom and can set the tone and guide students to higher levels of proficiency. It is important to think about each of your students individually and focus on how to capitalize on their strengths. Pairing the teacher in the classroom with a student to directly think about their individualized learning goals with the (R) reflect permits a more systematic focus on will and skill. Will refers specifically to the inclusive classroom teachers' will to reflect on their own classroom practices and on their own beliefs (e.g., race, gender, culture) and behaviors (e.g., positive interactions, opportunities to respond, use of research-based instructional practices) to identify needs for professional development and growth. Skill refers to a teacher's own knowledge about research-based practices and best teaching methodologies and instructional tools. We highlight that there are many other initiatives and practices which take place within the context of the classroom. It is important to think about all of these other practices and determine how to seamlessly integrate differentiation into your classroom. What is going to be the amount of time for students to work toward a goal in your classroom, and if they need extra support or intervention how will this be provided? What are going to be reasonable but ambitious and meaningful goals for your students with ED?

Next, we much consider the content. In many inclusive classrooms this is the general education curriculum and grade-level standards. When we combine this component with (E) evaluate the curriculum, we see that a deep knowledge of the curriculum is essential. We must know what the curriculum looks like in previous grades as to differentiate missed skills (e.g., bundling in opportunities to develop these skills into instruction) but also what the expectations are of the next grade level knowing that students will end

Table 8.1   REACH Graphic Organizer for Differentiating Instruction

(R) Reflect on Will and Skill	(E) Evaluate the Curriculum	(A) Analyze the Learners	(C) Craft Research-Based Lessons	(H) Hone in on the Data

instruction with the critical concepts and skills to be successful in the future. In fact, it may be important to understand a baseline of where your students are at or what knowledge and information they know and have retained, as some students may not fully understand concepts, some may have forgotten, and some may have mastered them. Knowing students' current performance levels gives us insight into how to help them reach the curriculum (e.g., this is where they are at, this is where we need to go, and this is how we can do it).

We must also consider the learner itself, (A) analyze the learners. We need to think about each student's experiences and what background experience they have to access the topic, and what background knowledge may still need to be given. We also need to consider each individual students learning preferences and the conditions that make them feel comfortable and enjoy accessing knowledge and demonstrating their understanding. Understanding specific student abilities and preferences allows you to be more systematic when considering the implementation of peer instructional strategies, group-based projects, and even considering engagement and format for instructional presentation. These considerations are particularly critical for students with ED, because they may engage in off-task or disruptive behavior in response to academic instruction or demands that they perceive as averse. One way to analyze learner characteristics and think about specific considerations within the classroom is to consider the use of accommodations to help students meet the instructional barriers and provide a differential boost to access curriculum. However, please note that many students with ED will need more than instructional and assessment accommodations, such as specialized instruction and supports. It should also be noted that educators need to assess the effectiveness of accommodations, rather than assuming that they are effective. The Center for Adolescent Research in schools created a guide to help address these issues: https://pbismissouri.org/wp-content/uploads/2019/09/CARS_G uide_2019.pdf.

In the link you will see a systematic format for evaluating a student with disabilities needs and selecting an accommodation which will help students to better access content within their general education classroom.

After understanding the learner and their specific needs, it is easier to focus on the instruction itself and its format: (C) craft research-based lessons. In a typical inclusive classroom there would be remediation, enrichment, and instruction, and as classroom teachers we must balance all of these students in a cohesive classroom structure. We must address differing abilities and think about what research-based practices we want to use to teach content to each group. We need to think about how we are using methods to address each learner and what evidence we have that our instructional format has proved effective. Technology and other assistive technology resources can be effective to help provide evidence-based learning approach to students of multiple abilities since the technology can help assist in how content is presented and even the pace at which it is taught. An example may be an electronic reading program that has text that covers the same topic but can be presented at a variety of reading levels. The text can be differentiated so that it is matched to that student's reading performance level.

When considering the inclusive classroom and these instructional approaches it is important to take a step back and consider the environment as whole. How can you shape the environmental features in the room (e.g., student desk arrangements) to encourage each individual student's needs? This may mean that the environment in the classroom changes frequently to meet the curricular format but also the individual student needs to make the environment encourage learning. In regards to research-based instructional methods, students with ED are likely to benefit from instruction that is explicit (e.g., includes expert teaching modeling), provides opportunities for active engagement (e.g., opportunities to actively respond, opportunities to correctly respond to questions), provides opportunities to receive feedback, incorporates student interests, and includes contingencies for reinforcing effort, task completion, and self-regulation (McKenna, Adamson, and Solis, 2019).

Finally, assessment is a critical component for understanding how students are progressing and if any instructional changes need to be made, or (H) hone in on the data. Understanding that the rate of learning may be different for students, or that some students may need presentation of materials multiple times, allows for teachers in inclusive environments to better access their students understanding. Learning and abilities in a classroom are constantly changing, and a student's abilities may have them being shifted throughout content areas into the instructional grouping which is going to support their individualized needs. Keeping record of where students are at but also being flexible to in your consideration to ensure that students are getting exactly what they need, when they need it, will allow more students to access content and be able to achieve. Table 8.2 provides a brief example of using this framework.

When providing instruction, general education teachers may rely on whole group instruction (e.g., teaching the entire class the same content at the same time) and independent practice (e.g., students working on their own at their desks or at a table). Teachers may rely on these practices because they are easier for them to manage: when the entire class is doing relatively the same thing, teachers may believe that this is an effective way to prevent the occurrence of challenging behaviors or to limit the number of challenging behaviors they have to manage. This can occur even when general education instruction is co-taught, such as when co-taught classes rely on the one teach-one assist method of co-teaching (e.g., general education teacher leads the class in instruction and the special education teacher uses active supervision to identify students who are in need of one-to-one support). However,

Table 8.2   Sample REACH Graphic Organizer for Differentiating Instruction for an Individual Student

(R) Reflect on Will and Skill	(E) Evaluate the Curriculum	(A) Analyze the Learners	(C) Craft Research-Based Lessons	(H) Hone in on the Data
Teacher understands phonemic instruction and the use of these tools to support student understanding through concrete practice.	Curriculum is focused on using direct instruction and practice finding each sound and blend to create words. Key features: Partner work Matching Worksheets Computer game for word patterns	Tomas prefers working in partners and groups. He has some basic understanding of CVC words but struggles with complex patterns.	Lessons will be taught with repeated practice and with skills built upon each other. Peer Assisted Learning Strategies will be utilized for assignments.	Baseline assessment of CVC words: 9/10 CCVC words: 1/10 CVCC words: 1/10

it is impossible to differentiate instruction effectively when teachers rely on whole group instruction and independent practice. When differentiating instruction, teachers must use different instructional formats and grouping methods.

General education teachers are encouraged to incorporate small group instruction into their differentiated lessons. Although challenging, general education teachers can provide small group instruction in the absence of a co-teacher. A typical lesson starts off with some form of whole group instruction. To make this instruction as effective as possible, teachers should incorporate explicit instructional methods (modeling/demonstrations, with clear verbal explanations). Explicit instruction is critical to the success of students with learning difficulties such as students with ED. However, even when whole group instruction is explicit, teachers should consider this merely a "presentation" of information, which may be unclear to students with learning difficulties such as students with ED. The presentation may be unclear due to receptive language difficulties, difficulties sustaining focus and attention on what is salient in the environment (e.g., the instruction), task avoidant behaviors, and gaps in prerequisite skills and knowledge. Instead of transitioning the class into independent practice, teachers can plan to have students work with preselected partners or groups while she/he works with a small group of students. This small group of students can consist of students with ED and other students (both general education and special education) who have learning difficulties. Teachers can also include higher-performing students in small group instruction so that students with learning difficulties do not feel like they are being singled out in a negative way. During small group instruction, the teacher can provide additional explicit instruction that re-teaches what was presented during whole group instruction and explicitly teach prerequisite skills that students may be lagging in. The teacher can also respond to student questions and provide them support as needed. Small group instruction also serves as an opportunity for teachers to provide immediate explicit feedback to students as they complete an academic task. After receiving small group instruction, students can join the remainder of the class in partner or small group work.

Although this instructional sequence does complicate classroom management, it can be accomplished. All students need to be taught the expectations and procedures associated with partner and small group work (e.g., teach the expectations and procedures using the same methods that are used to teach academics: teacher modeling, guided practice, independent practice). Students must also be provided feedback on their ability to meet these expectations and follow these procedures, as well as to receive consistent reinforcement when they comply. Teachers can support these efforts by linking this to a classwide or school-wide expectation to "Be Responsible."

CLOSING THOUGHTS

This mnemonic and your understanding of the research base of instructional practices for diverse learners can be utilized to create a framework for supporting students with ED in your inclusive classroom. Combining supports with an environment conducive to learning creates a classroom where students are more likely to achieve. Using assessment to guide this process creates a road map where teachers can see where they are starting, where they plan to go, and how they are going to get there. These principles should be the foundation of lesson planning and unit structures. There should be consistency across supports, all aspects of instruction, and classroom management to help each student be able to access their fullest potential.

Chapter 9

Using Technology to Support Inclusive Instruction

Placement of students with disabilities in a general education classroom does not guarantee that students will sufficiently benefit from instruction and services provided in this setting (see Kauffman and Badar, 2016; Solis, Vaughn, Swanson, and McCulley, 2012). The appropriateness of special education services is determined by the degree to which students actually benefit (e.g., free appropriate public education) and not by the location in which they receive instruction and support (e.g., least restrictive environment (LRE); McKenna and Brigham, 2019). This proves particularly true for students who receive special education services for emotional disturbance (ED). Students with ED may perform challenging behaviors that can adversely affect skill development and their ability to access instruction. As a result, students with ED may have underdeveloped prerequisite skills that are necessary to sufficiently benefit from general education instruction. When planning inclusive instruction for students with ED, teachers need to identify and consider the specific skills that students must have some degree of proficiency in to successfully complete assigned tasks. When prerequisite skill deficits are identified, teachers have to consider which to explicitly teach and which skill deficits to address through the use of modifications and accommodations (see Bryant, Bryant, and Smith, 2016). To address gaps between the skills necessary to complete the task and student current levels of performance, teachers and related service providers should use a variety of strategies and supports to support learning and to prevent the occurrence of problem behaviors due to excessive or unsupported task demands.

In this chapter, we discuss how assistive technology (AT) can be used as an antecedent support (e.g., a proactive support, a way to adapt or adjust instruction) to promote task engagement and student learning. Before moving forward with this discussion, we would like to emphasize that students with

ED who are educated in general education classrooms are likely to require intensive behavioral and/or academic intervention to sufficiently profit from school (see Maggin, Wehby, Farmer, and Brooks, 2016; McKenna, Shin, Solis, Mize, and Pfannenstiel, 2019). AT is presented as a tool that should be considered as part of a comprehensive support plan that promotes the development of academic and behavioral skills and increasing levels of student independence.

ROLE OF AT IN SPECIAL EDUCATION

AT are devices and services that permit students with disabilities to be more independent (Dell, Newton, and Petroff, 2016). When developing a student's Individualized Education Program (IEP), teams determine if the student would benefit from the use of AT as an accommodation (e.g., changes to how a student learns) or a modification (e.g., changes to what a student learns or what a student is taught). This process involves the assessment of potential AT needs, selection of appropriate devices and services, and selection of contingencies for assessing their effectiveness (Bausch, Ault, and Hasselbring, 2015). In fact, an assessment of AT needs is best performed by staff with specific experience and expertise in AT assessment and experience and expertise with students with ED. According to the Individuals with Education Improvement Act (2004), an AT device is "any item, piece of equipment or product system whether acquired commercially off the shelf, modified, or customized that is used to increase, maintain, or improve the functional capabilities of a child with a disability" (34 C.F.R. § 300.5). An AT service is "any service that directly assists an individual with a disability in the selection, acquisition, or use of an assistive technology device" (29 USC 3002 (5)). Thus, an AT assessment performed by a qualified professional is considered an AT service. Devices on their own are insufficient, as services must be provided in concert with devices to ensure continued student access and student ability to use devices in an effective and efficient manner. In essence, devices must be appropriately maintained and students must be provided explicit instruction in their proper use. However, school teams may fail to consider the potential benefits of AT for students with ED, due to an emphasis on student behavior over learning. School teams may also fail to consider connections between access to effective instruction and supports that make instruction more accessible and student performance of challenging behavior. When students have their needs met, they are more likely to engage in positive behavior and to make academic progress.

Bryant, Bryant, and Smith (2016) provide a framework for adapting instruction for students with disabilities. When using this framework (e.g., ADAPT; Bryant et al., 2016) to consider why and how to differentiate instruction for students with disabilities, teachers can consider how AT can be used to address a student's learning difficulties. Table 9.1 is a planning tool based on an adaptation of this framework by Bryant and colleagues (2016). Teachers first consider the nature of the academic task that will be assigned. Specifically, teachers consider the types of tasks and skills students must perform with a degree of accuracy and fluency to successfully complete the assignment. The teacher then considers a student's current performance levels and skills to identify potential gaps between specific task demands and student competencies. Next, the teacher considers potential ways that AT can be used to address these potential gaps. However, it should be noted that AT is just one potential method for adapting instruction for students with ED that should be considered by teachers. For example, students with ED may also benefit from differentiated content, differentiated work products, and opportunities to participate in one-to-one, small-group, and peer-mediated instruction (McKenna, Newton, and Bergman, 2019).

Table 9.1 Framework for Determining Instructional Adaptations Including Assistive Technology

A	D	A	P	T
Ask what students must do to complete the assigned task.	Determine what prerequisite skills and knowledge students must have to be successful with the task.	Analyze/ consider gaps between student skills and knowledge and the skills and knowledge required by the task. Consider student performance on similar tasks.	Propose adaptations to instructional methods, content, materials, and behavioral supports to address each identified gap. Consider the use of different types of AT to address these gaps. Consider the appropriateness of using AT to promote student learning and success.	Provide instruction using the selected adaptations. Test student response to selected adaptations including AT. Analyze work products. Discuss work products with students to identify difficulties to address.

Source: Adapted from Bryant, Bryant, and Smith (2016).

Examples of AT

AT can be used to support student access and performance on a variety of academic tasks that students frequently are required to complete in general education classrooms. Adapting general education instruction (e.g., providing appropriate accommodations and modifications, integration of positive behavior supports with academic instruction) is important to ameliorate the adverse effects of a student's disability or skill deficits. In the following section, we describe examples of AT supports that teachers can employ with students with ED. The following AT are described: electronic text and text to speech, speech to text, word processors with spell-check, word prediction, and computer-based graphic organizers.

Digital text and text to speech. Digital text is an electronic version of a written text. Digital text can be used in a variety of ways. Digital text can be selected or adjusted so that it aligns with a student's independent reading level, thus making it more accessible to students. Carefully accounting for text difficulty is important for students with ED, as students can engage in challenging behaviors in response to academic tasks that are too difficult (perceived or actual difficulty; McKenna, Adamson, and Solis, 2019). Teachers can also highlight key parts of text (e.g., main idea) within a passage to focus student attention on the most salient or important information. This feature can be used to build a degree of success into a reading task: for example, instead of having to read through a longer selection of text to make an inference or to identify text evidence, students can read a shorter selection of text that has the necessary information. Key vocabulary can also be highlighted to support explicit vocabulary instruction that occurs during reading (e.g., the highlighting draws the student's attention to a previously taught vocabulary word used in context, which could then initiate peer-to-peer discussion, student-to-teacher discussion, or some form of written response).

Digital text can be used along with text to speech programs. Text to speech programs convert digital text into audio/sound so that students can listen to content rather than read it. Text to speech may be particularly helpful for students who experience difficulties with decoding (e.g., using knowledge of letter-sound relationships to read/sound out words), reading fluency, and reading comprehension difficulties or students who are resistant readers (Schmitt, McCallum, Hale, Obeldobel, and Dingus, 2009; Wood, Moxley, Tighe, and Wagner, 2018). In fact, research has shown that text to speech can improve the comprehension of students with ED, with the text to speech condition being more effective than an independent silent reading condition (Schmitt et al., 2009; please note: we do not recommend using independent silent reading with students with ED because it may limit student access to teacher directed instruction and provides a low level of student accountability;

see Bettini et al., (2020) and McKenna et al., [2019]). Thus text to speech technology could potentially be used to support comprehension of narrative and content area text. Some text to speech programs also highlight individual words and/or sentences as they are read aloud by the computer. However, students may need to use different applications or programs for different text formats (e.g., Word documents, web pages, pdf documents). School teams are also cautioned about relying on text to speech programs in the absence of reading instruction and intervention with students with ED who are also struggling readers. Students with lagging skills need more instruction that targets them, not less. Students with ED who are struggling readers should also be provided intensive reading intervention that addresses their specific reading difficulties (e.g., phonological awareness, decoding, fluency, vocabulary, comprehension; Garwood, Ciullo, and Brunsting, 2017; McKenna, Kim, Shin, and Pfannenstiel, 2017).

Students with ED can also use text to speech when revising and editing their writing with a word processing program. For example, when using the text to speech function in Word, students can listen to the audio of their writing to check to see if some parts are unclear or if parts need additional elaboration and/or explanation. However, students with ED require explicit instruction in methods for revising and editing their writing in order to maximize the potential effectiveness of this strategy, including the use of revising and editing checklists. When using text to speech software, teachers may find it beneficial to give students a choice between reading the text and listening to it/following along. Planning instruction so that students with ED have opportunities to make choices is considered a generally effective practice for improving student behavior and task engagement (Landrum and Sweigart, 2014; McKenna, Adamson, and Solis, 2019).

Speech to text. Students with ED may experience a variety of difficulties when writing (Gage, Wilson, MacSuga-Gage, 2014), which is critical to success in general education classrooms. Speech to text programs convert a student's spoken statements into written text. Students with ED will need explicit instruction (e.g., modeling, guided practice, independent practice upon demonstrating competency during guided practice) and support on how to use speech to text during each phase of the writing process (e.g., planning, drafting, revising). This type of instruction would be considered an AT service. Speech to text programs have the potential to improve student motivation to write because students may experience the program as novel. Speech to text can also help with any fine motor difficulties that students may experience, or serve as a scaffold for students who are not proficient in keyboarding.

Word processors with spell-check. Word processors with spell-check can be used to address motor difficulties that adversely affect handwriting or to make writing activities more novel or interesting for students with ED.

However, to maximize the potential benefits, students need opportunities to develop keyboarding skills so they can type with a degree of accuracy and fluency. When students with ED are not proficient at typing, speech to text programs can be used along with word processors and spell-check to promote writing fluency.

Word prediction. Word prediction software can be used along with word processors and spell-check to improve writing fluency, spelling, and vocabulary use. As students are typing, word prediction programs predict what word the student intends to use next, using information such as a word's spelling and sentence syntax to make a prediction. Some word prediction programs also permit teachers to create or add to a dictionary of vocabulary terms. This is particularly helpful when students are required to use specific concepts and terms in their writing, such as when writing in content area classes. Prior to instruction, teachers can add the target vocabulary words and their student-friendly definition.

Computer-based graphic organizers. Students with ED can use computer-based graphic organizers to plan their writing products. Computer-based graphic organizers are an effective tool for improving writing performance and content area knowledge (Ciullo and Reutebuch, 2013). However, it is important that students with ED are provided explicit instruction (e.g., teacher modeling) and guided practice (e.g., practice with teacher support) in how to complete computer-based graphic organizers and use them to produce a writing product (Ciullo and Reutebuch, 2013). Without this instruction and support, computer-based graphic organizers are likely to be used ineffectively and/or lead to the performance of challenging behavior. Table 9.2 provides an overview of some commercially available and free examples of AT. In the following section, we make recommendations for planning and implementing AT with students with ED.

CONSIDERATIONS FOR PLANNING AND USE

1. It is important for teachers and students to know how to use the tools and their different features. Prior to using AT with students with ED, teachers should practice using the specific program or application with the specific tasks that students will complete (e.g., go through the process that you intend the student to go through and provide yourself sufficient practice so that you can teach the process to the student). Teachers must be fluent in the use of AT so that they can focus their efforts on teaching and supporting students with ED instead of troubleshooting or focusing on their own skill development. Student skill fluency is

Table 9.2 Assistive Technology Resources

Resource	URL	Description
Read&Write	https://chrome.google.com/webstore/detail/rea dwrite-for-google-chro/inoeonmfapjbbkmda foankkfajkcphgd?hl=en-US	An extension for Google Chrome; provides text to speech, speech to text, vocabulary support, and word prediction; summarizes text to improve readability; compatible with Google Docs formats.
Read and Write Gold	https://www.texthelp.com/en-us/products/re ad-write/	Screen reader; compatible with Firefox and Chrome; provides text to speech, speech to text, and various writing supports.
Natural Reader	https://www.naturalreaders.com/	Converts text files and documents to MP3 files.
Bookshare	https://www.bookshare.org/cms/	Extensive online library of digital texts.
Read Works	https://www.readworks.org/	Online library of digital texts; online literacy performance tasks and assessments.
Simple Mind Plus	https://simplemind.eu/	Program for making mind maps to brainstorm and organize ideas/thoughts.
Inspiration	http://www.inspiration.com/	Computer-based graphic organizers, concept maps, mind maps, and outlines.
Kidspiration	http://www.inspiration.com/Kidspiration	A version of Inspiration for students in grades K-5.
ReadWriteThink	http://www.readwritethink.org/	An online library of graphic organizers and structured writing tasks.

developed through AT services and continued practice. Students require direct and explicit instruction on all aspects of using the tool, from start to finish, to maximize the tool's potential effectiveness and minimize potential behavioral difficulties. Explicit, systematic instruction in the use of AT to complete specific tasks may be particularly important for students with ED, who may experience heightened stress and/or anxiety when having academic difficulties or when they experience challenges using new or unfamiliar tools such as AT. Teachers may find it helpful to perform a task analysis of the assigned task (e.g., create a list of the sequential steps that must be followed to successfully complete the task) and use this information to create a task checklist. Teachers can demonstrate how to complete each step in the checklist and check off each step as it is completed. Teachers can then provide students with ED guided practice as they attempt to use the checklist to complete the assigned task that was just modeled.

2. It is important for teachers to know in advance when certain AT applications or features are incompatible with the format that is used. The idea is to avoid potential "glitches" when using technology, which could potentially lead to student anxiety and/or stress. For example, at the time of this writing, speech text in Read&Write (Texthelp Ltd, 2020) is not compatible with some programs that are used to create computer graphic organizers in Google Docs. Teachers can identify compatibility issues that need to be addressed by first using the selected applications to complete the activities that will be assigned on their own before assigning them to students with ED. In sum, become fluent in their use and the different ways they can be applied and identify potential barriers before using them during instruction.

3. Teachers should talk with students with ED regarding the academic and behavioral difficulties they are experiencing and discuss how specific AT may be beneficial. Present different acceptable and potentially effective AT options to students with ED and involve them in the process of selecting what AT to use and in what instructional situations or performance tasks. This can help students with ED take some ownership/responsibility and can help improve overall motivation.

4. Teachers should have ongoing conversations with students with ED regarding their experiences using AT. Teachers should provide additional explicit instruction as an AT service and make informed adjustments to how AT is used, as well as the AT that are selected based on student perceptions and performance. Skills related to the proper use of AT should be explicitly retaught when skill deficits are identified. As with the instruction of any skill, teacher may find it advantageous to

reinforce student efforts (e.g., behavior-specific praise, token economies) to use AT appropriately as well as their successes.

5. Teachers should keep parents/guardians informed of what AT their children are using and how they are using it. Teachers should encourage parents/guardians to permit their child to use AT at home when it is appropriate. Teachers should also encourage parents to practice using the AT that their children use so that they can become more familiar with it and provide support at home when necessary. To assist parents/ guardians in their efforts to support the use of AT at home, teachers should provide parents/guardians demonstrations on how to use AT and how their child can use it to complete specific academic tasks. Since time is often limited and can often be an issue, teachers could make video recordings as they model use of AT and share these videos with parents/guardians. Teachers can also provide parents/guardians links to online resources on the use of AT.

6. When selecting AT with students, consider the demands of commonly assigned academic tasks, the prerequisite skills and competencies necessary to successfully complete them, and the student's current level of performance in these skills and competencies. Teachers should then consider how AT can be used as an accommodation or modification to address gaps between student performance and necessary performance. The ADAPT framework by Bryant et al. (2016) serves as a great planning tool for selecting AT, and for structuring discussions with students with ED about the potential benefits of AT.

7. When students display a pattern of challenging behavior when required to complete specific academic tasks, teachers should consider the overall task demands as well as the individual tasks that must be performed to complete the assigned task. Overall task demands as well as the steps taken to complete the task may be triggering to students with ED due to perceived or real skill deficits or a lack of motivation. Tasks or aspects of tasks that may be challenging and perhaps triggering to students with ED may include, but are not limited to, reading for understanding, reading large amounts of text at one time, spelling, handwriting, planning a writing product, revising a writing product, and identifying text evidence to support conclusions or contentions. Maintaining attention and work productivity may also be triggering for students with ED. Teachers should consider potential ways that AT can be used to address behavioral difficulties, as well as effective ways to integrate positive behavior supports such as earned breaks and reinforcement of student effort and accomplishment (e.g., behavior-specific praise, token economies).

8. Connectivity to the internet may adversely affect the ability to use some AT devices. It is important for teachers to develop procedures for addressing connectivity issues should they occur and for using other options that do not rely on an internet connection in the event these issues cannot be quickly addressed. Teachers are encouraged to discuss with their district's technology experts about how they intend to use AT during instruction and to be proactive in identifying potential issues that they can help resolve.

FINAL THOUGHTS

In this chapter, we discussed how AT can be used as an proactive, antecedent support to promote engagement and student learning. It is critical to consider AT as a part of comprehensive support plans for students and to consider how the use of AT can assist with student independence and the continued development of academic and behavioral skills.

Chapter 10

Daily Progress Reports and Behavioral Contracts to Support Inclusive Education

Even the most experienced teachers and the most highly structured classrooms have students that need an additional layer of support. This additional layer of support may be individualized to address specific needs and involve a consistent focus on determining why challenging behavior is occurring and how to limit or prevent its occurrence. We create classroom strategies to help guide these students toward success. We do this with a consideration about the function of the student's behavior (e.g., the reasons why the behavior occurs, the needs that the behavior meets). However, even when we have strong systems in place we need additional tools that are more focused on the individual including higher rates of reinforcement specifically targeted and meeting the individual's needs. In this chapter we will discuss interventions that can be used to specifically support these high-need students within inclusive settings.

Research continues to show an ongoing relationship between academic failure and problem behavior (Simonsen, et al., 2015). It is not uncommon for students to be excluded from inclusive settings when challenging behavior interrupts their ability to function in the classroom, or for schools to rely on strategies that result in students receiving limited opportunities to develop academic skills and to interact with their non-disabled peers (Brigham, Ahn, Soon, and McKenna, 2016). In fact, not all students who receive special education services for emotional disturbance (ED) are best served in general education classrooms, due to insufficient prerequisite skills and knowledge, the nature of the academic and social demands in this setting, and the limits to which instruction and supports can be sufficiently specialized and consistently implemented for students to be successful in general education classrooms (see Kauffman and Badar, 2014). However, decisions related to a change of placement should not be considered until school-teams have considered all reasonable options and approaches. When universal methods (e.g., maximize structure and predictability, post teach, review, monitor, and reinforce expectations, active supervision, explicit feedback, opportunities to respond, behavior-specific praise, precorrection; see Simonsen, Fairbanks, Briesch, Myers, and Sugai, 2008) of support prove insufficient for preventing the occurrence of challenging behaviors and for promoting positive engagement with the curriculum and peers, additional supports should be used to focus on specific behaviors that are hindering success. In this chapter we will examine some individualized supports which focus on the use of daily progress reports (DPR), a comprehensive system for using DPR, and behavior contracts.

PRINCIPLES OF SUPPORT

Understanding the complexities of student needs requires us to examine our classroom environment and even our own instructional behavior more critically. We are members of the environment and have the capability to impede or develop a student's power to learn and act appropriately in the classroom (e.g., we can't control students, but we can create environments that make it more likely that they will be successful). A clear understanding of how to target specific behaviors that are incompatible with success makes our instruction more pointed and targeted on the task at hand. We must have specific targets for our student, have a shared understanding of an appropriate level of performance, have an accurate way to capture this progress, and a system for evaluating the environmental components that may help or hinder success. Let's break down each of these pieces and think about what this looks like and what impact each piece has on student performance.

First is a specific target behavior for our student. Understanding the function of behavior and competing pathways is critical for identifying replacement behaviors (e.g., behaviors that students can perform that are prosocial and meet the same need as the challenging behavior). However, just demonstrating the replacement behavior in some instances or school contexts is insufficient. A replacement behavior is the behavior which serves the same purpose for a student (i.e., attention, avoidance, etc.) but is socially acceptable for the classroom environment. For students with ED to be successful in inclusive environments, they need to demonstrate replacement behaviors at a level of consistency that is somewhat comparable with their peers within that environment. Thinking about replacement behaviors is step one in thinking about how to provide behavioral support. When doing this, you will want to determine what behaviors you would like the student to perform more frequently in the educational environment.

Many times when we think about demonstration of replacement behaviors, we may think that the goal should be 100 percent or to demonstrate these behaviors at all times. In fact, if we consider our own behavior, we are unlikely to perform a given positive behavior 100 percent of the time, no matter our level of experience, the training we have received, and how thoughtful and conscientious we are. We are all fallible to some degree. If we sit back and think about the performance of even the highest-achieving students in a classroom, they do not typically demonstrate their positive behaviors all of the time. A high-achieving student may be so excited about an answer that they shout it out. This behavior, if done too frequently, is a challenging behavior for the classroom environment. However, in most cases, this high-achieving student would be reminded to "remember to raise your hand" or "be sure you give everyone a chance to answer" as a response and then instruction is continued. Perhaps the teacher may even ignore the shout-out and recognize the correct response, since this is a student who is high achieving and not a student who performs challenging behavior in the classroom. Therefore, it is more common to consider a student proficient with a behavior if it is seen as a rate similar to that of their peers (e.g., use peer performance as a possible end goal or something to strive for over time for students who receive special education services for ED). Another way to determine performance criteria is to actually watch peers and get observable samples of the rate and display of behavior. For example, during a typical sixty-minute class, a teacher can collect frequency counts on the number of times a randomly selected student calls out during a fifteen-minute time period. At the end of the fifteen minutes, the teacher can randomly select another peer to observe and then repeat the process. By doing this over the course of a few class periods, teachers can obtain information on how often students in the class call out (e.g., determine what is normative behavior for calling out during instruction). This helps identify what is the performance of a successful student in the classroom and what level of proficiency does our targeted student need to assimilate within the classroom community. This is helpful so that students with ED are not held to excessive behavioral expectations, or expectations that are greater than what their peers are held to. This concept is step two in providing behavior support. We want to know how much we are aiming to see the replacement behavior and what is a reasonable target for the student based on how often they are currently displaying the problem behavior.

Next, we must have an accurate and efficient way to capture progress. For example, a teacher has been tracking the times a student was off task and out of their seat during instruction using simple tally marks on her instructional clipboard. The teacher reported that almost every time independent work was given, the student was wandering around the classroom and disrupting others. When we started discussing some possible antecedent (changes to environmental conditions that are predictive of problem behavior, changes to conditions that occur before the problem behavior) and consequence strategies (the manner in which peers and adults respond to problem behavior when it occurs) that could be put into place, we also needed to address this measurement system. Having documentation that the challenging behavior was happening almost every time independent work was assigned was valuable for identifying independent seatwork as an issue, but if we kept that same data collection method we may not obtain an accurate understanding of student response to support strategies. In this classroom, almost every student got up at one time or another during independent work. Some students got up to go to the restroom, which was a classroom procedure. Some went to sharpen pencils or went to get materials that were necessary to complete a task. All of these students also were off task to some degree within almost every instructional period. Through our conversation we discussed how the real measure of this behavior was not in the number of times that it was occurring but how long the students were out of their seat for. We needed to use duration recording (e.g., determine how long the student was performing these behaviors in a typical class). For the student who performed challenging behavior, they were out of their seat for in excess of twenty minutes going from one distraction to another. Many of the other students were not, as they were out of their seat for two to three minutes completing their task and then returned to their seat and the task at hand.

Another way that we could have tracked the student's behavior would be to look at the amount of work that was completed during the instructional period. The students who were out of seat for a short period of time were able to complete their assignments and typically still had time for an independent activity (e.g., a form of reinforcement used by this teacher). For the student with challenging behavior, he was not completing his assignment and therefore almost never had reinforcement that was directly tied to his task completion.

Both methods for tracking behavior (e.g., the duration of time out of seat and evaluating assignment completion) would have been more accurate than the tally mark system (frequency count) that was used in capturing a better understanding of the problem. However, even within these two examples of data collection, there is one that requires no additional effort on the part of the teacher to get a better understanding about the impact or improvement of strategies: evaluating assignment completion. Assignment completion is task that the teacher already did as part of her day-to-day responsibilities. She graded completed work and made additional notes about the student. She had a system already in place to identify how this student was making progress in response to strategies that would be put in place. Therefore, this data collection method was selected for efficiency. Determining how you are going to collect and record data to track progress of behavioral support is step four.

How specifically are you going to track progress and is it feasible to record using the methods that you select?

Finally, we must have a system for evaluating the environmental components that may help or hinder success. There are multiple ways in which monitoring behavioral progress can be tracked but understanding behavior change takes time means that we must constantly be monitoring and examining student progress to see if adjustments need to be made to reach our target. We should have an end goal in mind, and then focus on how we can help the student reach that goal within the time frame in which we have identified. By evaluating our data through analyzing student progressing or decreasing trends we know if we need to make any adjustments in our strategies, try something new, or if what we are doing most likely is working but maybe needs a booster to ensure a student meets our goal within our time frame. Another consideration about the success of a strategy may be to observe students within other settings where strategies were not taught to see if students had generalized behaviors (e.g., performance in untrained settings) into multiple environments. To do this you, use the same criteria for which you have been observing students within the training environment and the same data collection format. If you change either of these pieces, this could take away from the reliability of your data collection (e.g., keep this consistent so you can make comparisons). Compare results within both environments and see if there are additional supports that you can put into place in the untrained setting to boost student performance. Sometimes just a visual or nonverbal cue as a reminder can solve this issue, but at times it may require methods similar to those used in the trained setting.

All of these components are critical to the success of interventions and supports within the inclusive environment. Appendix A includes a data collection form that educators may find useful for identifying common characteristics and environmental factors associated with a student's challenging behaviors. For the remainder of the chapter we will discuss two structured supports for inclusive classrooms and how they can be used to help students that insufficiently responded to universal practices.

DAILY PROGRESS REPORTS

Having a scheduled time to give students specific feedback while using a visual to support discussions about success and challenges to solve is one effective type of individualized behavior support. One way to complete this in the classroom, which can easily be modified for any student age, is through the use of DPR. At times, DPRs may be referred to as points sheets, smiley charts, behavior tracking forms, and so on. Although all of these versions have different names, their purpose is the same: to give educators a way to track student performance across environments and to have data-based discussions with students and other professionals. DPRs are typically broken up into intervals based on time or schedule (e.g., class period). This permits students to receive feedback before any instructional change or on a set schedule. It also allows for students to get one-on-one interaction with an adult which increases the opportunity for praise and reinforcement and relationships development. Finally, it also gives students multiple chances throughout a day for success. Typically, DPRs assign a target behavior(s) for students to focus on. Staff then monitor these behaviors to identify a student's level of performance. The actual measure of performance is not as critical as having all adults in agreement about the measurement system and feedback is given to students at a regular interval (e.g., consistently).

Interventions like these serve two needs related to student success. One, students receive individualized feedback from adults at set times. This encourages attention and praise from adults and can serve as a consequence strategy for attention-seeking students (e.g., students who perform challenging behavior to receive attention by participating in check-ins). In addition, the use of DPRs gives students a visual representation of their day. They are able to see in what classes or periods of time they performed well and the time periods in which they were less successful. Having students monitor their progress and meet with adults even if they did not do well within a class period gives students the opportunity to take accountability for their performance. It provides them an opportunity to have ownership of their own behavior change when they are successful. The use of self-monitoring and using a DPR as a visual representation of where students are succeeding and where they may be having trouble can also help to have targeted conversations and interventions to continue to assist with increases in student performance (Peterson, Young, Salzberg, West, and Hill, 2006).

BEHAVIOR EDUCATION PROGRAM

DPRs are a critical component within the behavior education program (BEP), or more commonly referred to as check-in/check-out (Crone, Haken, and Horner, 2010). This program has revolutionized the use of DPRs. It provides a system and structure that is consistent across settings and has been validated as an effective practice for improving student behavior (Maggin, Zurheide, Pickett, and Baillie, 2015; Mitchell, Adamson, and McKenna, 2017).

Core components of the intervention include clearly defined behavioral expectations and rules, pre-corrections for meeting behavioral expectations (e.g., statements that correct misbehavior before they occur), high rates of feedback and reinforcement for demonstration of desired behavior, use of data to monitor outcomes, and a system for school-to home communication. These components take the system of DPRs and give a model of exemplar presentation. Exemplar presentation includes focus on having strong universal systems, understand the behavior desired for performance, provide a structure for adults to provide consistent feedback to students but also the format and language in which adults should give feedback. Individuals should make feedback constructive in nature and not reprimanding students for problem behavior and instead treating it as a chance to move forward and to continue to progress. BEP provides a clear focus for data and making decisions often including how to determine if a more intensive intervention is needed, or conversely how to scale back the intervention after prolonged periods of success. Finally, it also has a strong focus on building relationships beyond just the school setting and bringing the behavioral expectations into the home where similar constructive feedback can be given if needed or additional reinforcement for student success. Students can take DPR sheets home to celebrate successes with their family and to talk about struggles they have had and plan for a better day.

The use of the BEP is typically thought of as a tier two intervention for students that can be implemented for those students who may struggle to respond to just universal interventions. This intervention also takes specific function of behavior into account focusing on those students who receive reinforcement from attention and shifting previously given attention for problem behavior into positive attention for appropriate behaviors. Typically, implementation of the BEP is not just isolated to inclusive classroom settings but significant amounts of feedback do take place within theseinclusive settings. Appendix B includes resources to support practitioner use of DPR.

BEHAVIORAL CONTRACTS

Behavioral contracts are another format for providing specific feedback and attention to individual students. Behavioral contracts are just as they sound: a permanent product that documents an agreement between teacher and student about specific expectations and a predetermined proficiency level for them (Alberto and Troutman, 2013; Downing, 2002). The use of behavioral contracts should include five components for successful implementation: (1) description of expected behavior, (2) the conditions in which the behavior will be demonstrated, (3) criteria for acceptable performance, (4) reinforcement that will be given, and (5) dates for review.

The description of expected behavior should be tied directly to classroom universals but also have a specific focus on what behavior(s) are impeding this student from being successful and how can we directly target these for change. The description should not be ambiguous for students and provide a clear understanding of both contracting individuals about what the behavior must look like. Sometimes, providing lists of examples and non-examples can assist in this process.

When creating conditions in which the behavior will be demonstrated both individuals should understand exactly when the behavior is expected to be displayed and in what format, which directly ties back to the description. The student should be directly taught about the behavior and the conditions surrounding it. As mentioned previously, when addressing criteria, it is important to take into account what level other classroom peers are performing at, and create a tangible goal for the student commensurate with their peers. Criteria should be directly tied to reinforcement and it should be explicit about when criteria are met what type of reinforcement will be given and there should be specific focus on the ensuring that reinforcement is such that it can be given immediately to the student.

Criteria should be measurable and completely objective and agreed upon before the plan is put into place. In some circumstances where substantial growth is needed for the student to achieve their goals, specific benchmarks may be needed, which can make reinforcement more likely while still documenting behavioral improvements. Finally, the plan must be systematically reviewed for any adjustments that may be needed for student performance. Having documented times preset for review allows for all parties participating in the contract to reflect on how things have been working and make any needed changes. It is critical that these contracts are used consistently and that when designing the plan that both the teacher and student are able to give feedback and direction on what they feel like is reasonable. This input allows for student buy-in and assurance that each part understands their roles and responsibilities within the terms of the contract.

Using a behavioral contract gives a unique format for the teacher and student to come together on a plan where each gets ownership and understanding over the behaviors demonstrated. In addition, it allows for students and teachers to support each other and hold each other accountable for negotiated supports and structures. Having a clear goal in mind and setting up points of feedback allows for all educators to understand what is at stake and how to help a student achieve it (See Appendix C).

BUILDING ONTO CURRENT STRUCTURES

Although the DPR and behavior contract strategies are designed to help assist students in the next level of required support they also provide a format for ensuring that we haven't given up hope on students when they begin to struggle within inclusive environments. Students and teachers together are working collaboratively to make sure that there is a shared understanding of the expectations and that both individuals are working together to reach these goals. Both of these strategies have the potential to rebuild or strengthen student/teacher interactions and reformat possible negative statements to be more constructive for encouraging positive behaviors. When implementing these systems, they should always be done in tandem with previous interventions and supports. These systems are designed to build onto the current structure and enhance intervention for the student.

APPENDIX A

Teacher: Class:	Time / Location (if not in the classroom)										
DURATION (ex. # of Minutes)											
BEHAVIORS	Not engaged in assigned task										
	Disruptive Non-Verbal Behaviors: *i.e. swinging arms*										
	Disruptive Verbal Behaviors: *i.e. making noises*										
	Inappropriate interaction directed at peer: *i.e. Name calling*										
	Inappropriate interaction directed at teacher: *i.e. talking back*										
ACTIVITY	Unstructured Activity										
	Structured Activity										
	Transition										
	Academic – independent work										
	Academic – group work										
	Academic – teacher led discussion/lecture										
	Down time / wait time										
	Difficult task										
TRIGGERS	Asked to perform a task										
	Given repeated directions										
	Engagement with a peer										
	Peers respond or encourage student										
	Peers ignore										
	Provoked by peers										
	Teacher working with others										
	Told "no" or "wait"										
POSSIBLE FUNCTION	GAIN adult attention										
	GAIN peer attention										
	GAIN desired item/activity										
	GAIN sensory input										
	AVOID adult										
	AVOID task/demand/request										
	AVOID peer interaction										
	AVOID sensory input										
	UNKNOWN										
CONSEQUENCE	Redirection/Warning										
	Safe seat										
	Buddy Room / Alternative Location in Building to Work										
	ISS/OC										
	Debrief										
	Loss of Privilege										

Directions:

Please complete a column each time a behavior occurs.
• Write the time in the space provided. (& indicate if the behavior occurred in a location other than the
  classroom)
• Please mark ALL that apply in the column. (For example, the "activity" may be a "structured", "group
  work" and "difficult task". You would mark all three of these.)
Please make additional notes on back if the behavior/activity/trigger/function/or consequence is not captured
  by the possible choices on the form.

Thank you in advance for your time and attention this. The results will help us better refine programming
  to support this student.

APPENDIX B

Daily Progress Reports (DPRs)

2 ways to use DPR
You need to decide how the DPR will be used before you start so that you can communicate its purpose to all the people working with the student.

- Collect data

The DPR is a good way to get information if you are just wanting data about a student's day and what times of day are better and worse and which goals they are most successful with.

- Intervention

The DPR works as an intervention if an adult checks in with the student after each class period to discuss what score the student should get and why. The student gets frequent adult feedback and 1 on 1 adult time regularly throughout the day. Another piece making this an intervention is tying the daily score to a reward.

Training
With every plan, you need to make sure everyone using the DPR knows how to use it. This means adults and kids.

- Teachers/staff

Make sure they understand when they should be filling out the DPR and the importance of the quick and accurate data. If this student is needing the adult to check in with them - explain that to all the adults working with the student. You will probably need to send out reminders of the importance and value of checking in with the student.

- Parents

Make sure to explain what the DPR is to the parents - why you are collecting the data, what data you are collecting, and how you are going to use the data. It's important to remind parents that we are looking for the sheet to be a positive experience and their support is crucial! We are also looking for the student to meet their goal, not have a perfect day. We don't want kids getting in trouble at home when they meet their goal, but maybe don't get a 100%.

- Students

Make sure students know why you are collecting the data, what data you are collecting, and how you are going to use the data. If you are going to have a reinforcer tied to their score, make sure to figure out what is most motivating for them. Don't assume you know - ask the kids! See reinforcement surveys if needed.

Checking in and out with students
To get students started, it is common practice to have them check in with an adult in the morning to get their sheet and get their morning pep talk. This gives the student a chance to talk about anything on their mind and know that someone is keeping tabs on their day. Then, at the end of the day, these students will check out with an adult. It's a chance to talk with an adult 1 on 1 about their day and either celebrate or make a plan for how tomorrow will be better. If a student has a reward tied to meeting their goal, after check out time is a good time to provide this.

DPR scale

- Ideally the DPR scale used should be consistent across the building.
- A bigger scale creates more accurate data
- A 0-3 or 0-5 scale is most common.
- Adding in a "0" can ensure a student gets no credit when they go home

Rating Scale	
5 – Great Job	No Reminders
4 – Good Job	1 Reminder
3 – Sort of	2 Reminders
2 – Struggling	> 2 Reminders
1 – Try Again	Out of Classroom/ISS
0 – Stop & Think	Sent Home/OSS

Target Behaviors

You need to come up with usually 2-3 target behaviors you'd like to collect data on using the DPR. Having a general term related to school expectations such as safe, respectful, and responsible is a good place to start. Making sure to define what each area means for the individual student.

As you collect data, over time you may realize that the student gets a 100% for safety every day, so it's really respectfulness and responsibility that you need to focus on. You can adapt the DPR to meet this need.

Safe
Hands & Feet to Self, stay in my assigned area

Respectful
Listen when someone speaks

Responsible
Follows Directions, get my work done

Using the data

The DPR tells us so much good information! Let's use it effectively! Make sure to keep the DPR daily so that you can go back and look for trends. If a parent wants to see the sheet, make them a copy!

- Graphing

We need to make sure we are graphing the info regularly so we can determine what's going well, what's not going well, and where changes are needed.

Using the pre-made Google Sheets graphing tool in the Document Library, you can easily set up your data collection and start getting in the habit of entering the info regularly.

- Interpreting

The most common way you will look at data is the daily percentage the student achieves; however, this is not the only way to look at data. You can look at how the student is doing during different times of day, different classes, different teachers, and on their different target behaviors. Interpreting this data can help you make informed decisions about needed changes/interventions.

APPENDIX C

Student: _____ Date: _____

School: _____

Directions: Fill in the top row of the report chart with today's schedule (i.e., reading, math, science, etc.).

At the end of each activity, circle the corresponding point value (0-5)

Rating Scale	
5 – Great Job	**No Reminders**
4 – Good Job	**1 Reminder**
3 – Sort of	**2 or 3 Reminders**
2 – Struggling	**> 3 Reminders**
1 – Try Again	**Out of Classroom/ISS**
0 – Stop & Think	**Sent Home/OSS**

Safe *Hands & Feet to Self*	5 4 3 2 1 0	5 4 3 2 1 0	5 4 3 2 1 0	5 4 3 2 1 0	5 4 3 2 1 0	5 4 3 2 1 0	5 4 3 2 1 0	5 4 3 2 1 0	5 4 3 2 1 0
Respectful *Listen when someone speaks*	5 4 3 2 1 0	5 4 3 2 1 0	5 4 3 2 1 0	5 4 3 2 1 0	5 4 3 2 1 0	5 4 3 2 1 0	5 4 3 2 1 0	5 4 3 2 1 0	5 4 3 2 1 0
Responsible *Follows Directions*	5 4 3 2 1 0	5 4 3 2 1 0	5 4 3 2 1 0	5 4 3 2 1 0	5 4 3 2 1 0	5 4 3 2 1 0	5 4 3 2 1 0	5 4 3 2 1 0	5 4 3 2 1 0
Targeted Behavior **#1**	5 4 3 2 1 0	5 4 3 2 1 0	5 4 3 2 1 0	5 4 3 2 1 0	5 4 3 2 1 0	5 4 3 2 1 0	5 4 3 2 1 0	5 4 3 2 1 0	5 4 3 2 1 0
Targeted Behavior **#2**	5 4 3 2 1 0	5 4 3 2 1 0	5 4 3 2 1 0	5 4 3 2 1 0	5 4 3 2 1 0	5 4 3 2 1 0	5 4 3 2 1 0	5 4 3 2 1 0	5 4 3 2 1 0

Safe-Respectful-Responsible	**Targeted Behavior #1**	**Targeted Behavior #2**
_____/_____ = _____%	_____/_____ = _____%	_____/_____ = _____%

Student: _____	Date: _____	**Rating Scale** 5 – Great Job 4 – Good Job
School: _____		3 – Sort of 2 – Struggling 1 – Try Again\Out of Classroom\ISS
	Criteria for Rating Scale Scores	0 – Sent Home\OSS

Safe *Hands & Feet* *to Self*	5 – Exceeds Expectations – NO Reminders 4 –Meeting Expectations – group pre-correct, 1 reminder, keeps hands, feet & body safe. 3 – group pre-correct, one-on-one prompt, < 3 reminders for personal space 2 – > 3 reminders, does not keep hands, feet and/or body safe but not a safety concern 1 – student's behavior is a safety concern and/or received numerous reminders, out of room buddy room/office (ISS) 0 – Student is sent home or not in school due to OSS
Respectful *Listen when* *someone* *speaks*	5 – Exceeds Expectations – NO Reminders 4 –Meeting Expectations – group pre-correct, listening appropriately 3 – group pre-correct, one-on-one prompt, < 3 reminders for listening attentively 2 – > 3 reminders, does not listen, mildly disrupting learning environment 1 – not listening after several redirects, continual disruption of environment, out of room buddy room/office (ISS) 0 – Student is sent home or not in school due to OSS
Responsible *Follows* *Directions*	5 – Exceeds Expectations – NO Reminders 4 –Meeting Expectations – group pre-correct, 1 reminder to stay on task and/or following directives 3 – < 3 reminders for on task and/or following directives, some tasks completed 2 – > 3 reminders for on task and/or following directives, few tasks completed 1 – does not follow directives, all tasks are incomplete, out of room buddy room/office (ISS) 0 – Student is sent home or not in school due to OSS
Targeted Behavior(s)	5 – Great Job 4 – Good Job 3 – Sort of 2 – Struggling 1 – Try Again\Out of Classroom\ISS 0 – Sent Home\OSS

APPENDIX D

Brandon's Behavior Contract

Mrs. Jones, the teacher will give Brandon a point to add on his "Self Management" chart each time he does the following:

- Follows teacher directions the first time asked.
- Handle conflicts using safe strategies he has learned rather than leaving the classroom.
- Expresses his feelings in a calm, quiet voice without making threats or using impolite words of gestures.
-

Behaviors and Conditions

When Brandon has collected 10 points from Mrs. Jones, he may choose one option from a menu of rewards that he and Mrs. Jones create together.

Criteria and Reinforcers

The student, Brandon, helped to create this agreement.
He understands and agrees to the terms of the behavior contract.

_____
(Signature of Student)   Date

The teacher, Mrs. Jones, agrees to carry out her part of this agreement. Brandon will receive points each time he fulfills one or more of the behavioral goals. Brandon will also be allowed to collect his reward immediately when he has earned enough points for it.

Reasonable Negotiations

_____
(Signature of Teacher)   Date

Brandon will begin this contract on this date 1/7/20 to help in assuring his success and be reviewed on 3/15/20.

⟵ Date for Review

Chapter 11

Function-Based Thinking to Support Inclusive Instruction

Imagine that you are trying to let everyone around you know how you are feeling but do not have the words/language to articulate what is going on or how you are feeling. Or, you have the words/language but are unable to express them when you feel heightened levels of stress or anxiety. Imagine that the only way that you can let these feelings and/or thoughts be known is through your behaviors, acting out and responding to your environment and every individual (or, certain people) you come in contact with. You have no way (real and/or perceived) to advocate for what you want besides your actions. This is how children communicate with their surroundings to get their needs met.

A child at a very young age is inherently taught this interaction and our bodies are designed to respond. Consider an infant who feels hungry because they need to eat or child who feels great discomfort because they have a soiled diaper. This infant learns that by expressing their discomfort through their physical actions, such as crying, that an adult will respond and take care of their need (e.g., feed them, change their diaper). This form of communication is developed during infancy and then expanded upon as people grow through their direct interactions with their surroundings.

The relationship between behavior and environmental conditions is well established by the time children reach school age, and the means for communication is typically well established and ingrained in behavioral responses. For many children, this pattern of communication is considered appropriate and is typical of the developmental age (e.g., respecting adults and following school rules). For some children, this pattern may have been warped in some capacity where pathways to communication rely on problem behaviors within the school context (e.g., tantrums or aggression; Smith and Sugai, 2000). These problem behaviors are typically specific factors that increase a student's likelihood of experiencing exclusionary disciplinary practices (e.g., suspension), resulting in the loss of instructional time and lower levels of academic achievement (Simonsen, et al., 2015). Creating a new pathway, a prosocial and positive one, for students to communicate their needs and to have them met without the performance of problem behaviors is an everyday challenge for educators. Educators can create and maintain class environments that promote the occurrence of positive behaviors, but they cannot guarantee that this will occur for all students all of the time (Mitchell, Adamson, and McKenna, 2017). Gaining an understanding of why challenging behaviors occur and the environmental conditions that predict their occurrence is essential to this effort.

UNDERSTANDING BEHAVIOR AS A FORM OF COMMUNICATION

It is critical to analyze the patterns of communication (e.g., behavior) into what challenging behavior or behaviors the student is demonstrating and directly compare these problem behaviors to the behavior educators would like the student to perform (i.e., replacement behavior). This is done to ensure the behaviors meet the same need for a student and their communication (e.g., serve the same function or purpose as the challenging behaviors). This process is referred to as the competing pathways model of problem behavior (Alberto and Troutman, 2013; see figure 11.1). Making this positive pathway (top path in figure 11.1) the first choice for students when they have something to communicate (e.g., need, want, experience of stress and/or anxiety) requires significant work to ensure that all environmental conditions and supports are working in tandem to make this choice efficient and effective (e.g., by figuring out how to structure the environment, we can make this pathway more likely for students). To prevent the occurrence of problem behaviors and increase the likelihood that students perform the desired positive behavior, educators must make adjustments to the class environment, teach students new skills, reinforce student performance of new skills, and change the way they respond to students when they perform challenging behaviors. In essence, changing student behavior involves changing teacher behavior.

A foundational principle of behavior analysis (which is the focus of this chapter) is that students communicate with persons in their environment to meet two basic needs, referred to as the "function" of problem of behavior (see figure 11.1): to obtain something in the environment or to avoid or escape something in the environment (Alberto and Troutman, 2013). Within these two potential goals of problem behavior, there are three subcategories: sensory, attention, and tangible items (see table 11.1). These goals of behavior

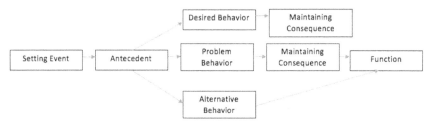

Figure 11.1   Competing Pathways Model of Problem Behavior.

are called functions of behavior and serve as the foundation for identifying the reasons why problem behaviors occur and how we can adjust the environment and teach skills to promote the occurrence of prosocial behaviors. The competing behavior model helps us understand why a student used the form of behavioral communication that they did (e.g., performs a challenging behavior in a specific school context). It also helps us to determine what changes we can make to the class environment, what behaviors we can teach that can compete with the problem behavior (e.g., replacement behaviors; McKenna, Flower, and Adamson, 2016), and encourage positive behaviors that will meet the same student need. Prosocial behaviors that compete with problem behaviors are those behaviors that meet the student's need or needs in a more effective and efficient manner than the problem behavior or problem behaviors.

Students typically have one primary function that they are trying to communicate through their behavioral language. It is our job as educators to assist students within their language development and create positive pathways of communication. This is particularly critical for students who receive special education services for emotional disturbance (ED), who may have a functional expressive language disorder (e.g., unable to use language to express their needs during times of heightened stress and/or anxiety). Students with ED may also have deficient language skills that are not situational (Nelson, Benner, Cheney, 2005). Determining what students are trying to communicate through their challenging behavior and using this information to change it to an appropriate behavior is not easy, as the negative pathway may be

Table 11.1   Functions of Problem Behavior

Obtain something in the environment	• Sensory • Attention • Tangible item
Avoid or escape something in the environment	• Sensory • Attention • Tangible item

ingrained in students and is likely an efficient means of communication and getting needs met. In essence, the negative pathway becomes an automatic response by the student to conditions in the class environment. However, we can adjust both environmental supports to prompt the positive behavior, the events or environmental conditions that predictably take place before a problem behavior occurs (antecedents: conditions that tend to be present before the occurrence of problem behavior, conditions that predict the occurrence of the problem behavior), and the environmental response to the problem behavior (maintaining consequences: the way teachers and/or students in the environment tend to respond to the problem behavior).

Consider the following example. We have a student in our classroom who is consistently shouting out for the teacher's assistance during independent seatwork. We could hypothesize that this behavioral communication is an attempt "to get" adult "attention." In fact, when we consider the manner in which the teacher responds to shouting (reprimands the student, answers the student's question, reminds the student to raise his/her hand), we see that the student in fact receives adult attention when he/she shouts in class, and this attention comes in the form of the teacher reprimanding the student, answering the students question, or redirecting the student to the task at hand. To develop a competing pathway, we first need to consider what behavior is typical and more acceptable in a classroom to obtain teacher attention. In this situation, raising a hand and waiting for the teacher to call on you is a common behavior "to get" adult "attention." Our job now is to change the environment in the classroom to make the problem behavior of shouting out ineffective for obtaining adult attention and increase the likelihood that the student will demonstrate the positive behavior of hand raising when they need assistance or when they have a topic relevant question. We can address this situation by adjusting the antecedents of the behavior (conditions that occur before the problem behavior and that predict the occurrence of the problem behavior) and the consequences within the environment (conditions and actions that occur after the problem behavior and make the problem behavior effective and efficient at meeting a student's need). Figure 11.2 is a completed competing pathways model for this hypothetical scenario.

First, let's focus on adapting the antecedents. By proactively structuring the class environment for student success, teachers can prevent the occurrence of challenging behaviors and devote more time to providing academic instruction. One way to change antecedents is to think about the work that is presented to the student. Perhaps the work is too difficult and that is why the student is requesting teacher attention? Are there possible accommodations or modification we can put in place to make the work less aversive? Are there accommodations and/or modifications that are written into the students Individual Education Program (IEP) that are inconsistently provided

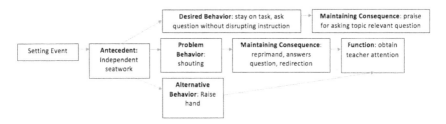

Figure 11.2   Competing Pathways Model for Scenario.

or implemented in an ineffective manner? We could also think about creating a system where, at the beginning of independent seatwork, our first stop is to give this student attention in the form of checking in to make certain he/she understood the directions and to ask the student if they have any questions before beginning. We could also help the student get started with one of the first items or tasks during independent seatwork. This strategy provides the student with attention before shouting out occurs, and ensures that they have the necessary tools to begin the independent assignment.

Conversely, we can also think about the consequences of behavior (e.g., how adults and students respond to challenging behavior). With shouting out, the student has probably become quite effective at requesting adult attention and it is given to him by the teacher. We can manipulate this consequence by ensuring that adults, for the problem behavior of shouting out, provide no attention (e.g., planned ignoring). This makes the problem behavior ineffective for obtaining teacher attention and creates an environment that requires the student to demonstrate the positive behavior of hand raising and waiting to be called on before they receive teacher attention. Combining both antecedent and consequence manipulations increases the likelihood that we, as educators, can change student behavior. But, we must be consistent and planful with our behaviors and how we shape the environment to increase our chances of seeing students demonstrate the behavior we are after.

Function-Based Thinking

Using the function of problem behavior to help determine our responses to them is a concept commonly referred to as function-based thinking (Hershfeldt, Rosenberg, and Bradshaw, 2010). Function-based thinking gives school personnel tools for understanding why problem behaviors occur and provides a framework for their remediation. Function-based thinking is not the same as functional-based assessment as it is less comprehensive and has been demonstrated as easier to adopt within inclusive environments (Sugai et al., 2000).

There is no one conventional form for determining functional-based thinking, but there are multiple recommended practices or steps that should be included. There are also many structured and unstructured methods for understanding and interpreting the results. Analyzing and considering key concepts contained within the competing pathways model for students with ED is a good starting point. First, there should be a statement of what behaviors are hindering student success, a method to collect data on the challenging behavior when it occurs to identify the relevant antecedents and consequences that predict and help maintain the occurrence of the challenging behavior, time to analyze this data to determine the function of this problem behavior, selection of a functionally equivalent replacement behavior (e.g., a more appropriate behavior that meets the same need as the problem behavior), consideration of adjustments to antecedent (e.g., instructional methods and materials, etc.) and consequences (e.g., contingencies for prompting and reinforcing the occurrence of replacement behaviors), and a specific plan to monitor the plan's effectiveness (Hershfeldt, Rosenberg, and Bradshaw, 2010). When developing this plan, teachers should focus on ecological factors present within the learning environment (Sheriden and Gutkin, 2000). A student's cultural norms should also be considered as an influencing factor for problem behaviors. For example, students should know and understand if there are any classroom norms that may be different from what they were taught within their own homes and if so make concessions and accommodations if there are strong cultural beliefs around behaviors.

For a more structured approach (e.g., an approach that is more consistent with a functional behavioral assessment), teachers can use a form such as the Functional Assessment Checklist for Teachers and Staff (FACTS, March et al., 2000). This assessment for function-based thinking takes approximately thirty minutes to complete and generate hypothesis statements about the motivation for the problem behavior and what antecedents and consequences may exist which may be encouraging this problem behavior (e.g., conditions that appear to predict the occurrence of problem behavior). This assessment can help individuals directly identify what conditions predict problem behavior (e.g., what tends to be going on in the environment immediately before the problem behavior occurs) to better identify how to address the function. The data collection form in Chapter 10 Appendix A can also be used to support this process (e.g., identification of the function or functions of challenging behavior, and antecedent and consequent conditions that are commonly associated with their performance).

When determining how to best support individual student's needs within inclusive environments it is critical that classroom teachers take into account broad school systems and supports as well as their own context and instructional tools (Adamson, McKenna, Mitchell, 2018). Tiered systems of support such as Positive Behavioral Interventions and Supports (PBIS) and Response to Intervention (RTI) can be identified as full school structures that create proactive measures to increase student success. These supports should not be discounted, however, they can be enhanced through a similar philosophy at the classroom level that focuses on prevention of problem behaviors, creates a systematic support, and also highlights the use of classroom-based interventions.

Whole Class Supports

Creating an inclusive environment that encourages student achievement and offers a variety of behavioral supports is considered best practice for classroom management. Typically, these supports revolve around universal supports within the classroom, or supports that are provided to all students. Supports include expectations and rules, clear procedures, active supervision, behavior-specific praise, and effective error correction (Simonsen et al., 2015; Simonsen, Fairbanks, Briesch, Myers, and Sugai, 2008). Although these universal supports are not solely based on the concept of function of problem behavior, they are the foundation for a classroom's success.

In fact, before a classroom teacher should consider any more intensive intervention it is critical to understand the specific context of the environment and to ensure that all universal practices are implemented consistently. Ensuring consistency of universal supports sets the foundation and framework for an environment of support and inclusion (Adamson, McKenna, and Mitchell, 2019). Although analyzing your own classroom environment can be challenging, there are numerous lists of essential practices to support teacher implementation: https://pbismissouri.org/wp-content/uploads/2017/0 6/8.0-MO-SW-PBS-Tier-1-Workbook-Ch-8-Classroom-1.pdf.

In addition, many teachers use peer observation and feedback in their approach to analyze their classroom structure. Having another teacher come into your classroom and give you feedback on any observed universal supports provides a different perspective from someone who may be able to observe behaviors or issues that may be different from what you have observed. They also may be able to offer guidance and support in brainstorming through any issues identified in their observations, based on their experience in their own classroom (Kennedy, Hirsch, Rodgers, Bruce, and Lloyd, 2017). With this in mind, administrators are strongly encouraged to build in time during the school week for teachers to have discussions about instructional practices and supports, their implementation, and ways to better address the needs of classes and individual students (Bettini et al., 2020; McKenna and Parenti, 2017).

The Impact of Antecedents and Consequences

There are two common strategies for addressing problem behavior and neither has to be implemented in isolation. Controlling antecedents is the process of adapting contexts in which the behavior is most likely to occur. For example, consider a class where many students are frequently off task during independent seatwork. In this situation, teachers can remind the class what they should do if they need assistance. The teacher can also provide more explicit instruction through the provision of modeling and explicit feedback prior to engaging students in independent practice. Teachers can also use information on the current levels of performance of individual students to adapt independent work assignments so that they align with what students can actually do independently. When teachers create an intervention that focuses on antecedent changes, they are trying to adapt the environment and the specific events that have demonstrated to increase the likelihood of problem behavior occurring. For some students, when an antecedent to problem behavior is academic work, accommodations and modifications to the academic demands can be an effective. However, students with ED must be appropriately challenged academically, with instructional adaptations improving student access to effective instruction rather than limiting or preventing it (Brigham, Ahn, Stride, and McKenna, 2016). Using specific structures that may make the academic demands less aversive, through the provision of appropriately differentiated and supported instruction, can help students achieve success as well as prevent the occurrence of problem behaviors.

Another way to address problem behaviors is to focus on the maintaining consequences. As we mentioned before, behavior is the way students communicate. By making this form of communication (e.g., problem behavior) ineffective and inefficient for achieving the desired outcome, we are creating environments where students are looking for other ways to get their needs met. This sets the occasion for educations to teach the appropriate replacement behavior(s) and reinforce student efforts to perform them. For example, if a student is shouting out a teacher may not respond to the student, making this behavior ineffective, and instead wait for a hand to be raised or call on another student demonstrating the appropriate behavior.

CLOSING THOUGHTS

Understanding what students are trying to communicate through their behavior is critical to developing supports that are effective in inclusive settings. It is crucial for teachers to think systematically about behavior so that they can quickly determine an effective and efficient method to address problem behavior. Taking data and making data-based decisions ensure that the strategies selected are beneficial and are in fact improving student behavior.

Chapter 12

Trauma-Informed Support

Considerations for Students with Emotional Disturbance Who Have Experienced Trauma

By Felicity Post

Since the requirement of inclusive instruction for students diagnosed with emotional disturbance (ED), educators have been working tirelessly to meet their needs. Gone are the days when teachers are solely responsible for the academic growth of students, if, in fact, those days ever truly existed. Instead, educators are expected to tend to the social, emotional, and behavioral needs of students. As a result, educators must wear many hats to meet the vast array of student needs. In an effort to provide appropriate, academic instruction, educators must first consider a student's current level of academic and behavioral performance and what factors work to play a part. One major factor that has the potential to adversely affect a student's efforts to learn and grow is trauma. In this chapter, I will discuss the effects that trauma can have on the brain, the relevance of trauma in the classroom, and strategies to combat its potential effects.

TRAUMA AND THE BRAIN

Much research has been conducted on the brain over the last twenty years, which has allowed us a better understanding of the brain and how it functions. A better awareness of the effects of trauma on the brain has given insight into the role that exposure to trauma plays in childhood development. This awareness is critical for educators and caretakers working to provide supports for students who have experienced traumatic events.

Whenever exposed to extreme stress, the human body is forced to respond in a heightened state of alert known as *fight, flight, or freeze*. Students experiencing the need to flee may be those who, when exposed to a perceived threat, choose to run. They may run out of a particular area in the classroom, out of the classroom, or out of the building all together. They may also refuse to complete certain types of academic tasks, or participate in social activities. These are examples of escape-maintained behavior. Those who fight may lash out verbally or physically to both their peers and teachers. They may even inflict harm upon themselves when faced with situations they perceive as stressful. Students who freeze may become unresponsive and will tend to "zone out." They may appear to be avoiding stressful tasks or seem as though they are refusing to answer questions posed.

Because of our biological makeup, we, as humans, choose *flight* first. Our instincts cause us to want to avoid or escape danger. If escape is not a viable option, we will choose to *fight*. At times, we struggle to process what is currently happening around us. Thus, we will *freeze*. Regardless of the choice, our bodies were designed to be in this state only for a short duration and only when faced with extreme danger. When children are exposed to either complex or acute trauma, the brain shifts into this heightened state, which can lead to devastating results. When the brain is triggered by a real or perceived threat, chemicals are released into the body which allow us to "survive" the stressful events. In large doses, these chemicals are considered toxic and can severely impair development. When such a release occurs in the fetal, infant, or early childhood brain, serious disruptions to learning, memory, mood, relational skills, and aspects of executive functioning occur (Shonkoff and Garner, 2012).

The science behind the brain's response is an elaborate one. In his book, *The Body Keeps the Score: Brain, Mind, and Body in the Healing of Trauma*, van der Kolk (2014) discusses this response in great depth. For purposes of this chapter, we will explore a more abbreviated explanation. When in a state of stress, students are in the part of their brain that is designed for survival: the limbic area. This particular system is responsible for arousal, emotion, and the fight, flight, or freeze response. The limbic system is commonly referred to as "the downstairs brain" (Siegel, 2003). When this part of the brain is in control, a person's ability to learn and retain information is disrupted. Rather than allowing this part of the brain to have long-term control, it is preferred that the higher-functioning part of the brain, the prefrontal cortex, be calling the shots. The prefrontal cortex enables us to think, reason, and maintain flexibility. It is often referred to as "the upstairs brain" (Siegel, 2003). An even bigger responsibility of the prefrontal cortex is to regulate the downstairs brain and allow it to shift into survival mode only when the need actually arises.

When students are experiencing stress, their brains tend to shift "downstairs." Our brains were designed to be in this state for only short periods of time, for survival, and then revert back to a normal state of functioning. Unfortunately, students who experience continuing stress or trauma live in their "downstairs" brain. Our goal, as educators, is to help students gain a better understanding of the biological responses of the body so that, when exposed to stress, they are able to override their tendencies to go or stay "downstairs" and work to stay "upstairs." That way, they are able to respond in a logical, thoughtful, and intentional manner to the events in their current surroundings.

Relevance in the Classroom

Current research indicates that more children are affected by trauma than ever before. In fact, according to the National Survey of Children's Health (2011/2012) nearly thirty-five million U.S. children have experienced at least one type of childhood trauma. It is estimated that about 40 percent of American children will have at least one potentially traumatizing experience by age eighteen (Perry and Szalavitz, 2006). Estimates further suggest that at any given time, more than eight million American children suffer from severe, trauma-related psychiatric problems that could be diagnosed. It is estimated that approximately one in three will grow up with three or more adverse childhood experiences (ACEs), which can affect brain development, quality of the relationships, and the ability to manage one's self.

Teachers, despite their contact time with children, are not typically taught to identify or address the challenges that result from trauma experienced by their students. However, they face the impact that trauma leaves behind every day in their classrooms. While not every single student will have experienced trauma, the needs of the students who do have the ability to determine the success of the entire classroom of students.

The lack of preparedness of teachers has major implications in terms of producing desired results within the school system. Trauma creates an ongoing interference for students in their efforts to be ready for learning and contributes to chronic attendance problems. Even more worrisome, trauma is a major cause for the behavior problems faced daily by well-intentioned educators. "When children are oppositional, defensive, numbed out, or enraged, it's also important to recognize that such 'bad behavior' may repeat action patterns that were established to survive serious threats, even if they are intensely upsetting or off-putting" (van der Kolk, 2014; p. 88). When this trauma is unaddressed, it contributes to frustration, low job satisfaction, and burnout (Souers and Hall, 2016).

We, as educators, hold an enormous amount of power. While we are unable to prevent trauma, we are able to "give students the skills and strategies needed to manage the intensity through intentional teaching in a safe, predictable environment" (Souers and Hall, 2016; p. 34). The reality is that we spend a great deal of time with our students, sometimes upward of six hours per day. This time provides us with a huge opportunity to make a difference in the lives of our students. We have the ability to ensure that our students are safe, engaged, well-supported, and appropriately challenged, and, in order to do so, we must first look at our own efforts. After all, the level of student success that we can realistically expect depends upon our level of readiness to provide an environment in which all can thrive.

STRATEGIES

Because of the current state of our nation (see MacSuga-Gage, Ennis, Hirsch, and Evanovich, 2018) and the high prevalence of trauma, various approaches and strategies have been developed to increase our sensitivity and better prepare educators and society as a whole to meet the needs of students who have experienced trauma. Many educators, parents, and policymakers have acknowledged the necessity of a trauma-sensitive approach. At this point in time, however, being a trauma-sensitive school is a choice, not a requirement. Trauma sensitivity will look different from school to school, and educators must acknowledge and understand the educational impacts of trauma so that they can establish safe and supportive environments.

Awareness

A vast majority of teachers acknowledge that learning how to work with especially difficult students was not a main staple in their educator preparation program, and that they feel incredibly overwhelmed trying to figure out how to work with these students (Greene, 2008). Because of this very real concern, half of teachers leave the profession within the first four years and list students with behavioral challenges and parents as the main reason for doing so (Public Agenda, 2004; Skiba, 2000). This statistic alone makes a dramatic statement.

While efforts to create alternative paths for teacher education have become commonplace at many institutions, we must ask ourselves why the behaviors present in today's classrooms are driving teachers from the classroom in mass exodus. How could we even measure this phenomenon? Could a much more likely possibility be that it is not the children themselves who have changed but the world in which they live?

The realization that the world today has produced a population of students exposed to trauma more than ever before essentially opens a door of responsibility. Doing what has always been done is no longer sufficient. If we are to meet the needs of the current population of students, educators across the nation must step up their game. While the ideal approach involves the transformation of every public and private school into a trauma-informed institution, smaller steps can be taken in the meantime for educators looking for smaller scale alternatives.

Relationships—a Strong Foundation

A great deal of responsibility is placed upon the shoulders of educators. As every year passes, it seems as though we are asked to do more with less. Building relationships on top of everything else we are expected to do may seem like an unrealistic expectation. After all, if we considered all of the relationships that we were expected to build with students, families, and colleagues, the number alone may make the task feel insurmountable. However, building relationships is not only possible, it is how we, as interdependent human beings, function. It is how we support one another. It is essential to our individual and combined success. Establishment of positive relationships may also be critical to the academic performance of students with ED (see McKenna, Shin, Solis, Mize, and Pfannenstiel, 2019).

We, as educators, must work to adapt our relationships with students in ways that allow them to form a connection. We must be reflective and "real" with ourselves so that we can form authentic relationships with students that can lead to healing. These relationships must be safe and healthy. We must provide consistency, positivity, and integrity with every interaction. These relationships require a relentless pursuit of support for student endeavors, forgiveness when undesirable choices are made, and an unwavering belief that students will rise to meet our expectations. Essentially, we must make ourselves available and show up for our students.

Building relationships with students affected by trauma is a delicate undertaking. It requires a rebuilding of trust, a regaining of confidence, a return to a sense of security, and a reconnection to love. But healing and recovery are impossible without lasting and caring connections to others.

Teach

Children who have experienced trauma often establish patterns of behavior necessary to cope. Sometimes, the behaviors are healthy. Many times, they are not. We, as educators, must step in and teach students a healthier alternative for coping methods that we observe. This process is not particularly easy, welcome, or comfortable for students who have become accustomed to systems already solidly in place. Acknowledging and trying something new requires a student to become vulnerable, and this is a place no student who has experienced trauma particularly wants to be. No matter, we must help students gain an awareness of the stress response they display (e.g., behavior patterns) and actively teach them positive ways to respond. These efforts require us to hold students accountable in a way that does not negate the value of the relational experience. Rather than reacting in a way that adheres to a strict standard of behavior management, we must first validate and assure students of their safety. Once students are regulated, only then can the discussion begin which will allow the teacher and the student to explore alternative ways to manage the intensity of their response and then work to make needed change.

It Goes Both Ways

Relationships, regardless of who is involved, are a two-way street. If both people are not invested, the likelihood of the relationship's success is slim to none. Both parties must be all in, and must expect of each other only what they expect of themselves. Thus, we, as educators, cannot expect trust and transparency from our students if we are unwilling to give it in return. In other words, we must be sincere and authentic. Students can sense authenticity a mile away and may even push (e.g., test) to ensure the authenticity they suspect actually exists. This is especially true for students who have experienced trauma.

I Will Treat You All Fairly

Society is currently plagued with a self-imposed necessity to treat all children equally. While it is unclear where this need transpired, we must take a moment to examine what this means for students. No classroom roster contains a list of students who have experienced the exact same events throughout their lives. In fact, classrooms are an incredibly diverse mixture of young people who all carry their own unique baggage in terms of life experience. Why is it then that educators often feel the need to treat all of their students equally? This seems to become more apparent in terms of discipline. Rather than considering the needs of each unique individual, teachers are quick to dole out the same consequences to all students regardless. In such instances, the focus seems to fall more on being a "fair" educator and doing for one what we would do for all. However, this logic is flawed.

   Treating people fairly means taking their circumstances into consideration and giving them what they need to feel safe, nurtured, and able to grow. It does not mean ensuring that every single student gets the exact same treatment. In fact, educators are known for their ability to differentiate instruction. Teachers work with small groups of students to ensure that the lessons being presented to them are appropriate considering their level of skill, confidence, and ability. Yet, when faced with situations involving social and behavioral decision-making, this required approach suddenly becomes irrelevant. Rather than considering the ability, skill level, confidence, and, more importantly, experience, educators often forget that these elements are still in play.

Fair does not mean equal. Education as a whole has embraced this statement in terms of academic instruction but continuously fails in terms of behavior and social instruction. A few great examples to illustrate the impossibility of delivering true equality are as follows and are ones I use to illustrate this idea to my preservice teachers. If a student enters your classroom with glasses, does this mean that all students should be made to wear them? Or, if a student requires crutches to walk, must we supply a pair for all students? When you visit the doctor to have your appendix removed, would he or she follow the same protocol required if you had simply broken your arm? The obvious answer is no. Thus, rather than treating all students equally in terms of behavioral and social guidance, perhaps we should consider all factors in play before determining how to move forward just as a doctor would for his patients or as an educator would when planning reading and math instruction. Instead of welcoming students to the classroom with the following greeting, "Welcome to third grade! This year I will treat you all exactly the same," perhaps what we should be saying is, "Welcome to third grade! I promise to treat you all differently and to take into consideration all that is happening in your life before I make any kind of decision that will affect you."

Function

We, as educators, need to understand that every behavior has a purpose. Behavior is a form of communication established on the day each and every one of us is born. While many of the behaviors we display are automatic, many times we display behaviors in order to send a deliberate message. The purpose of a behavior is often referred to as the behavior's function. In order to determine the function of a behavior, a teacher must ask what it is the student is trying to communicate by the behavior that they are demonstrating.

There are three common functions of behavior that are referred to most throughout professional literature. They are to get or obtain, to escape or avoid, or for sensory purposes. While other functions may exist, these three are known to guide most human behavior. Having a basic understanding of the three main functions of behavior will allow educators a clearer path for what it is their students are trying to tell them. By understanding what a student is trying to say, the interventions we choose to implement will be much better designed to hit a specific target or meet a specific need.

An understanding of the functions of a student's behavior becomes even more critical when working with students who have experienced trauma. Because their mind has essentially become hijacked by an event that happened in the past, a student who has experienced trauma may not be able to articulate exactly what it is they need. Their energy is expended on suppressing the chaos happening within their bodies, and they are not able to be fully present in the here and now. It is up to us as educators to use the clues from the student's behavior to determine exactly what they may need and are trying to communicate as a result of the behavior they are displaying.

Feel It

Students who have experienced traumatic events struggle with identifying what exactly is happening within their own bodies. When presented with a stressful event, the student may disassociate or "space out" or go from zero to sixty in terms of anger in the blink of an eye. When this happens, students cannot identify the cause of their intense reaction. They are essentially out of touch with their bodies, which means they are unable to meet their own needs. Put simply, children who have been traumatized cannot describe their feelings because they have no idea what the physical sensations mean within their own bodies. Psychiatrists call this phenomenon alexithymia, which is Greek for not having words for feelings.

With this realization, we must work to help traumatized students become more in tune with their bodies. We must find out what students are asking for, help them make sense of that need, and teach them to express it in a way that is productive. Communication with students who have not experienced trauma is difficult enough. Communication with students who have experienced trauma is a whole new ball game. In the book *Fostering Resilient Learners: Strategies for Creating a Trauma-Sensitive Classroom*, Souers and Hall (2016) discuss six communication steps to use when communicating with students. They are as follows:

1. Listen
2. Reassure
3. Validate
4. Respond
5. Repair
6. Resolve

They go on to explain that teachers are often experts at steps 1, 4, and 6 but often skip steps 2, 3, and 5. This is unfortunate as these are crucial steps that enable both effective regulation and long-term relationships with students. By following these steps, educators are much more likely to explore alternative solutions that will lead to more positive and productive outcomes than those currently being chosen by the student.

Don't Take It Personal

Working with students who have experienced trauma exposes teachers to a barrage of less-than-desirable events. Students who are unpredictable, emotional, angry, and who can provide no explanation for their responses can quickly wear on a teacher's state of mind. Imagine being met with unpredictable behaviors on a daily basis. It is no wonder that this path leads many teachers to burn out. Somewhere, in the midst of the chaos, teachers must come to the realization that the behaviors displayed by students are not personal even if it feels as though they are. Educators must understand that in their efforts to create a safe, trustworthy, and productive work environment, students feel that they are able to respond in a manner that is true to their current state of being. This could very well mean an emotional response that is far from ideal. It just so happens that the educator is caught in the cross fire if only because of good intentions. If wouldn't matter who was standing at the front of the classroom, more than likely that teacher would be met with the same type of response.

Rather than wishing the situation were different, we can come to expect that chaos may very well ensue. Teachers must remind themselves that the volatile responses shown by their students are results of the traumatic experiences already in the past. Simply said, it is not about the educator. At the same time, teachers have a valuable opportunity in those moments to respond in a trauma-sensitive manner that can alter a student's reality for the better. Our goal as educators is to help students gain a clear understanding of how their bodies are responding to stress so that they can learn the tools and strategies to avoid going "downstairs" and instead respond in a way that is logical, thoughtful, and intentional. When we realize that a student's misbehavior is an attempt at managing the chaos within their own bodies and not because they are trying to annoy or hurt us personally, it helps us as teachers to realize what it is we are working with. If we simply take behaviors at face value, we will rob ourselves of the ability to figure out what is the driving force. It is imperative that we, as teachers, stay in our own "upstairs" brain so that we can stay in control and guide the situation at hand to a productive outcome.

Proactive versus Reactive

Teachers are often very skilled at planning ahead. After all, we are responsible for directing an orchestra of students, and this requires careful planning if we are to be productive and successful. In terms of managing behavior, however, we often set ourselves up for a much rougher course. At the beginning of every school year, well-intentioned teachers spend time determining which behavior management approach they will utilize over the course of the school year. Teachers gather incentives and whatever other materials are necessary to carry out the plan. Then the students show up. Despite best efforts, often times behavior systems designed to support our students do the exact opposite and, instead, create additional stress for students who have already met their stress threshold. On top of keeping their own chaos in order, students now have another expectation hanging over their heads. The pressure is simply too much. This leads to reoccurring behavior incidents that the very system we designed was supposed to eliminate. This phenomenon leaves many teachers baffled and at a loss.

What educators must understand is that simply designing a system for students whom you have yet to meet is not enough. Rather, educators must continue to be proactive throughout the course of the entire year, constantly making needed adjustments to an already-thought-out system. This is particularly critical for students with ED who are educated in general education classrooms, as this setting may present significant challenges for the student and teacher alike. It is also critical because the mere placement of a student in a general education classroom does not confer benefit that is "more than trivial" (e.g., the free appropriate public education [FAPE] mandate; McKenna and Brigham, 2019). As you learn about your students and pay attention to their responses within the classroom, you will quickly learn the intricacies that set students up to succeed and those that set students up to fail. It is the very expectations that set students up to fail that must be addressed.

Simply put, implementing interventions before a behavior occurs works to eliminate over the top reactions, gives students appropriate options for how to handle a given expectation, and keeps a situation from spinning out of control. By approaching your educational responses in this manner, teachers are being proactive rather than reactive. Additionally, teachers are working to individualize behavior expectations based upon each student as an individual. As a whole, the state of education is notorious for operating in a state of crisis and waiting until after an undesired event occurs before reacting. Rather than working to dig themselves out of a hole, teachers must be proactive and put positive supports in place that will increase the likelihood of student success.

Self-care

Teachers are well-known for being selfless and for making their students the number one priority. Teachers do not enter the education field if they care a great deal about money or personal recognition. Instead, teachers enter the profession because they want to make a difference in the life of a child and to leave a lasting imprint on the next generation. Teachers work day in and day out planning, grading, reflecting, collaborating, and ensuring the needs of their students are met. In the midst of the everyday hustle and bustle, teachers become a population at risk.

When considering all of the demands placed upon the shoulders of teachers, it is no wonder that many teachers are on a quick journey to burn out. Many preach self-care to their students but do not practice it. Self-care that occurs on the surface is not enough. A random massage, retail therapy, or an occasional night out with friends is not enough to sustain a teacher long term. Instead, teachers must realize the importance of tuning into their inner voice telling them what it is they need to continue down the path of teaching. Without doing so, teachers can easily succumb to the pressures placed upon them and find themselves as another statistic.

Daily, we hope students to show up in our classrooms and present their best self to the world. In fact, we expect it. It seems only fair that we pay our students the same courtesy. This means teachers must attend to our own needs, take a break when needed, set realistic expectations for themselves and their students, and that they provide themselves with healthy boundaries. Teachers must trust their intuition and be cognizant of the kind of teacher they wish to be. When teachers find themselves veering from the track on which they originally started, a trajectory adjustment is needed. In essence, everything teachers do for their students, they must also do. Teachers cannot, in reality, take care of anyone if they are unable to care for themselves (table 12.1).

CLOSING THOUGHTS

Trauma is not an event that simply took place in a student's past. It is that and so much more. Trauma is an event with far-reaching effects, and, in a split second, leaves its mark on the mind, the brain, and the body. Trauma bruises the past and tarnishes the present and future. It results in the reorganization of perception, and it creates a reality that is anything but ideal. It does not discriminate, and can essentially touch the life of anyone anywhere.

While educators have an individual responsibility to continuously educate themselves about the reality of trauma in their students' lives, the need for change goes far above and beyond what a single educator can do. Rather than being stagnant in a reactive state of being, entire education systems must step up to the plate ready to make systematic change.

It is apparent that the students of today are not the same as those who once sat in the classrooms of yesterday. If we are to keep up and ensure an appropriate education for the students who keep showing up, a paradigm shift is

Table 12.1   Summary of Proposed Strategies

Strategy	*Summary*
Awareness	Educators and caretakers must continuously educate themselves regarding the population of students with whom they work. Reading professional literature, attending workshops and conferences, as well as asking questions will help enhance knowledge in regards to trauma and its effect on student populations.
Establish Relationships	Constant effort must be placed on building relationships which meet the needs of the students served. Relationships must be consistent and positive and will look different for every student. One size does not fit all. Building relationships is an ongoing effort that never ends and goes both ways. Students will give what they are given in return. Transparency, sincerity, and authenticity are a must.
Teach	Help students gain an awareness of the stress response they display and actively teach them healthier ways to respond to events perceived as stressful. Students must be validated and reassured of their safety during the time they are learning because this is when they are most vulnerable.
Fair vs. Equal	Treating students fairly does not mean that every student gets the exact same thing. Rather, every student is an individual who requires a particular approach and set of supports in order to reach their maximum potential. Thus, educators and caretakers must ensure that each student is given what it is they need based upon a differentiated approach to instruction in academics, social interactions, emotional responses, and behavioral performance.
Function	All behavior is a form of communication, and educators and caretakers must work to understand what it is a student is trying to communicate through the behavior they display. The three most prevalent functions of behavior include to get or obtain, to escape or avoid, or for sensory purposes. Students who have experienced trauma cannot always articulate what it is they need so it may be up to educators and caretakers to figure it out. Determining the function of a student's behavior allows interventions to be more targeted.
Feel It	Students who have experienced trauma are not always able to recognize exactly what it is they are feeling within their own bodies. Instead, they experience alexithymia, which means a loss of words for feelings. Souers and Hall (2016) suggest the following six steps to better communicate with students regarding their feelings: listen, reassure, validate, respond, repair, and resolve.
Don't Take It Personal	Educators and caretakers must come to expect chaos when working with students to change responses that happen as a result of trauma. Because students are at their most vulnerable during this time, educators and caretakers will be exposed to behaviors that are less than ideal. Teachers and caretakers must recognize that this behavior would happen regardless of who was standing in front of the student.

(Continued)

Table 12.1 (Continued)

Strategy	Summary
Proactive vs. Reactive	Attention must be paid to the responses of students in an effort to intervene before behaviors happen. Once patterns of behavior are recognized, efforts to alter student triggers must occur. By responding in this manner, students are set up for the likelihood of a successful encounter as opposed to one riddled with undesired behaviors.
Self-Care	In order to rise to the ongoing challenge of working with students who display undesired behaviors, it is imperative that teachers and caretakers attend to their own needs. They must take a break when needed, set realistic expectations for themselves and their students, and provide themselves with healthy boundaries. Without doing so, the reality of becoming a statistic in terms of burn out is a much bigger possibility.

inevitable. Teacher education programs must take a step back and evaluate course expectations for preservice teachers. Those responsible for professional development and ongoing teacher training must choose wisely when deciding how teachers will spend their precious hours away from students. Policymakers must determine if budget cuts are a wise decision when preparing future generations who will be responsible for the well-being of society. Rather than eliminating critical supports essential for childhood development, perhaps consideration should be given to adding mental health supports in school and bolstering an already-broken system.

In the meantime, educators on the frontlines will continue doing the best they can with what they have. They will keep reading literature, attending professional workshops, asking questions, collaborating, and doing whatever they can to appropriately support their students. Additionally, supporting students who have experienced trauma goes far beyond just a classroom effort. Teachers, parents, and caregivers must work together tirelessly to ensure students are well-supported in every environment.

Chapter 13

False Promise of Learning Styles-Based Instruction

By John William Mckenna,
Reesha Adamson, and Eliza Bobek

Designing instructional practices to meet the identified needs of students is a best practice that supports student learning. In fact, it seems that understanding "how learning happens," for example, how students pay attention, how information is encoded and later retrieved, and how content can be applied to solve problems, is a necessary prerequisite skill for successful instruction. However, myths and misconceptions about learning and the learning process are very common. These "neuromyths" can be defined as a "misconception generated by a misunderstanding, a misreading, or a misquoting of facts scientifically established (by brain research) to make a case for use of brain research in education and other contexts" (OECD, 2002).

One of the most common neuromyths in education is that of learning styles, the idea that students learn best when they are taught in a mode that matches with their purported learning style. In fact, identifying a student's learning style and designing instruction to utilize this perceived strength is a popular and at times mandated approach in school practice. For example, Massachusetts mandated in 2012 that educators seeking to renew their teaching license must earn fifteen professional development points in "effective schooling for students with disabilities and instruction of students with diverse learning styles" (Massachusetts Department of Elementary and Secondary Education, 2017). Furthermore, preservice teachers are evaluated on the degree to which they are able to "accommodate differences in learning styles" (Massachusetts Department of Elementary and Secondary Education, 2018). According to proponents of learning styles, instruction should be based on specific methods that students best master content and skills and these methods align with a student's identified learning style. Learning styles-based instruction has gained popularity in part due to an emphasis on differentiating instruction (Landrum and McDuffie, 2010), with methods consistent with learning styles-based instruction presented as an effective method for meeting the diverse needs of students in general education classrooms.

WHAT ARE "LEARNING STYLES"?

There are multiple definitions of learning style (Landrum and Landrum, 2016). A review by Coffield, Mosley, Hall, and Ecclestone (2004) reported seventy-one different models of learning styles. One specific model operationalizes it as "a combination of environmental, emotional, sociological, physical, and psychological elements that permit individuals to receive, store, and use knowledge" (Dunn, 1983; p. 496). According to this conception, it is estimated that 20 percent to 30 percent of students perform best when instruction is auditory, 40 percent of students respond best to visual instruction, and 30 percent to 40 percent to tactual/kinesthetic, visual tactical, or multiple sensory methods (Dunn and Dunn, 1979). "VAK" is another learning styles framework that is likely to be familiar to educators. According to VAK, students are considered to be visual (V), auditory (A), or kinesthetic (K) learners (Geake, 2008). Additional terms associated with learning styles include analytic learner, global learner, reflective learner, left-brain learner, and right-brain learner (Landrum and McDuffie, 2010).

Once a student's learning style is identified, proponents recommend that educators adapt instruction to align with the student's learning style. For example, proponents may advocate for the use of visual representations of information for students who are "visual learners." Proponents may also claim that visual learners have difficulties benefiting from instruction based on lectures and the absence of visuals (Hoffler, Prechtl, and Nerdel, 2010). They may also claim that student learning is diminished when instruction involves only one perceptual area or modality (Dunn and Dunn, 1979). In fact, the benefits of learning styles-based instruction are considered by many to be an established fact (Newton, 2015). Although this approach may have intuitive and commonsense appeal, rigorous research does not support the use of this method to improve school performance.

Learning Styles as a Neuromyth

Learning styles and learning styles instructional methods are based on a "neuromyth," which is a misconception of the brain and its role in learning (Howard-Jones, 2014). Claims or statements related to "brain-based teaching" and "brain-based learning" are commonly encountered by school-based professionals (van Dijk and Lane, 2018). For example, educational curricula, activities, and games may be presented to educators and parents/guardians as "brain-based," which may increase the likelihood that the product is positively received (Bernard, 2010). Yet such claims are often based on misconceptions, beliefs, or anecdotal information rather than research evidence. In fact, beliefs based on neuromyths are common among educational professionals including general education and special education teachers (van Dijk and Lane, 2018). The truth is that learning is a complex process, and proponents of learning styles-based instructional methods, at best, greatly oversimplify if not completely distort this process. Learning involves making meaning of different types of information rather than just information that is presented through a sense or modality, preferred or otherwise (Newton, 2015).

What do we know about how teachers' knowledge of the brain and the learning sciences may affect their teaching and student learning? Some research has suggested that teachers' knowledge of the brain is limited and that neuromyths are extremely common (e.g., Pasquinelli, 2012). Why is this the case? It may be that having a surface-level understanding of the brain combined with the challenging complexity of neuroscience lends itself to oversimplification of information and processes. Add to this the difficulty in translating those findings into practical teaching and learning strategies and it is easy to understand the prevalence of neuromyths.

The learning styles myth is particularly resistant to change, unlike other myths. For example, one of the most well-known neuromyths include the "Mozart effect"—the idea that playing classical music to infants (even in utero!) and young children could make them "smarter." This myth has, of course, been debunked, and the public's belief in the myth has faded. Most now accept this to be a common "gimic" or "fad." Perhaps this is because it is tied to particularly products, and it's fairly easy for consumers to accept the idea that companies market products based on incorrect ideas. Intuitively, people are drawn to accepting the myth of learning styles-based instruction; the idea that people have different styles/ways of learning, after all, doesn't seem too far-fetched. Another reason is that it implies that everyone can learn, an idea that is easy to grasp hold of. However, there has been no empirical support for style-based instruction.

Assessment of Learning Styles

A prerequisite to learning styles-based instruction is the accurate identification of a student's learning style. If a learning style cannot be reliably identified, then it is impossible to plan instruction based on a student's specific learning style (Landrum and Landrum, 2016). Considering the number of different conceptions of learning styles, it is not surprising that there are many different assessments for identifying learning styles (Landrum and

Landrum, 2016). However, research has demonstrated that students cannot be accurately assigned to a specific learning style (Druckman and Porter, 1991). In fact, learning styles assessments have poor reliability (e.g., consistency of measurement) and validity (e.g., the assessment measures what it actually professes to measure; Coffield et al., 2004; Kirschner, 2017; Landrum and Landrum, 2016), which are two essential characteristics for any assessment used to inform decision-making. Learning styles-based assessments tend to be self-report measures, which have been shown to be highly inaccurate. Another concern is that learning styles assessments require students to be assigned to categories based on characteristics that lack an empirical basis (Kirschner, 2017).

Effectiveness of Learning Styles-Based Instruction

The second critical aspect of learning styles-based instruction is to establish the effectiveness of instruction that aligns with a student's preferred or identified learning style. To document the effectiveness of learning styles-based instruction, research studies need to demonstrate that changes in academic performance are due to learning styles-based instructional methods. Studies would need to show that when students are provided instruction based on their learning style, their gains in academic performance should also be greater than the gains or performance levels of students who were provided instruction that did not align with their learning style. In sum, research needs to compare the performance of students who received instruction that aligns with their learning style to the performance of students who did not. When making this comparison, we would expect the performance of the students who received learning styles instruction to be superior and for differences in academic achievement between the two groups to be statistically significant (e.g., the differences are unlikely to be due to chance). However, at this time, there is no research that compares student performance in this manner and demonstrates the effectiveness of learning styles-based instructional methods (Kirschner, 2017).

Proponents of learning styles methods tend to cite unpublished studies as evidence of effectiveness (Stahl, 1999). Much of this unpublished research was conducted at one university (Landrum and McDuffie, 2010). Systematic literature reviews, which are used to identify research-based instructional methods (McKenna, Flower, and Adamson, 2016), have evaluated the research base on learning styles methods. Pashler and colleagues (2009) identified four studies investigating the effects of learning styles-based instruction. Three of the four studies did not report positive effects and one study reported student gains. However, the study that reported positive effects involved high school students who were gifted and talented and not students with learning difficulties or disabilities. In fact, much of the information presented to educators as "evidence" of effectiveness is anecdotal (Kirschner, 2017), which cannot be considered research evidence (Cook, Cook, and Collins, 2016). However, rigorous studies (e.g., studies using research designs that permit some degree of causal inference between instructional methods and any changes in student performance) have investigated the effects of learning styles-based instructional methods. For example, studies have identified student learning styles, randomly assigned students to instruction that aligned or conflicted with their learning style, and then assessed student performance in response to the instruction they received (Constantidinou and Baker, 2002; Massa and Mayer, 2006; Cook, Thompson, Thomas, and Thomas, 2009; Rogowsky, Calhoun, and Tallal, 2015). In fact, studies in which students are randomly assigned to different conditions is considered a "gold standard" in research. In studies investigating the effects of learning styles-based instructional methods, students who received instruction that was consistent with their identified learning style did not outperform students who did not receive learning styles-based instruction. In sum, there is no empirical evidence supporting the use of learning styles methods (Newton and Miah, 2017). Furthermore, there is a need for rigorous investigations that document the effectiveness of this approach (Newcombe and Stieff, 2012) before its widespread use can be justified.

So why isn't learning styles-based instruction effective, despite its wide use and broad appeal? First, there is a weak relationship between student performance and reported preferences (Massa and Mayer, 2006). Preferences, which learning styles assessments tend to attempt to identify, do not predict the best methods for learning a concept or skill (Knoll, Otani, Skeel, and Van Horn, 2017; Clark, 1982). Complex skills or concepts cannot be effectively taught using one style or using methods consistent with a specific learning style. The best methods are determined in part by the skill or content that is being taught. When learning new skills and concepts, research has demonstrated that students can use multiple methods to solve problems, with visual methods equally effective as methods that are not (Schwartz and Black, 1999; Stieff, 2011; Stieff and Raje, 2010). In fact, adept problem solvers are flexible in their approach. In sum, students are able to use multiple means to learn and complete complex tasks and do not rely on one distinct set of strategies, methods, or modalities, as professed by proponents of learning styles methods.

Dangers of Neuromyths

False beliefs concerning hypothesized connections between the brain, learning, and instruction adversely affect school practice (Macdonald, Germine,

Anderson, Christodoulou, and McGrath, 2017; van Dijk and Lane, 2018). Teacher reliance on practices based on neuromyths may result in students having less access to research-based instructional methods (van Dijk and Lane, 2018). Consider the following example. Explicit instruction in phonics is an instructional practice supported by a substantial accumulation of rigorous, peer-reviewed research (Denton, Fletcher, Taylor, Barth, and Vaughn, 2014; Ehri, Nunes, Stahl, and Willows, 2001; McKenna, Shin, and Ciullo, 2015). As a result, this practice is recommended by the National Reading Panel (2000). However, proponents of learning styles-based instruction have stated that phonics instruction should only be provided to students who have a learning style that permit them to benefit from it (see Carbo, 2005). Again, rigorous and plentiful peer-reviewed research has demonstrated that phonics instruction is an effective reading instructional practice for students in general and not as an effective practice for students with a specific learning style. If an educator was to believe this false claim, students in need of explicit phonics instruction (e.g., an evidence-based practice) may receive instruction characterized by its complete absence or receive insufficient opportunities to participate in this type of instruction. To be clear, basing reading instruction on a student's learning style is an ineffective practice (Stahl, 1999), if not immoral. Furthermore, students may spend time engaged in instruction based on neuromyths (e.g., learning styles-based methods) rather than instruction that is research-based. Use of learning styles-based instruction is harmful to students because (1) it is a waste of precious instructional time and resources and (2) students may avoid pursuing areas they believe do not align with their learning style (Newton and Miah, 2017).

Why Do Neuromyths Persist?

There are a number of reasons why instructional practices based on neuromyths such as learning styles methods pervade education despite the lack of rigorous research supporting its use, and despite research showing it is ineffective. Confirmation bias is a tendency to positively view information that is consistent with one's beliefs and to negatively perceive information that conflicts with beliefs (Lord, Ross, and Lepper, 1979; Newton, 2015). When we hear things that we agree with, we tend to like it. When we hear things that we disagree with, we tend to dismiss it. In sum, we commonly desire information that confirms our belief and reject information that calls into question our beliefs. It is also difficult to challenge or change beliefs that are established (Koslowki, 1996). As a result, educators, such as some readers of this chapter, may continue to use learning styles-based instruction despite being presented evidence to the contrary (Newton and Miah, 2017). Proponents may hold on to their beliefs because of the appeal of a simple method (e.g., learning styles) to address a very complex problem (e.g., differentiating instruction to improve student achievement; Willingham, 2017). Learning styles-based assessment and instructional practices are also commonly taught to educators, which may also contribute to the prevalence of this belief (Willingham, 2017). In fact, educators are provided a substantial amount of incorrect information and recommendations regarding the effectiveness of learning styles-based methods (Newton, 2015). In addition to preservice teacher preparation and teacher professional development sessions, this information can be found in academic journals that purport to publish rigorous research studies. For example, a recent investigation reported that 89 percent of manuscripts on learning styles had a positive view of learning styles and learning styles-based instructional methods (Newton, 2015). Yet there is no research that permits causal inferences between the use of learning styles-based methods and differences in student performance that supports the effectiveness of learning styles-based methods for use with students with or without disabilities.

CLOSING THOUGHTS

Honoring students' individuality doesn't happen when we categorize them and assign them to particular groups, each requiring particular instruction. It's far more important for educators to match their instructional style and approach with the content and skills they are trying to teach. Obviously students differ, just not by learning style. Educators should plan instruction based on research evidence rather than "best practices" based on anecdotal information, misconceptions, and/or distortions such as neuromyths. Instruction should be based on practices that have a sound research base. Assessment of student performance and/or progress should be conducted with tools that have adequate reliability and validity. As previously stated, learning styles assessments do not meet these criteria: they are invalid and unreliable. Learning styles-based instruction also cannot be considered a research-based practice due to the absence of research documenting its effectiveness. As a result, we strongly recommend that educators refrain from using learning styles assessments and instructional methods despite their commonsense appeal and pervasive use. There is only so much instructional time in the school day and in an academic year. Schools and districts, unfortunately, have a finite number of resources to allocate. Instructional decisions and resource allocation should be based on research evidence rather than anecdotal information and misconceptions.

*For a video explanation of the dangers of learning styles-based instruction, enter the following search terms in your preferred browser of choice: "learning styles, TED talk."

*For additional information on research-based instructional practices and practices that lack a research base, visit the TEACHING LD Current Practice Alerts webpage.

*For additional information on research-based practices, visit the What Works Clearinghouse website. Here you will find a number of practice guides focusing on various instructional areas and student populations.

Chapter 14

Progress Monitoring in the Inclusive Classroom

How do you know if students are improving and benefiting from inclusive instruction? Can you just feel it? Does your mental health show it? Are you exhausted at the end of the day? These are just some of the questions that school-based practitioners answer to demonstrate if a student is making growth in their academic and behavioral performance. Though the impact of student behavior does at times influence our perception of change, a more impactful measure is one that is objective, can be demonstrated across time, and tracked for irregularities and patterns of growth or decline. In fact, anecdotal information, or information on teacher "perspectives," cannot be used to assess the degree to which students benefit from inclusive instruction (Hott et al., 2019; Yell and Bateman, 2017). A reliance on subjective information and summary statements of student performance violates a parent/guardian's right to actively participate in the Individual Education Program (IEP) process. Subjective information is also not useful and completely ineffective for guiding instructional and student support decisions. Schools and teachers need to use a variety of data sources to determine a student's current level of performance and their response to existing services (e.g., is the student benefiting from instruction and supports academically, behaviorally, and socially? Or, is student progress in some or all of these areas flat or declining?). Progress monitoring, an essential practice in inclusive instruction, is the systematic measure of student performance across time to make data-based decisions to refine instruction (Tillman and Johnson, 2017).

All too often, school-based practitioners spend their time and effort describing the adverse effects of challenging behavior on academic performance without a systematic approach for determining a student's current levels of performance and rate of progress. Historically, students who require additional instruction and/or specialized instructional methods progress at a slower rate than their typically developing peers and this growth may be hard to recognize in the short term. However, a variety of measurement tools and systems have been developed to address this issue. They give educators and parents/guardians quick "checkups" into the health of student's academic and behavioral growth, thus potentially limiting the amount of instructional time spent on assessment while simultaneously providing valuable information. When we visit a doctor, comprehensive body scans and blood work are not routinely completed. However, quick and efficient measures of our health are completed (e.g., temperature, blood pressure, heart rate, weight) to determine if there is an area that should be explored more in depth. These quick measures are similar to progress monitoring in educational settings, as they are performed to ensure that students are making the progress that is expected without an undue burden of time or effort unless specific concerns are identified.

FORMATIVE AND SUMMATIVE ASSESSMENT

One of the most common educational practices of evaluating student performance is through the use of formative and summative assessment. These assessment processes are fairly quick measures of the degree to which students understand the concepts being taught. First, let's focus on formative assessment. Formative assessment is performed to obtain information that serves as feedback on how to modify teaching and learning (Black and William, 2010). This format of accountability supports instruction by determining if we are teaching content and skills in a manner that students are able to understand. In fact, frequent checks for student understanding is a generally effective teaching practice that educators should leverage when providing inclusive instruction to students with Emotional Disturbance (ED). Two primary methods of formative assessment are self-report and permanent product analysis.

First let's consider self-report. I am sure we have all seen a classroom teacher ask at the end of instruction "Does anyone have questions?" This quintessential statement is often not a question at all but a statement implying the conclusion of teacher instruction. Even though this question may be rhetorical, it is a basic example of formative assessment. We know that although this is a basic method of formative assessment, it is not a method that teachers can rely on to determine if students with disabilities are making effective progress on their IEP goals. It is also insufficient to document their performance on general education curriculum frameworks. There are more in-depth and systematic ways that self-report can be used and give us more instructional guidance and clarity about student behaviors.

For example, students can self-evaluate their performance on teacher-assigned work product. Students can provide a list of characteristics or aspects of the completed assignment that they are proud of, as well as aspects of the assignment that were challenging. Students can be asked to provide additional information to explain why they were proud of specific aspects and why certain parts were difficult. Students can also provide information on the types of supports they needed to be successful, aspects they were able to do independently, and information on additional supports they believe would be beneficial next time they work on a similar assignment. These reflections can be completed in writing, or can take the form of discussions with a teacher serving as a scribe. In fact, teachers can complete a similar process with the student in which they point out specific aspects of the completed assignment they are proud of, aspects they thought were challenging to the student, information on how the student and teacher responded to the challenges, things that the student was able to do independently, and additional responsibilities the teacher believes the student can take on next time a similar task is assigned. These work assignments with student self-reflections and teacher reflections can then be added to the student's work portfolio, which can then be shared and discussed during a treatment and/or IEP meeting.

Another common practice is to use a thumb-up ("I understand it!"), thumb-sideways ("I am uncertain."), or thumb-down ("I don't understand it.") approach for students to self-report. This takes the "any questions?" prompt a step farther by requiring all students to submit a response and giving a variety of response choices. The teacher can then scan the room and estimate the percentage of students who self-report understanding what was just taught as well as the percentage of students who require additional modeling, explanation, examples, and/or practice. A more in-depth formative assessment that involves self-rating is to have students report their understanding on a rating scale. Student self-reports can then be confirmed by requiring students to explain the concept or demonstrate the skill to a peer.

Another example of formative assessment is using a permanent product to guide student understanding. An example of this is asking a probing question about content knowledge and having students demonstrate their understanding in writing or orally. In classrooms, this can be done through a basic instruction technique such as an "exit slip" at the end of a lesson which can guide the next day's instruction, curricular goals, or even pace of content presentation. Exit slips can take a variety of forms from a multiple-choice quiz, open-ended questions, or even reflections on content presented. However, they should be done in a manner that is quick and easy for students to complete in the last few minutes of an instructional time period.

Technology has helped make formative assessment more efficient and perhaps more engaging for students (e.g., Plickers, Poll Everywhere, Kahoot,

Socrative, Quizlet, etc.) by providing educators a means to determine response patterns without any additional analysis. Using an opportunity to respond (OTR) questioning system for students to demonstrate understanding is another permanent product that teachers can use to determine student understanding. This provides a quick assessment, through a more traditional quiz approach where students demonstrate their understanding. These tools give students a way to each interact with content and demonstrate their knowledge through competition with each other and demonstration of the content. Many programs also score student responses automatically, generating a classwide report of proficiency.

Summative assessments are much more of an evaluation in nature. Instead of providing information that is used to inform instruction, they are more cumulative in nature and evaluate performance on intended learning outcomes (Dixsen and Worrell, 2016). The documentation of this competence is typically demonstrated through a culminating project, assessment, or paper. It could also be measured through more formal evaluation such as state and national tests of academic performance. This measurement tool is critical for comparison of students across groups but does little to impact instructional changes because the assessment occurs at the end of a unit of instruction. However, information on student performance on end of unit assessments is important, as it provides an indication of how the student is performing on grade-level content and curriculum standards.

Curriculum-Based Measurement

Instruction in general education classroom focuses on grade-level content and the development of higher-order skills to promote college and career readiness. With this in mind, it is important to frequently measure student performance using valid (e.g., they measure what they intend to measure) and reliable (the information obtained has degree of accuracy or consistency) measures to determine the degree to which students with ED are benefiting from inclusive instruction. In fact, research suggests that curriculum-based measures (CBM) can be used to inform inclusive instruction and to determine its effectiveness (Fuchs, Roberts, Fuchs, and Bowers, 1996; Powell-Smith and Stewart, 1998). However, it should be noted that this research is not specific to students with ED, and this research was not conducted in classrooms that provide instruction based on current college and career readiness standards or the common core. CBM measures provide information on student performance levels and growth in foundational skills in reading, mathematics, and written language (Deno, 2003). More recently, CBM have been developed to assess content area knowledge through the use of vocabulary matching (Lembke et al., 2017). These measures serve as proxies for student performance on more complex and involved assessments such as end of unit or end of year assessments in their respective areas.

CBM can be performed using systematic and commercially available measures of performance (e.g., DIBELS, easyCBM) to measure broad constructs of performance or more individualized lesson-specific assessments. These measures are such that if checked consistently and across time, student growth in curriculum areas can be determined over time (e.g., students are assessed using comparable forms of the measure over time, with performance entered in a graph). It can give a more valid measure of overall student understanding than one formative assessment or any individual content. Also using these methods, especially when using commercially available materials, there are standard growth rates that have been determined which can highlight if there is need for concern and additional monitoring.

Keeping these processes in mind allows for the direct understanding of student learning and rate of progression. It also gives information to consider about student progress and if more intensive instruction is needed to remediate any concerns. For example, students with low academic performance levels and flat rates of progress when provided inclusive instruction on its own may need more intensive intervention to make effective progress in school. Intensive intervention may take the form of supplemental small group instruction, or supplemental one-to-one instruction. However, for some students, more intensive intervention may take the form of a more highly specialized classroom setting rather than inclusion plus supplemental intervention. Conversely, it can also demonstrate how quickly a student is acquiring knowledge and if there should be enrichment or additional activities built into instruction to ensure students are continuing to be challenged and having their individual needs addressed.

Simple Progress Monitoring and Data Collection

All too often while teaching we would look back at our list of items to accomplish for the week and reflect on our "best-laid plans" which were often overshadowed by unexpected and pressing crises. Many times, we would continue lesson plans to the next week and shuffle individualized assessments and data collection in order to complete the timeliest tasks first. This philosophy and organizational structure was what we assumed was a reality of the classroom. There was always more to accomplish, and we found ourselves consistently prioritizing and rearranging. However, we discovered that this scenario could play out in alternate ways. And, it does not have to take place in the way we were allowing it to.

With some mindful reorganization and planning on our part, we can set up our classrooms using an organized process that we revisited and revised at the beginning of each year, quarter, month, and sometimes week. These adjustments create a systematic structure for data collection and progress monitoring that allowed us to be efficient, timely, and share responsibility with all of the other adults with access to our classrooms and students. In turn, this allowed students to take ownership of their own learning and progress and provided opportunities for self-monitoring. Data was the cornerstone for us as teachers to make informed decisions about student progress. Below are some of the strategies that we incorporated across our classrooms to ensure efficient and succinct data collection that accurately captured the progress and growth of every child in our classrooms.

Training

Jumping into data collection with necessary knowledge and know how it is all too often an assumption of someone in our profession. In reality, the knowledge base required for effective data collection requires careful and well-thought-out considerations for purposeful implementation. Data collection training and basic familiarity is a first step for every adult that is going to be in a classroom in order to ensure shared responsibility of the process. The most basic forms of direct data collection often used for monitoring of academic and social behaviors include frequency, duration, and latency. However, these are not often the best tools for use in the classroom. More complex systems can allow for efficient data collection including using an interval recording system. This type of recording allows measurement across multiple individuals and gives a more accurate snapshot of observed behavior. Another way to complete efficient data collection is through indirect data collection, such as permanent products of academic behaviors. This can be a valuable tool for monitoring academic progress as it allows the adults to monitor student performance with a produced product, such as a completed worksheet or even a computer-based tool which records performance. Expecting that all adults in a classroom have knowledge of these systems allows for each individual to be able to efficiently understand what data they are collecting as well as the specific planning and process for measurement.

Having a simple series of morning meetings or planning sessions with paraeducators and other staff allow for individuals to disseminate this knowledge and create a unified plan for implementation (e.g., who will be assessed, what will be assessed, when the assessment will occur, and how skills will be assessed). Other important consideration to emphasize to all individuals involved in the process is that data collection should just be a quick snapshot of behavior. Typically, a ten-to-fifteen-minute direct observation of student behavior or an estimate of student behavior using Direct Behavior Ratings (DBR; von der Embse, Scott, and Kilgus, 2015) and probes of academic performance is sufficient. DBR data may be particularly feasible for general education teachers who teach in the absence of a special education teacher or paraprofessional, because this process involves estimating academic engagement and disruptive behavior after teaching a lesson, rather than collecting data while teaching a lesson. In regards to student behavior, direct observation or DBR allows for a quick glimpse of the child to be observed in their natural environment. Such observations may be an overrepresentation of problem behaviors on some days and an underrepresentation on others, but, with enough observations, a fine balance can be attained. Another consideration and common pitfall are long, lengthy written notes for data collection. These are not only time-consuming in their conception but take a significant amount of time to analyze and understand whether or not a change is occurring in the behavior being observed. Finally, it is critical for special education teams to consider data collection during IEP team meetings. Creating goals and objectives for monitoring student academics and behavior that are measurable is the first step, but they also should be created with efficient and effective data collection in mind. As you are planning goals and objectives, a progress management plan for a student should also be created with mindfulness on how data will be collected and documented and what specific individuals will help implement this plan.

Materials

This seems like a basic process, but having easy access to a stopwatch, timer, clipboard, schedule (discussed later), and even possibly an interval alert system can create consistency of data collection. Typically, in our classrooms we had tasked an individual with organization of all materials for data collection and had created "data stations." These stations included all materials for the adults but also included student self-monitoring and recording sheets for students. This allowed for shared ownership of the process and for students to be accountable for their progress along with adults. Having tools printed, devices charged, and items organized increased the likelihood that the process went smoothly. We also graphed our data weekly to ensure that we were implementing interventions that were showing positive results. Since some of our data was paper data, we also had binders organized by student names to ensure that all of the data was organized and kept in the same spot so all members of the IEP team had access to it.

Schedule

Another basic process but one that is probably the most critical is the creation of an efficient schedule. Thinking about all of your students' goals and objectives and any other criteria that you would like to record and creating a succinct system for data collection is critical for success. We suggest planning data collection first by thinking about which goals and objectives need to be measured independently such as a specific replacement behavior, and which goals could be measured in a group format such as reading fluency. Typically, your classroom schedule for instruction is already grouped across instructional goals, so the organization of your data collection schedule should parallel (e.g., Lee, Vostel, Lylo, Hua, 2011). Then create a grid and assign specific days and times for each goal. Make sure that your instruction matches the format that is selected, and be sure to assign an adult to oversee each data collection period.

After you have a schedule for data collection, think about your data collection time to ensure consistency, specifically with the criterion of performance that you stated within your goals and objectives (e.g., three out of five days, 70% of the time). This ensures parallel construction of your data collection schedule with your IEP goals and process and allows for streamlined measurement systems. Creating a schedule also allows you to be systematic about what dates and times you are collecting data and build it into your instructional planning. This allows you to be efficient in the creation of a system where multiple data collection processes can be occurring simultaneously (e.g., permanent product of academic written work, momentary time sampling of student academic performance, and direct observation of the frequency of replacement behaviors).

Responsibilities

Data collection should never fall on just one individual within a classroom or school setting. The most effective classrooms have multiple individuals who are all tasked with data collection responsibilities to ensure that in one's absence another individual can seamlessly pick up and seamlessly continue collection. In some schools, an "all-hands-on-deck" approach is used to ensure that data collection occurs and is done correctly. All adults are vested in seeing student improvement and gives shared understanding of student growth and development across accountability systems. Having adequately trained individuals for data collection also allows for easier collection when maintenance or generalization data collection occurs outside of the context. It also allows for specific probes of the performance of skills outside of the context by having individuals that can monitor performance in varied settings. This allows for more mindful planning of goal modifications and additional performance criteria for mastery of academic and social skills and behaviors.

Problem-Solving and Celebrations

An important step in the data collection process is understanding that problems will arise! Even those "best-laid plans" can at times be thrown a curve ball. This is typical when you are working in settings where multiple individuals are involved and multiple systems are in place. Some of the most common issues to develop a plan for are individual absences of both adults and students, unexpected disruptions in the schedules like assemblies and activities that remove students from the classroom, and problems with the collection itself including training and organization.

Preplanning what to do when a problem arises and thinking about potential obstacles helps to create a clear process where no one is surprised or frustrated about anything that may come up to disrupt data collection. Having a change in the schedule may also be an opportunity for data collection that we had not thought of. Would data from an assembly be valuable data for this student? Sometimes thinking outside of the box for data collection may give you another look in a setting you had not thought of. Just as important as problem-solving is creating a time for celebrating accomplishments. These celebrations shouldn't just be on student performance gains but should also focus on the success of efficiency, reliable data, the creation of a manageable schedule and succinct data collection and recording that doesn't affect instructional time periods. Planning celebrations and problem-solving any issues and potential issues again helps with consistency across individuals and understanding of a system for success.

Recording, Synthesizing, Analyzing, and Evaluating

Finally, data collection is not something that is done in isolation. It is critical to have a system where data is organized and evaluated for instructional planning and considerations. It is crucial that this process is just as efficient as the data collection process itself. Planning responsibility of input and evaluation ensures that instruction toward goals and objectives are efficient and can be used to make considerations for modifications and adaptations in instruction to ensure performance criteria are met and that progress toward the goal is being made. Creating trend lines (e.g., a student's projected rate of progress over time, based on the trend of their previous performance) for data measures and goal performance lines gives all individuals, including the student and other educational decision makers, a specific guide for progress. It allows for mindful planning for lessons and creates a standard of performance that can be replicated. The most successful classrooms know where a student has come from, where they are currently performing, where they are going, have a specific plan on how to get there, and know how long it will take. In essence, this is our job as special educators and how we best impact our student performance and our classroom expectations.

Revisiting data on a consistent basis with all adults on a student's team and reporting on progress and instructional plans allows for shared ownership and responsibility in student growth. It also allows to have conversations across adults about trends and patterns within data and helps everyone to stay up to date on progress and the impact of supports and accommodations. It may be helpful at times to have multiple adults collect data to ensure all are staying consistent on data collection or to troubleshoot any issues which may arise. Having strong collaborative discussions and focus creates a data-driven culture within a classroom that can be easily replicated across environments, and in other settings and environments. This data-driven mindset and organization helps create systems where students and adults each know their role in the process and shares a community of support. Powerful outcomes can come from mindful planning and the structure of cohesion.

Disseminating Data Across Stakeholders

Overall, within school settings there are typically multiple individuals who must be part of a data evaluation teach for students. There is no student who is educated individually by only one person. Even if a student spends all of their time with one teacher, there is still administrative oversight which is given and hopefully a level of collaboration and problem-solving across individuals to improve outcomes for inclusive environments. Having defined systems to house data and make data-based decisions across individuals helps to expedite this process.

There are many formats from low-tech (e.g., file cabinets) to high-tech (e.g., systematic data entry and analysis systems) which can help organize data. However, beyond the organization and storage of data creating consistent thresholds for intervention is critical to cohesive success across a classroom, grade level, and school. Decisions and support for intervention and enrichment should not be made unilaterally and by one individual. A careful consideration of student progress, or lack thereof, can help determine the best avenue of support and what decisions are made.

These decisions and support should also expand outside of just the educational setting and should involve direct support from parents and guardians. Remember: sharing data on student performance is central to parent/guardian participation in the IEP process. Having an approach where all stakeholders have access to the data and can assist with decision-making helps to strengthen support for student achievement. A residual effect is that trust is built across stakeholders to support that child's best interest are in mind and that all team members are working together even though differing opinions may exist. This approach and consideration of data by all individuals also helps to align each individual's goals and ensure that all resources and supports are being given to assist with intervention and goal acquisition.

CLOSING THOUGHTS

Looking back on all that you and your students have accomplished throughout the school year can be quite a rewarding experience. However, this cause for celebration can be overshadowed if a consistent system of progress monitoring is not documented consistently or effectively to see your student growth. With some of these simple considerations and processes, a culture based around growth can be developed. The celebrations and understanding of student gain and the instructional planning around student struggles allow all adults to know how to help students achieve and give specific influence to all individuals involved and invested with a student to see attainment of success. These approximations toward the performance criteria can at times become lost in the struggles. Efficient systems help to document for all stakeholders critical growth and the plan for success.

RESOURCES FOR PROGRESS MONITORING

National Center for Intensive Intervention: www.intensiveintervention.org
This organization offers free tool charts to assist schools with the selection of research-based progress-monitoring measures. They also provide additional information (training modules, webinars) on using progress-monitoring data to inform decision-making. This is an incredible resource on progress monitoring. When selecting progress-monitoring measures, consider looking at this website first.
easyCBM: www.easycbm.com
Developed by the University of Oregon, the website offers free progress-monitoring measures in reading (e.g., letter names, letter sounds, fluency, comprehension, etc.) and mathematics (numbers and operations, geometry, measurement, algebra, etc.) as well as additional resources on their fee-based site.
Teaching LD, Expert Connection on CBM: https://www.teachingld.org/questions/12
This online resource provides additional information on developing and administering vocabulary matching assessments, as well as an overview of research on their use.
IRIS Center training module on assessment and progress monitoring: https://iris.peabody.vanderbilt.edu/module/gpm/cresource/q1/p01/#content
Developed by Vanderbilt's Peabody College, this free training module compares and contrasts the different types of assessment. It provides recommendations for initiating efforts to monitor student progress and additional resources.

Direct Behavior Ratings (DBR): dbr.education.uconn.edu
Developed by NEAG School of Education at the University of Connecticut, this website offers free resources (e.g., training, assessment) for assessing student academic performance and disruptive behaviors.

Plickers: https://get.plickers.com/
Plickers is the free card activity that allows you to create giant QR codes which when turned different directions register as different responses. A teacher uses their device to scan the room and record answers which are tied to individual students' cards.

Poll Everywhere: https://www.polleverywhere.com/?ref=PIW0qgbZ&campaignid=1624296850&adgroupid=63462208002&keyword=poll%20everywhere&matchtype=e&device=c&keywordid=kwd-304786950627&gclid=CjwKCAjw8ZHsBRA6EiwA7hw_sT5wp4MxMR9ela1fzp4KcQI9UtzYVZDRnxbkSNQd3lIQyHPV9cZ0GRoChewQAvD_BwE
Poll Everywhere is used to get instant classroom feedback from a variety of self-made questions. Individuals enter responses on their own devices which then show answers on the teacher's device.

Kahoot: https://kahoot.com/b/
Kahoot is an interactive quiz game which can be played by individual students or groups in a game show fashion. Answers are timed and results and scores are displayed on the teacher device.

Socratrive: https://socrative.com/
Socrative uses quiz questions as a review for student understanding at the class- , individual-student- , or question-level using this interactive program.

Quizlet: https://quizlet.com/
This program makes simple learning tools that let you study any content. Students can use flash cards, games, and other learning tools within at school or home.

Chapter 15

Collaboration in Inclusive Instruction

"There seems to be students who are placed wrong and nobody seems to know anything about them. It is hard to advocate for students when no one knows, when there is no communication with each other." Secondary grade special education teacher who provides instruction in an "inclusive," general education classroom.

*

"I would say ½ the kids have IEPs, so I think the most challenging thing is keeping track of everybody's different educational needs and making sure that we are adequately supporting all of the different kids, especially since I am a special ed teacher." Secondary grade special education teacher who teaches in "inclusive," general education classrooms.

*

The quotes above were obtained during a research study investigating the provision of special education services to students with disabilities who were educated in a large urban school district (McKenna, Brigham, Parenti, and Hott, 2019). As you can see, both teachers expressed concerns regarding collaboration, communication, and appropriately serving students with disabilities in general education classrooms. For students with comorbid learning and behavioral difficulties such as students with emotional disturbance (ED), collaboration, communication, and the selection and delivery of appropriate supports is imperative. A failure to do is likely to compound the learning and behavioral difficulties associated with this disability, as well as adversely affect the relationships and coordination between and among stakeholders that are necessary for inclusive instruction to be successful (e.g., the needs of individual students are addressed, as indicated by academic and behavioral progress that is more than trivial; see Kauffman, Wiley, Travers, Badar, and Anastasiou, 2019; Weiss and Glaser, 2019).

In this chapter, we provide an overview of important considerations for planning and delivering inclusive instruction for students with ED. We specifically focus on practices and considerations for effective collaboration between and among various stakeholders. First, we provide recommendations for collaboration between school-based practitioners and parents and guardians. We discuss parents and guardians first because it is absolutely critical to the potential success of inclusive instruction, as well as a requirement for the provision of a free appropriate public education (FAPE). Next, we discuss the importance of student access to and the coordination of multiple research-based supports that are provided by high-qualified professionals. Lastly, we discuss additional considerations for planning inclusive instruction and collaboration among outside service providers.

PARTNERSHIPS WITH PARENTS AND GUARDIANS

Schools/districts are strongly encouraged to expend all available resources and efforts to create, develop, and sustain positive relationships with the parents/guardians of students with ED. Students are acutely aware of the quality of these relationships, with students being more likely to accept instruction and support from those school staff who have a positive relationship with their parents and guardians. Team members, including the parents and guardians of students with ED, must work together to collaboratively plan and problem solve, both of which are much more easily accomplished when positive relationships have been established. However, as you know, school-parent/guardian collaboration can be challenging, with misconceptions between stakeholders having the potential to adversely affect collaboration and communication, and thus adversely affecting service delivery and student outcomes. For example, some school staff may have a deficit perspective of parents/guardians, believing that they are the primary cause of the students behavioral and/or learning difficulties at school. Parents/guardians should not be scapegoated under any circumstances, nor should collaboration difficulties be used as an excuse to disengage with parents/guardians or to stop the process of delivering services, assessing their effectiveness, and making timely adjustments to improve their effectiveness (e.g., "well, if the parents/guardians are not going to do this, then I might as well not do XYZ"). With this in mind, schools are reminded that parents/guardians of students with ED are equal partners in planning and assessing the effectiveness of inclusive instruction. Every parent and guardian has strengths, just like every teacher and school administrator, and they should be identified, acknowledged, and leveraged. For example, the Supreme Court of the United States (SCOTUS) affirmed the role of parents as equal partners in their opinion in *Endrew F.* (U. S. Department of Education, 2017). To foster active and positive collaboration with parents and guardians, we offer the following recommendations:

1. For at least some parents/guardians of students with ED, a phone call from school is a sign that there is yet another problem that needs to be addressed. This is due to a tendency for parents/guardians to only receive a phone call from school when there is a problem. For students who engage in frequent and persistent challenging behaviors such as students with ED, there have likely been many opportunities for such calls from school. Only receiving negative correspondence or "bad news" from school can wear any parent/guardian down. To address this issue, schools are encouraged to call parents/guardians when their child experiences even a small success at school. This type of school-home communication can break this cycle of negative feedback and correspondence (e.g., "here we go again . . ."), and may open up parents/guardians to having a refreshed relationship with school in those instances in which this relationship is fractured. Having conversations with parents/guardians about these small successes also serves as a foundation for when more difficult conversations need to happen, such as when there is a problem at school that needs to be addressed. In essence, contacting parents/guardians about even small successes, and doing this repeatedly over time, lays the groundwork for these more challenging conversations. When you enter these more challenging conversations, you may be perceived as someone who has a more complete understanding of their child because you noticed the strengths/gains and you took the time from your busy day to tell them. You also may be perceived as someone who not only "likes" but actually cares about their child and how they perform in school. Furthermore, you may be more likely to be perceived as an educator that understands the parent/guardian's perspective and the challenges they face as a parent of a child with ED who must simultaneously manage all of the other challenges associated with adult life. In sum, be proactive and start the process of establishing open lines of communication by calling parents/guardians about even small successes. Examples may include, but are not limited to, trying something new, persisting with a difficult task, raising their hand in class, asking for help when help was

needed, earning a high percentage of points in a school day, asking a topic-relevant question, an observed act of kindness toward another student or staff member.

2. Schedule meetings on days and at a time of day that is convenient for parents/guardians. Parents/guardians may have multiple responsibilities that they need to juggle, giving them limited flexibility in their day-to-day schedule. For example, parents may have responsibilities associated with having more than one job, have other types of meetings to attend, have meetings for other family members, and responsibilities associated with caring for other family members. Parents/guardians may also have previously missed time from work to go to school to discuss school difficulties, which may place their current employment in jeopardy. For example, parents/guardians may have had to unexpectedly take time off from work to deal with an incident at school, and this can create stress for them at work and at home. To address these difficulties, schools may need to schedule meeting before or after regularly scheduled school hours. Although this is an additional burden on faculty, schools are likely to have more resources available to them than a parent/guardian. Demonstrating this type of flexibility in scheduling also strongly expresses a commitment to collaboration with parents/guardians and of the school's belief that parent/guardians have an important and necessary role in inclusive instruction. In essence, "give a little" so that you can potentially get much more in return, as well as to avoid potential issues in the future. Give respect to get respect in return.

3. When first planning inclusive instruction for students with ED, it is essential to obtain parent/guardian information about what problems and issues they think are most important to address. This type of information is typically obtained during an Individualized Education Program (IEP) meeting, when discussing the vision statement and discussing how the student's disability adversely affects school performance. However, these types of conversations should occur more frequently for students with ED, as students achieve additional successes, have new experiences in and out of school, and as new challenges occur. Failure to do so may alienate parents/guardians, which would adversely affect collaboration moving forward. For example, it is important for schools and parents/guardians to have a shared understanding of the problems and issues that are most important to address. When disagreements occur, it is important to make certain that planning includes contingencies for addressing those issues and concerns that are considered most salient to parents/guardians. When creating a hierarchy of problems and issues to address, schools should discuss with parents/guardians how each problem and issue impacts the vision statement in IEP. When discussing services and

supports, school personnel are encouraged to provide information on how they support the achievement of specific aspects of the vision statement. Since the vision statement drives all special education and related services, challenges, issues, services and supports, and successes (no matter how small) should be viewed and discussed within the context of the vision statement.

4. When collaborating with parents/guardians, school personnel and outside service providers should avoid using terminology that is considered professional jargon. School professionals should avoid using words that persons without professional training in education, special education, social work, psychology, and so on are less likely to be familiar with. Professionals should simplify their verbal discourse (e.g., use easily understood vocabulary, use plain language) because parents/guardians are unlikely to have the professional background and training of school-based practitioners. In instances in which a team member uses terminology that may be confusing to parents/guardians, team members should interrupt the flow of the conversation and restate what was previously said using language that is more easily understood by those without professional training. In these instances, it is important to assume that parents/guardians do not understand what was just said rather than asking them if they understand, because parents/guardians may not feel comfortable admitting that they were confused. Assume that this is a situation that has to be fixed, and that you are the professional to fix it. Professionals are also urged to frequently check for understanding and to have frequent stop points for parents/guardians to ask questions, to share their perspective on the issue currently being discussed, and their knowledge of the student and/ or situation. Periodic summarization of key information, action items, and persons responsible for completing them should occur throughout parent/guardian school meetings. A summary of the meeting should also occur just before ending each meeting, with parents/guardians and team members provided an opportunity to clarify and/or refine this summary to make certain that it accurately represents actual events and discussions. School teams are encouraged to discuss possible dates for the next meeting just prior to the close of each meeting. To facilitate discussion of dates for future meetings, parents/guardians and school staff should be reminded to bring their calendars with them to the meeting so that this information is available to them.

5. Parents/guardians are equal partners in the selection of services, as this is a key component of IEP development. In fact, SCOTUS has affirmed their position as equal partners in this process. When making informed decisions regarding services and supports, it is important to select those that are considered culturally appropriate and acceptable to parents/guardians

(Cohen, Linker, and Stutts, 2006). Services and supports should align with the values of the student's culture and community (Kourea, Gibson, and Werunga, 2018). Consideration of the student's culture should inform the manner in which general education instruction and supports are planned and delivered (Cartledge, Gardner, and Ford, 2009). When developing the IEP, inclusive and culturally responsive teaching practices are recommended for students who are culturally and linguistically diverse (Grant and Sleeter, 2008). It is also important that school-based professionals do not misinterpret culturally relevant and accepted behaviors as problem behaviors, as teachers who are from the majority culture and who are unfamiliar with a student's culture may be prone to making this error (Green and Stormont, 2018). In fact, such misinterpretations can result in students being incorrectly identified as having an emotional or behavioral disorder (see McKenna, 2013; Raines, Dever, Kamphaus, and Roach, 2012). Parents/guardians are sources of valuable information on cultural and behavioral norms. School-based professionals can develop an understanding of the cultural backgrounds of their students and their families by engaging in conversations regarding connections between school expectations and norms and the expectations and norms of the student's culture to prevent misconceptions. Conversations also help identify expected school behaviors that should be targeted through direct instruction. For example, school-based professionals can provide concrete examples of common challenging behaviors that have been observed, describing the school contexts (e.g., environmental conditions such as tasks, peers, and adults) in which they were observed. Professionals can then ask parents/guardians if they consider the behavior to be a challenging behavior in this specific context. Conversations can then progress to identifying replacement behaviors (e.g., raising hand to ask a question, taking a break, making choices during independent seatwork) to be taught that promote success in the classroom and that are also culturally relevant and acceptable.

Initial Planning

Initial planning should be based on a comprehensive assessment of student strengths and areas of need (Cohen, Linker, and Stutts, 2006). All students have strengths, including those who are formally identified with ED. However, the performance of challenging behaviors may make these strengths less visible to school-based professionals. Assessment should incorporate informal (e.g., interviews, interest inventories) and formal (observation, standardized assessments, behavioral checklists, transition planning checklists) assessment methods. School teams should also consider the use of functional behavioral assessment (FBA) to identify contextual factors that predict problem behavior, as well as potential malleable factors to target in student support. The use of FBA to develop an individualized behavior plan based on the reasons why challenging behaviors occur is a research-based practice for improving the school performance of students with ED (Gage, Lewis, and Stichter, 2017). FBA data should be collected in contexts in which students with ED are successful as well as those that they experience difficulties. Assessment data collected in settings in which students are successful may provide "lessons learned" for adapting the environment in settings in which they experience difficulty.

A comprehensive understanding of the student's current level of academic performance is necessary to effectively plan inclusive instruction. This data is necessary to ensure that students with ED have sufficient competency in the prerequisite academic skills necessary to profit from inclusive instruction. We make this recommendation because some students with ED may have significant academic deficits (e.g., large gaps between their performance and that of their peers or grade-level performance), and these deficits may trigger the performance of escape-maintained behaviors which cannot be effectively addressed through the use of modifications, accommodations, and positive behavior supports. Skill deficits may cause students with ED to experience high levels of anxiety and/or stress. The pace of instruction may be too quick and the content of instruction too abstract for these students to benefit from general education instruction on its own. Valid, reliable, and current information on a student's academic performance is also necessary to identify those who need supplementary academic intervention (e.g., tier 2 or tier 3 instruction in addition to high-quality general education instruction) in addition to inclusive instruction to achieve FAPE mandates. Students with ED who are served in general education classrooms may require supplementary intervention and instruction (e.g., small group, one to one) in reading, writing, mathematics, and study skills. Supplemental intervention may also be needed to improve student behavior (e.g., social skills instruction, cognitive-behavioral interventions, check-in check-out, etc.). It should be noted that supplementary intervention and instruction is in addition to general education instruction rather than a replacement for general education instruction.

Student Involvement

School-based professionals and parents/guardians should meet with the student to discuss their interests and future goals. In general, it is critical that students with ED attend and actively participate in their planning meetings. Having students initially attend to discuss strengths and interests provides an opportunity for students with ED to develop the skills necessary to take a more active role. From our experience, this can and should be done with even young children with ED. Skills related to self-determined behavior are critical to the success of students with ED both in and outside of school (Carter, Lane, Crnobori, Bruhn, and Oakes, 2011). Initially, students with ED may only be ready (due to anxiety, insufficient experience, insufficient preparation, age) to sit in the meeting for a brief period of time, with a smaller subset of the overall team (e.g., a smaller group of adults, which should always include the parents/guardians). Adults present may then take turns to make one positive comment about the student. The student can then be asked to name and explain one area of personal growth or a recent experience of success. If student discussion is too difficult, a teacher could ask the student to name and explain an area of personal growth or a recent experience of success and dictate the student's response. The student could then bring this dictated response to the meeting and ask an IEP team member to read it for them. The team then gives the student one goal to work on, explaining its importance and steps that the student and the team can take to achieve it. Prior to having the student join this part of the meeting, team members should discuss what positive statement each will make and come to a consensus on a meaningful and realistic goal for the student to focus on. As students with ED become more comfortable attending meetings in this manner (e.g., attendance then progressing to partial participation), the number of adults present for this part of the meeting should increase, as well as expectations for student participation. For example, the student could participate in a discussion with the team about a goal to focus on, with a team member leading this discussion. The student could also lead a discussion about an appropriate goal to work on. The student could also be required to come to the meeting with a draft vision statement, written with an appropriate level of adult support. Regardless of the manner in which the team decides to increase the level of student participation, it is important for the student to be informed of this increased expectation prior to the meeting and with sufficient advance warning and time for adults to provide supports and instruction that is necessary to promote student success. Role play of the IEP team meeting can serve as a practice opportunity for student participation prior to the actual IEP meeting.

In general, services should be selected so that they incorporate student interests and focus on developing skills that are necessary for achieving the vision statement as well as the student's future goals. In the initial meeting, school staff and parents/guardians should identify potential team members to include in future meetings, based on the direct services and supports they can potentially provide, as well as the type of expertise that they can share in the form of ongoing consultation.

Multiple Supports and Interventions

Effective treatment and remediation of ED requires multiple interventions and approaches. It is essential that students with ED have access to evidence-based practices and interventions (Cohen, Linker, and Stutts, 2006; McKenna, Solis, Brigham, and Adamson, 2019). Unfortunately, research evidence is infrequently used to inform school practice and instructional decision-making (Cook, Cook, and Collins, 2016; Hurley et al., 2010). Conversations about school practice and student support should have more statements that begin with "the relevant research suggests" than "I think." Students with ED should have access to appropriate academic, behavioral, and mental health supports (Hunter, Elswick, and Casey, 2018; McDuffie, Landrum, and Gelman, 2008; Mitchell, Kern, and Conroy, 2019). Collaboration among team members should have a heighted focus on academic instruction to prevent and address the occurrence of problem behaviors and their effect on teaching and learning (see Kauffman, 2003). Academic instruction and supports are necessary to prevent achievement gaps from increasing as well as to narrow them. To coordinate services, clear expectations for service providers are required, as well as effective methods for accurate and ongoing communication with all partners (Cohen, Linker, and Stutts, 2006). Expectations should explicitly state the frequency and type of communication (e.g., biweekly e-mail updates; immediate communication of concerns) with other team members, frequency and types of assessment to monitor student progress, and persons responsible for providing specific services and conducting specific assessments. With this in mind, it is advantageous to have one person assigned as a case manager who can serve as a central point of communication, as well as someone who can periodically check to make certain that services, supports, assessments, and communication are occurring as planned and in an effective manner. In regards to case managers, it is important that they have sufficient time and expertise to manage these responsibilities. In some instances, this will involve removing other responsibilities from assigned case managers. Overall workloads for case managers must be carefully managed so that they can effectively perform their duties.

Planning and Delivering Co-taught Instruction

Students with ED may benefit from general education instruction that is co-taught, as it can provide access to content area instruction as well as professionals with expertise in adapting instruction and explicit (see Weiss and Glaser, 2019). When planning co-taught instruction, professionals should consider the full range of co-teaching models of instruction and student support. These include one teach one assist (one teacher leads instruction, one teacher provides support), parallel teaching (students are divided into two groups, with each teacher leading instruction with one of the groups), alternative teaching (one teacher leads the class, while another teacher provides instruction to one student or a small group of students), team teaching (teachers share responsibility for providing instruction to the whole class, both teachers are equally responsible for instruction and behavior management), and station teaching (students divided among different stations, with two stations being led by teachers and students working independently in the other stations).

Unfortunately, research suggests that the one teach one assist method tends to be the most commonly used in school practice, with limited use of the other models. This reliance on the one teach one assist model of co-teaching is likely to limit the potential effectiveness of co-taught instruction for all students including those with ED. To address this potential issue, teachers who are assigned to co-taught teaching arrangements must be provided ongoing professional development in co-teaching methods (Shin, Lee, and McKenna, 2016; Weiss and Glaser, 2019). Professional development should include methods for planning, delivering, and assessing the effectiveness of co-taught instruction. Professional development should include opportunities to observe expert co-teachers plan and delivery co-taught instruction. In essence, schools are encouraged to leverage their district- and building-level expertise in co-teaching. Scheduling and manageable workloads are also important consideration for co-taught instruction, particularly when it is used to serve students with ED. Co-teachers need consistent and adequate time to discuss instruction and how specific co-teaching arrangements can be used to support students with ED on specific academic tasks and the manner in which positive behavior supports will be employed. Furthermore, co-teaching teams should have opportunities to discuss barriers to effective co-teaching, methods for addressing them, and the implementation of specific teaching practices during co-teaching. In essence, a community of co-teaching practice is an important resource for teachers who are assigned to co-teach.

Co-teaching can improve classroom and behavior management, if both teachers are appropriately trained and supported (McDuffie, Landrum, and Gelman, 2008). Co-teaching can be used to support the planning and provision of opportunities for students with ED to practice social skills that are taught in intensive intervention. For example, more frequent and consistent prompting and reinforcement of student use of social skills may occur in co-taught classrooms, due to the presence of two teachers to fulfill this responsibility. Co-teaching arrangements may also permit students with ED to receive more frequent and consistent error correction and reteaching (e.g., modeling) of social skills in the natural classroom environment, as long as teachers are adequately trained, supported, and have manageable workloads.

However, co-teaching should not be used to replace intensive intervention because co-teaching is not an evidence-based practice and many students with disabilities, including students with ED, are likely to need intensive intervention in addition to high-quality general education instruction that is delivered through carefully planned and delivered co-teaching (see Hunter, Elswick, and Casey, 2018; Mitchell et al., 2019; Smith, Poling, and Worth, 2018; Weiss and Glaser, 2019).

Use of Paraeducators

Paraeducators can potentially be a resource for providing inclusive instruction to students with ED. However, school teams should be aware that potential benefits have limits because paraeducators are ill-equipped to provide high-quality academic instruction and to integrate positive behavior supports into instruction. Although paradeducators cannot replace instruction and support provided by highly qualified general educators and highly qualified special educators, they can be trained and supported to carry out important responsibilities.

Paraeducators' access to training is essential to their effectiveness (Maggin, Moore-Partin, Robertson, and Oliver, 2009). Paraeducators should have clearly defined roles in the classroom (e.g., specific responsibilities are assigned), with training provided on how to successfully carry out each assigned responsibility. If trained and supported, paraeducators can deliver scripted lessons and curriculums. However, developing and adapting curriculum, materials, and behavioral support plans should be performed by the classroom teacher, as paraeducators have insufficient training and expertise to perform this duty. However, it is appropriate for paraeducators to assist with the implementation of behavior support plans and to provide support during academic instruction. Training should consist of a discussion of the importance of the responsibility, modeling how to perform the responsibility, and ongoing performance feedback on implementation of the responsibility. Regularly scheduled meetings between the classroom teacher and paraeducator should occur to discuss performance on assigned responsibilities. Meetings can also be used to reteach/model skills in need of refinement and to discuss issues related to collaboration and support implementation (Maggin, Moore-Partin, Robertson, and Oliver, 2009). Meetings should also be used to provide paraeducators updates on important information about students that is necessary for them to know how to effectively carryout their responsibilities. As paraeducators demonstrate their ability to perform specific duties, additional responsibilities should be added.

Paraeducators should be provided behavior-specific praise for instances in which they complete their assigned responsibilities and have their efforts continually encouraged. Paraeducators should also be periodically reminded of the importance of their role to the success of inclusive instruction for students with ED. These methods may promote active engagement if not enthusiasm for continuing their support efforts. Although paraeducator training is likely to be performed by the general education teacher or the co-teaching team (if the paraeducator is assigned to a co-taught class), these professionals may lack sufficient training in how to support paraeducators (Maggin et al., 2009). As a result, teachers should be provided training in effective methods for supervising paraeducators.

Related Service Providers

It is likely that a number of related service providers will be involved in the provision of inclusive instruction for students with ED. Related services may provide direct services to students, coaching to teachers and/or paraprofessionals, or consultation services to the team. Selection of related services for students with ED should be based on a comprehensive evaluation of student needs and strengths as well as the needs and strengths of those teachers who work with the students.

Students with ED should be evaluated for speech and language difficulties, as research suggests that many have expressive (e.g., use of oral language) and/or receptive language (e.g., comprehending oral language) difficulties that are not addressed (Armstrong, 2011). Speech and language pathologists can help with the development of IEP goals that focus on using expressive language skills to communicate feelings, needs, and wants and to interact with others in a positive manner (Armstrong, 2011). Thus, the importance of collaboration with speech and language professionals, either as a direct service provider or as a consultant, should be considered, as indicated by a comprehension assessment of skills in these areas (Armstrong, 2011).

Related service providers may also provide instruction and support that focuses on the development of social skills and critical school survival skills (e.g., asking for a break, raising hand and waiting to be called on when one has a topic-relevant question or comment, etc.). Related service providers should work with the classroom team to identify times and activities that can be used to teach and reinforce social and school survival skills. Related service providers in these areas can also provide suggestions for promoting the generalization and transfer of skills taught in supplemental social skills interventions (Armstrong, 2011). Social skills support may be provided by a school psychologist, a special education teacher, a social worker, or any other school-based professional with prior experience and expertise in this area.

Social workers often collaborate with teachers (Hunter, Elswick, and Casey, 2018), particularly in the planning of inclusive instruction for students

changes (e.g., decrease in medications, starting of new medications, ending of medications) when assessing student response to interventions and supports and determining their (Blair, Torelli, and Symons, 2016).

CLOSING THOUGHTS

Students with ED have comprehensive needs that should be addressed by a comprehensive, multidisciplinary team. Teams need to function at their best to do their best for students with ED. As they say, "it takes a village." We hope that you find these suggestions and considerations helpful in your efforts to provide beneficial opportunities to students with ED.

Chapter 16

Abandoning Readiness

By Maria Kolbe, Inclusion Facilitator

I think about my first IEP meeting as a special educator quite often. I was teaching in an urban district in the northeast, and it was my first year as a lead teacher of a substantially separate classroom. I sat at the head of the conference room table with neatly stacked piles of itemized agendas, behavior graphs showing downward trends of challenging behaviors, and more data than could possibly be shared within one meeting. By any traditional definition, the meeting regarding a student with a diagnosed emotional disability, Renee, was a success. The team of school employees and parents left with a clear vision of the goals for this engaging, funny, and bright child: to decrease challenging behaviors, increase self-regulation skills, and increase her stamina for non-preferred tasks.

However, the reason this IEP meeting sticks in my mind is not because of the success I felt at the end of the meeting. Instead, I wish I could take what I know now and transport back in time, interrupting each time the word "readiness" was used as a rationale for lack of exposure to academic concepts. I would stop myself from touting behavioral decreases that were not linked to functional engagement in challenging tasks as an achievement. I wish I could go back and change Renee's IEP goals to be academically based, to remove statements in the document regarding the team reevaluating her readiness for inclusive experiences and more challenging academic content contingent on a decrease in interfering behaviors. I would speak about presuming competence in Renee's abilities, how consistent adult interactions based on phonological or numerical foundation skills (yes, with her behavior reinforcement system in place) could shape her identity as a learner and result in greater regulation gains.

Renee's family moved shortly after the meeting, and I have often wondered about the trajectory I set Renee on in her new district. Despite Renee's above average intelligence, a special educator receiving the IEP we proudly created was given a vision of a student incapable of engaging in academic tasks, a student that needed to achieve a long list of lagging emotional regulation skills before being able to engage with conventional schooling. This lens was appropriate to me at that time, since when Renee was in my classroom academic expectations were minimal for her and all interventions or curricula experiences were behaviorally driven and isolated by design. Renee was often presented with basic academic materials, such as letter-sound correspondence activities, 1:1 correspondence work, or letter tracing sheets, tasks based on skills she had already mastered. These types of activities were the core of her academic curriculum, with significantly lower academic expectations in relation to her intellect and ability, justified at the time based on her emotional and behavior deficits.

It is difficult for me to write that in her year in my classroom, Renee did not receive systematic access to grade-level literacy or math curriculum. I could not have told you what the grade-level curriculum standards were, or what the core-learning concepts were for her grade level. I certainly knew her discrete IEP objectives with academic content based on skills she had shown previously, as well as her rates of maladaptive behaviors at any given point of the day. Our focus was on Renee having safe hands during morning meeting (not actually engaging in morning meeting), completing a three-step task such as a stamping activity without environmental destructions (not teaching her the skills needed to complete a three-step literacy task), and using a functional communication response in the absence of challenging behavior (instead of focusing on engaging academic content that could actually hold her attention). Generalizing behavioral objectives to other content, settings, and teachers was something to be discussed once "mastery" was truly achieved.

Twelve years later, I have learned that I was not completely wrong about Renee. She needed programming with a strong behavioral foundation, with a focus on her lagging regulation skills. However, that was only half of what Renee needed. Both these elements should have been the "how," not the "what." In my first year of teaching, behavioral interventions and regulation skill instruction were the whole programming package, there was no bigger, contextual "what" to align our values about the student's potential. I was waiting for some undefined, subjective measure of behavioral success before opening the door to rigorous academic programming for Renee for her to be "ready."

Within my work in three school districts, I have seen again and again that without a rigorous "what" to align all programming and drive staff expectations, students with emotional disabilities can be on an endless loop of low expectations, deficit-driven interventions, and isolation from grade-level curriculum experiences. And, once this has been set in motion, with expectations becoming increasingly removed from neurotypical individuals, how can a student possibly be expected to get him or herself out of this loop? I certainly hope Renee found her way off the merry-go-round I originally started for her.

I now know that at that time I was stuck within a linear view of educational programming for students with emotional disabilities. I was convinced that behavioral stability with a robust toolbox of strategies needed to be present before exposure to rigorous academic concepts and schooling that is more conventional could be implemented. However, I have experienced three serious problems with this school of thought.

First, there is an inherent contradiction here. Emotional regulation skills and adaptive behaviors are not finite, they are not achieved and then built upon the way decoding, mathematics, or fine motor skills are obtained. Regulation and behavioral skills are environmentally dependent, meaning mastery should be defined as the successful application to events throughout the student's life. Any definition of behavioral "mastery" that leads a special educator to take the leap to expose students to more challenging tasks and contexts is subjective by definition, and should not be used as a final arbiter in opening the door to higher standards for the student. Instead, academic blocks can be a highly effective environment to embed regulation skill instruction and application. Students often have a much higher rate of acquisition of the regulation skills across multiple academic settings when instruction in adaptive and regulation skills are woven into the fabric of the student's academic tasks. The contextual instruction of emotional regulation and adaptive skills within academic blocks allows for a measurement of success that is aligned with settings and environments that the student will encounter throughout their academic career and beyond. Additionally, the measurement of "mastery" becomes refocused to a much more functional and adapted view: the student's ability to self-regulate and utilize adaptive strategies in a variety of ever-changing, often-challenging situations and settings.

Second, the majority of individuals with emotional disabilities have average to above average academic ability. There is often nothing within the student's cognitive profile that indicates that they should be exposed to less rigorous or lower academic content. Certainly, differentiation of the process or product will usually be required, in addition to embedded therapeutic accommodations. But, differentiation of content should not be considered for an individual that does not have an innate intellectual deficit. Unfortunately, many students with emotional disabilities have their content dramatically differentiated, creating large gaps in the student's knowledge that only grow wider and deeper with time. These gaps exist not because of inherent learning deficits but because of lack of exposure to content. At the core, this decision by compassionate and dedicated educators to reduce exposure to academic content when the student's disability does not warrant the restriction is a denial of the student's educational rights, with lasting impacts to students throughout their schooling career and beyond.

Third, there is a self-fulfilling prophecy aligned with this approach. Often, students with primarily behavioral and therapeutic programming will be given challenging academic expectations in small increments with behavioral objectives as the goal. For example, an expectation may be for a student to attend a science class while staying safe for ten minutes or stay for five minutes of a reading group. In these examples, the focus is not on the differentiation needed for students to engage in the academic content meaningfully and successfully. Time limits indicate an inability to experience prolonged success or establish the student's identity as a member of the activity and as a learner in general. It should be no surprise that the student will usually blow out of the activity in a dramatic fashion, a minus on the data chart for the day, to be tried again tomorrow with the same approach and probably the same result.

Instead, I have seen tremendous growth in students when behavioral and therapeutic programming exists cyclically and simultaneously within grade-level academic expectations. Students have often shifted to less restrictive settings, dramatically increased their frustration tolerance and stamina for challenging tasks, and have become truly successful students and members of their community. A programming package for students with significant emotional disabilities that holds them to the same academic expectations as neurotypical peers is not without its challenges and obstacles. There are expansive barriers to this work being implemented, even once the intent is present. The pervasive concept of "readiness" can seem woven in the fabric of special education, posing a particular challenge in the changing of mindsets to be able to implement this work. However, the growth I have witnessed in many students has been nothing short of remarkable, resulting in students' trajectories completely changing tracks, with students finding an anchoring identity as a learner and member of a school community. This became possible when school teams abandoned concerns of readiness and made grade-level academic expectations the unifying focus of the student's day.

THE "WHAT" OF SCHOOL

Imagine yourself at a weekly consultation meeting for a student with an emotional disability. I have sat in hundreds, and they typically start with a reporting of the laundry list of outrageous things the student did over the past week, with other updates mixed in. This reporting out serves an important purpose, to give each person at the meeting a picture of the student's week, but more importantly to allow for staff working daily with the student to be validated by stating the challenges of the week, knowing others have heard their experiences and concerns. Once this tapers down, I usually lead with one of my go-to questions: "So, what differentiation do we think will be needed for the upcoming unit in (fill in the blank)?" "How did the four parts of the literacy block go this week?" or "How is everyone here feeling about the structure of the math block for the student?"

For a student's team at my current school, these questions about the student's academic blocks would be easily answered, and the rest of our consultation would focus on how to maximize the student's engagement with these academic blocks until we meet again as a team. BCBAs, social workers, general educators, special educators, and support staff would leave the meeting with the few behavioral or therapeutic elements they would be focusing on to help the student reach the shared goal: the student showing their knowledge on the core-learning concepts of their grade-level units of study. New checklists would be laminated, a new coping strategy may be prepared to be introduced to the class, the visual clutter on worksheets would be reduced, and the iPad would be fully charged with the all-powerful Temple Run game ready to go.

Given that the meeting started with the team discussing natural consequences when lewd profanity is screamed at a teacher in front of the class, to an outsider these academically driven questions can seem inappropriate, or at the very least, not the priority to discuss. However, this is the easy part. Or, at least the straightforward part, really the only part of the process that is. Everything changed for my students with emotional disabilities when I embraced my role as a general educator first to determine the "what" of my students' days, then taking my knowledge as a special educator to help them get there (the "how").

So, what does this look like? If the student is in fourth grade, the expectations for your school district or county that fourth-grade teachers use to design their schedule for the day can be used as the student's schedule. This will generally contain something to the effect of a ninety-minute literacy and writing block, seventy-minute math block, forty-five-minute science/social studies block (alternating days), and minutes for recess, lunch, a special, and activities such as morning meeting. When I was transitioning to this model, I certainly did not start with implementing all of these blocks within my substantially separate classroom simultaneously. Instead, I started with the expectation that all students would be fully engaged in a ninety-minute literacy block, showing their knowledge of six grade-level core-learning standards by the end of the month.

No content modifications have taken place in this approach, and each student will be held to their grade-level ELA expectations. The special educator has not had to create a separate pacing guide or different curriculum altogether, picking and choosing standards based on a wide range of subjective reasons. I have found that, instead, following the grade-level guide for curriculum implementation takes a huge burden of planning off the plate of the special educator. Staying connected to general education content is admittedly easier if the special educator's classroom or role is situated within a public school setting. However, even without that reference, the school district's curriculum guides by grade level are certainly available to out-of-district schools or collaboratives. If nothing else is taken from this chapter, this would be my biggest piece of advice. Align your work with students with emotional disabilities in the framework of the state standards and the minute allocations of their grade level, regardless of the student's least restrictive environment. Presume academic competence in your students, and then put on your special educator hat to guide implementation of the plan.

With the grade-level ELA learning standards known and a ninety-minute literacy block structure expectation, the implementation is where clarity ends and individualization occurs. Although there is certainly variation among districts, a balanced literacy approach would generally include word study (explicit phonics instruction, spelling, grammar), a mix of shared, independent, and modeled reading, differentiated reading instruction based on the student's reading ability, and writing. I highly recommend this structure or a similar one, depending on the structure the school district you are in or are affiliated with uses. From here, the knowledge of each individual student will help with the long list of environmental accommodations that will certainly be needed for the student to be successful.

Table 16.1 is a sample ninety-minute literacy block for a hypothetical student named Daniel in third grade, a student with nonexistent frustration tolerance and an ability to jump from behavior 1 to behavior 10 in his behavioral repertoire in seconds. Daniel's typical engagement in anything at the time of his starting school in my classroom was one or two minutes before cognitive distraction would be needed to help him maintain a somewhat regulated state. Therefore, our design of his literacy block began. The minutes were not changed based on Daniel's behavior, the structure would stay the same for the entire month. Although the learning standards addressed in the blocks were third-grade standards, everything else could flex to Daniel's interests and profile. His writing task was a journal to the school secretary, someone he could not get enough of. Although the word "study" followed the Wilson Fundations approach, soccer was woven into each activity as much as humanly possible. The guided reading group used nonfiction texts about the grossest animals on earth. Strategy points were given out liberally for any instance of something that could resemble positive self-talk or a different regulation strategy, translating to a trade-in for preferred activities before

Table 16.1   Sample Initial Literacy Block Structure: Ninety Minutes

	Expectation	Staff Ratios
15 minutes	Guided reading group	Small group: Teacher-led
10 minutes	Technology-based literacy instruction	Individualized: Minimal teacher proximity
15 minutes	Word study	Small group: Teacher-led
15 minutes	Gross motor break and snack	
15 minutes	Applied writing task	Small group: Teacher-led
10 minutes	Break of student's choice	Minimal teacher proximity
15 minutes	Student choice: Reading fluency curriculum or shared Reading	Individualized: 1:1 with a teacher

lunch. Assessments were woven in, but assessments on completion of the learning goals of the activities.

Certainly, the implementation of this literacy block structure was not pretty. The first day, I have a distinct memory of the iPad being thrown at my head as we attempted to transition the student from block two to block three. Engagement was minimal during the first week, with new creative ways to avoid the tasks being tried each day (my least favorite was pulling the fire alarm in the hallway). I was put in the role of advocate to others in the building that were questioning his placement in my classroom at all, that maybe a substantially separate classroom in a public school was not restrictive enough for him. When I explained what we were doing when the behavior occurred, I was told I was expecting far too much of him. And, they may not have been wrong. However, the truth was that the student had years of behavioral patterns working against my plan. He had learned, as many students with his profile do, that explosive behavior is the perfect way to escape demands and not have to sit with the uncomfortable feeling of not knowing exactly what to do with a task. When their baseline feeling is often one of discomfort or anxiety, why would anyone seek out situations that made the feeling worse?

We stayed consistent in our expectations, and after two weeks of extreme difficulty, something began to happen. Daniel would walk over to the word study station while we were writing words in sand, watching until he saw I noticed. He asked me why another student got to trade in for points early, expressing interest when I explained it was because the student beat his fluency cold read score by twenty words. By week four, Daniel was completing all tasks in his literacy blocks, although not without the roller coaster of emotions that was part of who he currently was. After another month of Daniel showing his knowledge on the learning standards of the literacy block (notice the indicator for success was not zero rates of challenging behavior), a similar math structure was added for him. We saw a similar spike in behavior, but this time it only lasted one week. Over time, we shifted his structure to be in thirty-minute learning chunks, and the following year, he was in a general education classroom for literacy and math with the support of one of our special education aides.

Daniel's story is a successful one but rings true regarding my experiences in working with students with emotional disabilities. Daniel found an identity as a learner, something that became a cornerstone of his identity. I am sure he is still himself, still highly dependent on his environment and the regulation state of those around him to allow himself to utilize strategies to maintain his own regulation. I would assume he is still utilizing a positive behavior support plan to engage with more difficult parts of his day and is still finding ways to walk the line of insulting teachers without getting in "actual trouble," as he would say. However, I anticipate that he has been able to continue to generally access grade-level curriculum concepts, exposure that will lead to him passing state assessments in high school and receiving a high school diploma. From there, I am not sure what the future will hold for him. However, he will not have been limited by educator views of what he was capable of doing. This leads us to my least favorite question to be asked.

"BUT, IS THE STUDENT READY FOR THIS?"

The dreaded concept of readiness. I could fill pages and pages with my feelings about readiness standards in special education but will attempt to be succinct here. Readiness can be defined in many different ways, but in special education, I so often see readiness used as a vague, overgeneralized term to justify the restriction of a student's setting, services, or curricula.

Before jumping into my feelings on this topic, I should share that I truly am a behaviorist in my core. I believe my training and experience with applied behavior analysis has been crucial to the success my students have achieved, and that a behavioral foundation of programming for any student with emotional disabilities is critical to their short- and long-term success. I have continuously experienced the shaping of more prosocial behaviors using ABA approaches, and understand the need to build on students' successes when determining next steps for increasing expectations. I believe research-based interventions and data-driven decisions should be at the center of programming for all students, including neurodiverse students.

However, if this is all true, then why is the question of readiness so problematic? Certainly, a sequence of skills that build upon itself is central to education as a whole. We teach short vowels before introducing vowel digraphs. However, in my experience, readiness as a barrier to access is uniquely applied for neurodiverse individuals. Take language acquisition for example. A parent would never be told to speak to their baby in only one-word utterances until the child exhibited the ability to eat finger foods, point to request wanted items, and self-soothe when crying. The parent would be appalled if they were told their baby did not show the readiness skills to be exposed to complex language structures because of the inconsistency of their baby to request by pointing. Of course, developmental pediatricians make no such claim, instead encouraging language to be used far beyond a child's current understanding. In fact, exposure is the key to skill acquisition for a child to learn language, just as exposure is the key to learning, well, pretty much anything.

Yet, when determining programming for neurodiverse individuals, limiting exposure in the name of readiness is deeply woven into our practice. Any deficits in functioning can be cited as reasons for limiting exposure, which is the real danger of using readiness as a gatekeeper of exposure. I have observed that applying contrived readiness standards to students with emotional needs is not about the student at all. It is often the result of two main barriers in our current educational system: adult perceptions and discomfort with students that present with behavioral needs and overall structural rigidity. These two barriers are by no means minor, but the system will not change until individual educators take on these barriers at their own schools, showing that external forces do not need to dictate a student's educational outcome.

I know what you may be thinking. That you do not know the students I have personally worked with, but I cannot possibly be talking about your students: students with sexualized behavior, seemingly indiscriminate aggression, and zero stamina for paper and pencil tasks. That there is no way that a ninety-minute literacy block expectation would not result in the police being called. That the student you are thinking of (the one that keeps you up at night with worry) has none of the prerequisite skills to be in a group learning situation, let alone a writing group. That you couldn't imagine making a curriculum plan with grade-level learning targets, that you just hope and pray for your student to get through another year without being hospitalized or being arrested. I understand all of these thoughts, as I have been right where you are.

However, this is where we as a profession must take a step back and reevaluate why we drive into work each day. I'll give you a hint; it is probably not for the money. I would guess most special educators would agree that they are in the profession to help their students achieve their true potential, to help them find happiness and success in their lives. If our overall purpose is to assist our students in their journey toward a successful life, which of the following settings most resembles a workplace, subway, or grocery store? Environment A: a controlled, generally isolated environment with minimal demands, focusing on behavioral stabilization and skill building detached from generalized settings, or Environment B: a messy, unpredictable environment with high demands, focusing on behavioral and therapeutic strategies to find success in the dynamic and ever-changing environment. Our students live in Environment B, and the world that they are entering as an adult does not bear any resemblance to Environment A.

By looking at their profile on paper, it may be possible that a student with an emotional disability will never be truly "ready" to live in Environment B. However, it is coming for them, regardless of their fit for it. This is another reason why the concept of readiness is so dangerous in special education. I have found that a literacy block in an elementary classroom often has the same feel as a busy day at the Whole Foods down the street from my house: chaotic but purposeful, loud but focused, overwhelming but repetitive. Exposing students with emotional disabilities to grade-level academic standards should be done not just because of a federal mandate to provide each student to a free appropriate public education (FAPE) but also to prepare them for what comes next in their lives. To allow them to address their true deficits in an environment that really tests those regulation and behavioral muscles, all while educators are there to scaffold and support their success.

And, with that repeated success, something begins to happen. The student's identity and self-concept becomes defined as someone that can complete challenging tasks. Yes, with support, and yes, probably with an infuriating inconsistency. For our students with emotional disabilities, wouldn't the ability to complete highly challenging tasks, regardless of the details of the task, be the true definition of success? Yet, to implement this approach takes a tremendous leap of faith by the special educator, team, and school as a whole, because containment is being sacrificed in the name of longer-term success. The student is often initially very disruptive to the learners in the classroom, shows new behaviors not seen before, and enters into differing fight and flight modes throughout the day. That being said, I have never regretted shifting to this approach for a student. Accepting a loss of control is not something educators do well (myself included), but this leap of faith has been rewarded each and every time the team has jumped.

TAKING THE LEAP

Shifting a mindset for a student's programming starts first with the intent to do so by the special educator. However, I have learned is that the success of the shift will be defined by the greater team's investment in the new vision. This will require the special educator to become a tireless advocate for the student(s), shouting from the proverbial rooftops to ensure that the team is aligned in not shifting the plan when an increase in challenging behaviors inevitably occurs. I have also been part of very difficult conversations about the safety of other students in the classroom or in the school, and I wish I could offer a satisfying solution that would eliminate all potentially interfering impacts on other students.

The solution I can offer is one that I believe comes naturally with a newly aligned focus on grade-level curricula access. Once the "what" of the content has been determined and the team has shifted the conversation to how success will occur, teams have officially entered the land of environmental manipulation. I even worked with a BCBA once that had buttons made for her teams, EMs (Environmental Manipulators). What I absolutely love about this lens is that it sets the stage for endless flexibility, while putting educators in control, not of the student, but of the student's environment. When the second half of a literacy block has been unsuccessful for a week and a team is discussing what to do, the conversation shifts from "How dare she throw that chair!" to "What can we (as the environmental manipulators) shift for this week to increase success?"

This is not to absolve the student of responsibility for throwing the chair or to indicate it was the staff's poor planning or design that led to the chair being thrown. However, it does shift the conversation to address the lagging skill of the student, such as frustration tolerance deficits or minimal strategy use when challenging tasks are presented. This lens also takes away the personal nature of the student's behavior. The team can and should acknowledge their disappointment, along with any other feelings that were experienced. However, then the focus shifts to the lagging skill, and how the team is going to shift not the academic expectation but an element of how the student was working on it to increase their chances of success with the content.

I am convinced this work will never be easy. Just as I think I have something figured out, I encounter a student that requires me to expand my own toolbox. But, let me leave you with the student that is perhaps the biggest success story I have seen, but also the one that tested my resolve for two full years. To see the student now, it honestly does not align with my memory that they can be the same person. However, it was through the relentless high expectations of educators, endlessly supportive administration, and a very engaged family that allowed the student's transformation to occur.

Jackson walked into kindergarten at my school without any previous supports or services, and within five minutes, he had almost completely destroyed the classroom. Needless to say, my day was canceled and I became his 1:1 aide. He mostly grunted for the first week, communicating more often by throwing items, screaming at me, or crying. His dysregulation episodes could last for hours, including running around the building, often removing clothes as he ran. The building team quickly mobilized to support this student, and our district even sent additional resources to help the school team.

Over time, I learned Jackson was very bright, very articulate, and very interested in his peers. However, with minimal ability to wait, sustain attention, or experience any level of disappointment or frustration, we were struggling each day. The classroom teacher had the patience of a saint, even when I asked to turn her storage hallway into an individual work and break space for the student, and when we had to store all children's scissors away for when the classroom caddies were thrown. Just when we would make some traction in Jackson's engagement with academic concepts like his literacy block, it seems we would inevitably backslide into more unsafe behavioral episodes. The district supports stayed all year, and we continued on, with discussions of a change of setting happening often.

When we met with the family to discuss Jackson's progress and plans for the following school year, one element that kept coming up was how motivated he was by the social contingencies of the classroom. That is, the student actually did best when a task was previewed and pre-taught individually but could then be done within the classroom setting. The other students in the class became his coregulators, and in those moments, fleeting as they were, he shined. We felt as though we were able to see the true Jackson. It was our principal, in true fashion to her compassionate, child-centered style, who interjected to say that if this particular student needed to be anchored with a classroom setting and needed high academic standards, then she is ours, and we will adjust to her. The principal then asked me, in front of about fifteen people, including many other administrators, to articulate what the student would need from her environment to succeed. I took a deep breath, and did so, describing significant accommodations and differentiation in delivery and product. We adjourned the meeting with our newly shared vision.

Jackson started first grade with the same academic expectations as his peers but with a heavily modified schedule and day. He and I decorated the stairwell outside his class with his behavior therapist, and this became his safe space and workspace all rolled into one. His IEP reflected a partial inclusion setting, and he was outside the classroom quite often, sometimes by design and sometimes not. Although the school adjusted to hearing his dysregulation episodes, we were not seeing a decrease in behaviors that I had seen with my other students. In fact, it seemed that the frequency of interfering behaviors had been steadily increasing. Despite therapeutic interventions at home and school, the student's dysregulation episodes were still quite extreme, and could easily warrant hospitalization from an outsider's perspective. And yet, there were certainly gains happening as well. Jackson was now completing his literacy block successfully on most days. But, he continued to be isolated for chunks of his day, and my resolve with our model was breaking down. Perhaps my expectations really were too high for him.

After honestly sharing my hesitation with continuing the same model in second grade, the family and team decided to try until December of second grade and see what happened. I dreaded the start of the school year for this student, wishing I had pushed for a more restrictive placement where the expectations would be more aligned with his current functioning level, or that I had proposed a program with significantly lower expectations. I had my running shoes on for the first day of school, ready for what the day would bring. However, I would not need them. Jackson walked into his second-grade class, told his behavior therapist about his summer vacation, and sat at morning meeting. When Jackson started to yell out, the teacher firmly but unemotionally stated, "Stop. We do not yell out in the classroom. Do you have a question?" I held my breath as I walked toward the circle, ready for the inevitable destruction that was going to follow that redirection. Instead, Jackson shrugged and said, "I don't have a question," listening for the rest of the morning meeting without any of the dozens of interfering behaviors in his repertoire.

Jackson was still himself for his second-grade year, requiring a skill-based behavior support plan to incentivize strategy use, a 1:1 behavior therapist, and special educator support in his classroom multiple times a day. However, his adjustment to a grade-level academic expectations model with embedded behavioral and therapeutic interventions had happened. And yes, it was a two-year adjustment. At the time, I maybe would have said it was worth it, but years removed I can unequivocally say that it was worth the wait. Jackson's middle school programming currently includes a daily academic strategies class, counseling services, identified trusted adults in the building he can access as needed, and the same academic access as his neurotypical peers. He has deep friendships, and is even part of the popular crowd. He will say that he has trouble with his feelings sometimes, but he knows what to do now. He is on a trajectory to have the skills to pass his high school state assessments to receive a diploma. But more importantly, Jackson is on the path to enter the world of Environment B as an adult with years of successful experiences in a similar environment. He has been set up to be ready for what his adulthood holds.

Jackson's journey from his kindergarten self to now is certainly extraordinary, and not all examples are this dramatic. His story is shared here not just because of the success Jackson has found but also to illustrate the endlessly messy journey that is schooling for many students with emotional disabilities. Our schools are not set up for the flexibility that is needed for most students with emotional disabilities to be set on a path of long-term success, requiring special educators to carve those experiences for our students, often against significant resistance. In Jackson's example, there was no systemic resistance to the modifications he needed, which I have no doubt contributed significantly to his eventual success.

Thinking back to Renee and my first year of teaching, what I truly hope for her is that she crossed paths with a special educator that had the experience or instincts to step back from the discrete, isolated programming package I started for her. I hope that the educators in her world presumed competence in her academic abilities, and abandoned the use of behavioral deficits as a rationale to reduce her access to rigorous and more naturalistic settings and content. I hope that someone was thinking bigger picture about her life after high school, and shifted the team's mindset to one of supporting Renee to establish an identity as a learner that can complete challenging and novel tasks. That educators in her world have had experiences that have led them to the same conclusion that I have come to: that abandoning the concept of readiness and presuming academic competence in students with emotional disabilities is the only way to ensure their long-term success.

FINAL THOUGHTS

I look forward to a time in which this is an accepted practice in our field. In the meantime, we will all continue challenging ourselves to show our students their best selves, the ones neither of us can even see yet. Take the leap, I absolutely promise you will not regret it.

Chapter 17

Closing Commentary

Inclusive instruction has the potential to be effective for some, but all, students who receive special education services for Emotional Disturbance (ED). Inclusive instruction is effective when:

- Students are actively engaged in academic instruction.
- Students are actively engaged in the classroom's social environment.
- Students make effective progress toward the achievement of meaningful and ambitious goals.
- Progress is assessed using objective measures that are valid and reliable.
- The level of academic, behavioral, and social progress represents appropriate steps toward the eventual achievement of the IEP's vision statement.
- Decisions regarding instruction and support are based on the strengths and needs of the individual student, and not philosophies, beliefs, and policies that conflict with special education mandates related to the provision of a free appropriate public education.

Furthermore, inclusive instruction has the potential to be effective when:

- Contingencies are made to provide school-based practitioners with ongoing professional development in inclusive practices and research-based instructional and behavioral methods.
- Contingencies are made to provide school-based practitioners with performance feedback on their use of inclusive instructional practices and research-based instruction and behavioral methods.
- School-based practitioners have a consistently scheduled time to discuss student performance in response to IEP services with professionals with

similar and different types of expertise, as well as the real world implementation issues that they experience.
• School-based practitioners have the time to adapt instructional materials
  and methods prior to instruction, and when they have time to reflect on
  student response to the adaptations.
• School-based practitioners have the time to discuss what works, what is
  not working, and how to address what is not working (e.g., teach and work
  in a community of teachers, related service providers, and school leaders).

Equally critical, inclusive instruction has the potential to be effective when:

• Parents/guardians are not scapegoated, and when school-based practitioners are at least open to the idea that they can play a critical role in their
  child's success. What that role or roles are will vary from parent/guardian
  to parent/guardian, based on their personal circumstances.
• IEP teams reconvene when it appears that students are not making effective
  progress toward IEP goals.
• IEP teams, or a representative of the IEP team (e.g., a case manager), have
  regular communication with parents/guardians regarding instructional
  adaptations and methods and student progress-monitoring data.
• IEP teams identify potential outside partners and outside service providers
  and involve them in ongoing discussions about student performance and
  goal attainment.
• IEP teams continually revisit the Vision Statement, and discuss how goals,
  services, and supports contribute to the achievement of this vision.
• Students with ED are involved in IEP meetings in a developmentally appropriate way.
• IEP and transition services align with interests and skills of students with
  ED who are in the secondary grades.

Not all students with ED will be "ready" for placement in a general education, no matter how skilled the teachers are and how great the resources
are that are available to them. Placement decisions are not based on a "one-
size-fits-all" approach. However, all students with ED are "ready" to be
appropriately challenged academically, behaviorally, and socially by a team
of professionals who have knowledge of research-based practices and have
opportunities to collaborate with parents/guardians and the students themselves. Sometimes they will need to be challenged in dedicated school settings by professionals with specialized areas of expertise rather than a general
education classroom.

When appropriately challenging students with ED, sometimes the work
can get a little "messy," regardless of the educational setting. Students with

ED perform challenging behaviors that interrupt instruction and that at times may make us feel uncomfortable. Rely on your skills, and the skills and resources of your team. Embrace the messiness of the work as an opportunity to learn, and to establish an even stronger bond with the students and their parents/guardians. You are the ones that will make a difference, for that child, at this time. Through your unwavering efforts and dedication, you demonstrate that you are a source of stability, consistency, and care. Through your unwavering efforts and dedication, you create greater and more frequent pockets of student success, and develop links between them. Inclusive education for students with ED is challenging, but then again, you didn't get into this profession for things like fame and fortune! You likely did it because you want to have a positive impact on the lives of children, young adults, and their families.

We hope that you find this book as a source of support as you determine "what works" for your students, and under what conditions. We (e.g., John William McKenna and Reesha Adamson) welcome your feedback about this book, as well as opportunities to discuss any questions that you may have about the application of the ideas expressed to your students and your classroom(s). Furthermore, we welcome the opportunity to hear about the successes and challenges you experience when providing inclusive instruction to this student population.

References

5 Quick Ways to Assess Kids' Writing Progress. (2014). Retrieved from https://www.weareteachers.com/5-quick-ways-to-assess-kids-writing-progress/

Adamson, R. M., McKenna, J. W., & Mitchell, B. (2019). Supporting all students: Creating a tiered continuum of behavior support at the classroom level to enhance schoolwide multi-tiered systems of support. *Preventing School Failure: Alternative Education for Children and Youth, 63*(1), 62–67.

Ahmed, Y., Francis, D. J., York, M., Fletcher, J. M., Barnes, M., & Kulesz, P. (2016). Validation of the direct and inferential mediation (DIME) model of reading comprehension in Grades 7 through 12. *Contemporary Educational Psychology, 44*, 68–82.

Alberto, P., & Troutman, A. C. (2013). *Applied behavior analysis for teachers.* Boston: Pearson.

Anastasiou, D., & Kauffman, J. (2012). Disability as cultural difference: Implications for special education. *Remedial and Special Education, 33*(3), 139–149.

Anderson, J. A., Kutash, K., & Duchnowski, A. J. (2001). A comparison of the academic progress of students with EBO and students with LO. *Journal of Emotional and Behavioral Disorders, 9*, 106–115.

Archer, A. L., & Hughes, C. A. (2011). *Explicit instruction: Effective and efficient teaching.* New York, NY: Guilford Press.

Armstrong, J. (2011). Serving children with emotional/behavioral and language disorders: A collaborative approach. *The ASHA Leader, 16*(10), 32–34.

Arnold, D. H., Ortiz, C., Curry, J. C., Stowe, R. M., Goldstein, N. E., Fisher, P. H., . . . Yershova, K. (1999). Promoting academic success and preventing disruptive behavior disorders through community partnership. *Journal of Community Psychology, 27*, 589–598.

Bak, N., & Asaro-Saddler, K. (2013). Self-regulated strategy development for students with emotional behavioral disorders. *Beyond Behavior, 22*(3), 46–53.

Bausch, M. E., Ault, M. J., & Hasselbring, T. S. (2015). Assistive technology in schools: Lessons learned from the National Assistive Technology Research

Institute. In D. Edyburn (Ed.), *Efficacy of assistive technology interventions* (pp. 13–50). Bingley, UK: Emerald.

Baxter, K. (2019). My child talks nonstop: What can I do? Retrieved from https://www.understood.org/en/learning-attention-issues/child-learning-disabilities/hyperactivity-impulsivity/my-child-talks-nonstop-what-can-i-do

Beck, I. L., & McKeown, M. G. (2007). Increasing young low-income children's oral vocabulary repertoires through rich and focused instruction. *Elementary School Journal, 107*, 251–271.

Behizadeh, N., & Pang, M. E. (2016). Awaiting a new wave: The status of state writing assessment in the United States. *Assessing Writing, 29*, 25–41.

Bell, K., Young, K., Blair, M., & Nelson, R. (1990). Facilitating mainstreaming of students with behavioral disorders using classwide peer tutoring. *School Psychology Review, 19*, 564–573.

Bettini, E., Cumming, M., Brunsting, N., McKenna, J., Schneider, C., Muller, R., & Peyton, D. (2020). Administrators' roles: Providing special educators with opportunities to learn and enact effective reading practices for students with EBD. *Beyond Behavior, 29*(1), 52–61.

Bettini, E., Cumming, M., Merrill, K., Brunsting, N. C., & Liaupsin, C. (2017). Working conditions in self-contained settings for students with emotional disturbance. *The Journal of Special Education, 51*(2), 83–94.

Biemiller, A. (2001). Teaching vocabulary: Early, direct, and sequential. *American Educator, 25*, 24–49.

Black, P., & William, D. (2010). Inside the black box: Raising standards through classroom assessment. *Phi Delta Kappan, 92*(1), 81–90.

Breslau, N., Kessler, R. C., & Chilcoat, H. D. (1998). Trauma and posttraumatic stress disorder in the community: The 1996 Detroit area survey of trauma. *Archives of General Psychiatry, 55*, 626–632.

Brigham, F., Ahn, S., Stride, A., & McKenna, J. (2016). FAPE-accompli: Misapplication of the principles of inclusion and students with EBD. In J. Bakken & F. Obiakor (Eds.), *General and special education inclusion in an age of change: Impact on students with disabilities (advances in special education, vol. 31)* (pp. 31–47). Bingley, UK: Emerald Publishing Limited.

Brigham, F., McKenna, J., & Brigham, M. (2019). Memories of the warmth: Transition for students with emotional and/or behavioral disorders. In J. Bakken & F. Obiakor (Eds.), *Special education transition services for students with disabilities (advances in special education, vol. 35)* (pp. 35–52). Bingley, UK: Emerald Publishing Limited.

Brigham, F., McKenna, J., Lavin, C., Brigham, M., & Zurawski, L. (2018). Promoting positive freedoms for secondary students with emotional and behavioral disorders: The role of instruction. In F. Obiakor & J. Bakken (Eds.), *Viewpoints on interventions for learners with disabilities (advances in special education, vol. 33)* (pp. 31–53). Bingley, UK: Emerald Publishing Limited.

Brindle, M., Graham, S., Harris, K. R., & Hebert, M. (2016). Third and fourth grade teacher's classroom practices in writing: A national survey. *Reading and Writing, 29*, 929–954.

Brownell, M. T., Sindelar, P. T., Kiely, M. T., & Danielson, L. C. (2010). Special education teacher quality and preparation: Exposing foundations, constructing a new model. *Exceptional Children, 76*, 357–377.

Bryant, D., Bryant, B., & Smith, D. (2016). *Teaching students with special needs in inclusive classrooms*. Thousand Oaks, CA: Sage.

Burke, C. (2007). The view of the child: Releasing "visual voices" in the design of learning environments. *Discourse: Studies in the Cultural Politics of Education, 28*, 359–372.

Burke, M. D., Boon, R. T., Hatton, H., & Bowman-Perrott, L. (2015). Reading interventions for middle and secondary students with emotional and behavioral disorders: A quantitative review of single-case studies. *Behavior Modification, 39*(1), 43–68.

Burns, J. (2005). *Preliminary report-grant 790: Alternative education program*. Malden, MA: Massachusetts Department of Education.

Buta, M., Leva, D. S., & Visu-Petra, L. (2015). Who is the tattletale? Linking individual differences in socioemotional competence and anxiety to tattling behavior and attitudes in young children. *Early Education and Development, 26*, 496–519.

Button, K., Johnson, M. J., & Furgerson, P. (1996). Interactive writing in a primary classroom. *The Reading Teacher, 49*, 446–454.

Carbo, M. (2005). What principals need to know about reading instruction. *Principal, 85*(September/October), 46–49.

Carnine, D., Silbert, J., Kame'enui, E., Slocum, T., & Travers, P. (2017). *Direct instruction reading*. London, UK: Pearson.

Carter, E., Lane, K., Crnobori, M., Bruhn, A., & Oakes, W. (2011). Self-determination interventions for students with and at risk for emotional and behavioral disorders: Mapping the knowledge base. *Behavioral Disorders, 36*(2), 100–116.

Cartledge, G., Gardner, R., & Ford, D. (2009). *Diverse learners with exceptionalities: Culturally responsive teaching in the inclusive classroom*. Upper Saddle River, NJ: Pearson, Inc.

Cartledge, G., & Johnson, C. T. (1996). Inclusive classrooms for students with emotional and behavioral disorders: Critical variables. *Theory into Practice, 35*, 51–57.

Center for Adolescent Research in Schools. (2014). *Accommodation guide: The classroom-based interventions manual*. Bethlehem, PA: Center for Adolescent Research in Schools, Lehigh University.

Center on Response to Intervention at American Institutes for Research. (2019). Retrieved from https://rti4success.org/

Choi, Y. (2007). Academic achievement and problem behaviors among Asian Pacific Islander American adolescents. *Journal of Youth and Adolescence, 36*, 403–415.

Chong, K. (1993). Writing to learn mathematics: Strategies that work, K-12. *Arithmetic Teacher, 41*(3), 178–179.

Ciullo, S., Ortiz, M., Al Otaiba, S., & Lane, K. (2016). Advanced reading comprehension expectations in secondary school: Considerations for students with emotional or behavior disorders. *Journal of Disability Policy Studies, 27*, 54–64.

Ciullo, S., & Reutebuch, C. (2013). Computer-based graphic organizers for students with LD: A systematic review of literature. *Learning Disabilities Research & Practice, 28*(4), 196–210.

Coffield, F., Moseley, D., Hall, E., & Ecclestone, K. (2004). *Learning styles and pedagogy in post-16 learning: A systematic and critical review.* London, UK: Learning and Skills Research Centre.

Cohen, R., Linker, J., & Stutts, L. (2006). Working together: Lessons learned from school, family, and community collaborations. *Psychology in the Schools, 43*(4), 419–428.

Cole, C., Waldron, N., & Majd, M. (2004). Academic progress of students across inclusive and traditional settings. *Mental Retardation, 42*(2), 136–144.

Colvin, G. (2001). Designing classroom organization and structure. In K. L. Lane, F. M. Gresham, & T. O'Shaughnessy (Eds.), *Interventions for children with or at risk for emotional and behavioral disorders* (pp. 159–174). Boston, MA: Allyn & Bacon.

Conderman, G., & Hedin, L. (2015). Differentiating instruction in co-taught classrooms for students with emotional/behavior difficulties. *Emotional and Behavioral Difficulties, 20*(4), 349–361.

Constantidinou, F., & Baker, S. (2002). Stimulus modality and verbal learning performance in normal aging. *Brain and Language, 82*, 296–311.

Cook, A., Blaustein, M., Spinazzzola, J., & van der Kolk, B. (2003). *Complex trauma in children and adolescents* [White paper]. Los Angeles: National Child Traumatic Stress Network.

Cook, B., Cook, S., & Collins, L. (2016). Terminology and evidence-based practice for students with emotional and behavioral disorders: Exploring some devilish details. *Beyond Behavior, 25*(2), 4–13.

Cook, B., Landrum, T., Tankersley, M., & Kauffman, J. (2003). Bringing research to bear on practice: Effecting evidence-based instruction for students with emotional or behavioral disorders. *Education and Treatment of Children, 26*(4), 345–361.

Cook, D. A., Thompson, W. G., Thomas, K. G., & Thomas, M. R. (2009). Lack of interaction between sensing-intuitive learning styles and problem-first versus information-first instruction: A randomized cross-over trial. *Advances in Health Sciences Education, 14*, 79–90.

Cook, S. C., Rao, K., & Collins, L. (2017). Self-monitoring interventions for students with EBD: Applying UDL to a research-based practice. *Beyond Behavior, 26*(1), 19–27.

Council for Exceptional Children. (2014). Standards for evidence-based practices in special education. *TEACHING Exceptional Children, 46*(6), 206–212.

Countryman, J. (1992). *Writing to learn mathematics: Strategies that work in K-12.* Heinemann, 361 Hanover St., Portsmouth, NH 03801-3912.

Crone, D. A., Hawken, L. S., & Horner, R. H. (2010). *Responding to problem behavior in schools: The behavior education program.* New York: Guilford Press.

Curriculum Corner. (2017). Retrieved from https://www.thecurriculumcorner.com/thecurriculumcorner456/comic-strip-writing-templates/

Cutler, L., & Graham, S. (2008). Primary grade writing instruction: A national survey. *Journal of Educational Psychology, 100*, 907.

Dell, A. G., Newton, D. A., & Petroff, J. G. (2016). *Assistive technology in the class-room: Enhancing the school experiences of students with disabilities.* New York, NY: Pearson.

Deno, S. (2003). Developments in curriculum-based measurement. *The Journal of Special Education, 37*(3), 184–192.

Denton, C., Fletcher, J., Taylor, W., Barth, A., & Vaughn, S. (2014). An experimental evaluation of guided reading and explicit interventions for primary-grade students at-risk for reading difficulties. *Journal of Research on Educational Effectiveness, 7*(3), 268–293.

Dessemontet, R. S., Bless, G., & Morin, D. (2011). Effects of inclusion on the academic achievement and adaptive behavior of children with intellectual disabilities. *Journal of Intellectual Disability Research, 56*(6), 579–587.

Dimino, J., & Taylor, M. (2009). *Learning how to improve vocabulary instruction through teacher study groups.* Baltimore, MD: Paul Brookes Publishing Co.

Dixson, D. D., & Worrell, F. C. (2016). Formative and summative assessment in the classroom. *Theory into Practice, 55*(2), 153–159.

Downing, J. A. (2002). Individualized behavior contracts. *Intervention in School and Clinic, 37*, 168–172.

Druckman, D., & Porter, L. W. (1991). Developing careers. In D. Druckman & R. A. Bjork (Eds.), *In the mind's eye: Enhancing human performance* (pp. 80–103). Washington, D.C.: National Academy Press.

Dunn, R. (1983). Learning style and its relation to exceptionality at both ends of the spectrum. *Exceptional Children, 49*, 496–506.

Dunn, R., & Dunn, K. (1979). Learning styles/teaching styles: Should they...can they.. be matched? *Educational Leadership, 36*, 238–244.

Educator's Technology. (2012). Retrieved from https://www.educatorstechnology.com/2012/06/list-of-best-free-digital-storytelling.html

Elleman, A. M., Lindo, E. J., Morphy, P., & Compton, D. L. (2009). The impact of vocabulary instruction on passage-level comprehension of school-age children: A meta-analysis. *Journal of Research on Educational Effectiveness, 2*, 1–44.

Ellis, E. (1991). *SLANT: A starter strategy for class participation.* Lawrence, KS: Edge Enterprises.

Ennis, R. P., Harris, K. R., Lane, K. L., & Mason, L. H. (2014). Lessons learned from implementing self-regulated strategy development with students with emotional and behavioral disorders in alternative educational settings. *Behavioral Disorders, 40*, 68–77.

Ennis, R. P., Jolivette, K., & Boden, L. J. (2013). STOP and DARE: Self-regulated strategy development for persuasive writing with elementary students with EBD in a residential facility. *Education and Treatment of Children, 36*, 81–99.

Enri, L., Nunes, S., Stahl, S., & Willows, D. (2001). Systematic phonics instruction helps students learn to read: Evidence from the National Reading Panel's meta-analysis. *Review of Educational Research, 71*(3), 393–447.

Epstein, M., Atkins, M., Cullinan, D., Kutash, K., & Weaver, R. (2008). Reducing behavior problems in the elementary school classroom. IES Practice Guide. NCEE 2008-012. *What Works Clearinghouse.*

Ernest, J. M., Thompson, S. E., Heckaman, K. A., Hull, K., & Yates, J. (2011). Effects and social validity of differentiated instruction on student outcomes for special educators. *The Journal of International Association of Special Education*, *12*(1), 33–41.

Every Student Succeeds Act (ESSA), Pub. L. 114-95, § 1177.

Ewoldt, K. (2018). Productivity apps supporting higher order writing skills for secondary students with learning disabilities. *Intervention in School and Clinic*, *53*(5), 313–320.

Felitti, V. J., Anda, R. F., Nordenberg, D., Williamson, D. F., Spitz, A. M., Edwards, V., & Marks, J. S. (1998). Relationship of childhood abuse and household dysfunction to many of the leading causes of death in adults: The adverse childhood experiences (ACE) study. *American Journal of Preventive Medicine*, *14*(4), 245–258.

Fitzgerald, J., & Amendum, S. (2007). What is sound writing instruction for multilingual learners? In S. Graham, C. A. Mac-Arthur, & J. Fitzgerald (Eds.), *Best practices in writing instruction* (pp. 289–307). New York: Guilford Press.

Flannery, K., Fenning, P., Kato, M., & McIntosh, K. (2014). Effects of school-wide positive behavioral interventions and supports and fidelity of implementation on problem behavior in high schools. *School Psychology Quarterly*, *29*(2), 111–124.

Flower, A., McKenna, J., & Upreti, G. (2016). Validity and reliability of GraphClick and DataThief III for data extraction. *Behavior Modification*, *40*(3), 396–413.

Ford-Connors, E., & Paratore, J. R. (2015). Vocabulary instruction in fifth grade and beyond: Sources of word learning and productive contexts for development. *Review of Educational Research*, *85*, 50–91.

Foresman, S. (2000). *Scott Foresman reading*. Upper Saddle River, NJ: Pearson Education.

Freeman, M. S. (1998). *Teaching the youngest writers: A practical guide*. Gainesville, FL: Maupin House Publishing, Inc.

French, N. (2001). Supervising paraprofessionals: A survey of teacher practices. *Journal of Special Education*, *55*, 41–53.

Fuchs, D., & Fuchs, L. (1994). Inclusive schools movement and the radicalization of special education reform. *Exceptional Children*, *60*(4), 294–309.

Fuchs, D., Fuchs, L., McMaster, K., & Lemons, C. (2018). Students with disabilities' abysmal school performance: An introduction to the special issue. *Learning Disabilities Research & Practice*, *33*(3), 127–130.

Fuchs, D., Roberts, P., Fuchs, L., & Bowers, J. (1996). Reintegrating students with learning disabilities into the mainstream: A two-year study. *Learning Disabilities Research & Practice*, *11*, 214–229.

Fuchs, L., Fuchs, D., Compton, D., Wehby, J., Schumacher, R., Gersten, R., & Jordan, N. (2015). Inclusive versus specialized intervention for very-low-performing students: What does access mean in an era of academic challenge? *Exceptional Children*, *81*(2), 134–157.

Fuchs, L. S., Fuchs, D., Hamlett, C. L., Phillips, N. B., Karns, K., & Dutka, S. (1997). Enhancing students' helping behavior during peer-mediated instruction with conceptual mathematical explanations. *The Elementary School Journal*, *97*, 223–249.

Fuchs, L. S., Fuchs, D., Yazdian, L., & Powell, S. (2002). Enhancing first-grade children's mathematical development with peer-assisted learning strategies. *School Psychology Review*, *31*(4), 569–583.

Gage, N., Adamson, R., MacSuga-Gage, A., & Lewis, T. (2017). The relation between the academic achievement of students with emotional and behavioral disorders and teacher characteristics. *Behavioral Disorders*, *43*(1), 213–222.

Gage, N., Lewis, T., & Stichter, J. (2012). Functional behavioral assessment-based interventions for students with or at risk for emotional and/or behavioral disorders in school: A hierarchical linear modeling meta-analysis. *Behavioral Disorders*, *37*(2), 55–77.

Gage, N., Wilson, J., & MacSuga-Gage, A. (2014). Writing performance of students with emotional and/or behavioral disabilities. *Behavioral Disorders*, *40*(1), 3–14.

Gardner, D., & Davies, M. (2013). A new academic vocabulary list. *Applied Linguistics*, *35*(3), 305–327.

Garwood, J. (2018). Literacy interventions for secondary students formally identified with emotional and behavioral disorders: Trends and gaps in the research. *Journal of Behavioral Education*, *27*(1), 23–52.

Garwood, J., Ciullo, S., & Brunsting, N. (2017). Supporting students with emotional and behavioral disorders' comprehension and reading fluency. *Teaching Exceptional Children*, *49*(6), 391–401.

Geake, J. (2008). Neuromythologies in education. *Educational Research*, *50*, 123–133.

George, C. L. (2010). Effects of response cards on performance and participation in social studies for middle school students with emotional and behavioral disorders. *Behavioral Disorders*, *35*, 200–213.

Goodwin, A. P. (2016). Effectiveness of word solving: Integrating morphological problem-solving within comprehension instruction for middle school students. *Reading and Writing: An Interdisciplinary Journal*, *29*, 91–116.

Graham, S. (2013). *It all starts here: Fixing our national writing crises from the foundation*. Columbus: Saperstein Associates. Retrieved from https://www.zaner-bloser.com/products/pdfs/C3316_It_All_Starts_Here.pdf

Graham, S., Harris, K. R., Kiuhara, S. A., & Fishman, E. J. (2017). The relationship among strategic writing behavior, writing motivation, and writing performance with young, developing writers. *The Elementary School Journal*, *118*, 82–104.

Graham, S., & Hebert, M. (2011). Writing to read: A meta-analysis of the impact of writing and writing instruction on reading. *Harvard Educational Review*, *81*, 710–744.

Grant, C., & Sleeter, C. (2008). *Turning on learning: Five approaches for multicultural teaching plans for race, class, gender, and disability*. Hoboken, NJ: John Wiley & Sons.

Graves, M. (2007). Conceptual and empirical bases for providing struggling readers with multifaceted and long-term vocabulary instruction. In B. Taylor & J. Ysseldyke (Eds.), *Effective instruction for struggling readers, K-6*. New York, NY: Teachers College, Columbia University.

Graves, M. F. (2006). *The vocabulary book: Learning and instruction*. New York, NY: Teacher's College Press.

Green, A., & Stormont, M. (2017). Creating culturally responsive and evidence-based lessons for diverse learners with disabilities. *Intervention in School and Clinic, 53*(3), 138–145.

Greene, R. (2008). *Lost at school: Why our kids with behavioral challenges are falling through the cracks and how we can help them.* New York, NY: Scribner.

Gresham, F. M. (1995). Student self-concept scale: Description and relevance to students with emotional and behavioral disorders. *Journal of Emotional and Behavioral Disorders, 3*, 19–26.

Harris, K. R., & Graham, S. (1992). Self-regulated strategy development: A part of the writing process. In M. Pressley, K. R. Harris, & J. T. Guthrie (Eds.), *Promoting academic competence and Literacy in school* (pp. 277–309). New York: Academic Press.

Harris, K. L., & Graham, S. (1999). Programmatic intervention research: Illustrations from the evolution of self-regulated strategy development. *Learning Disability Quarterly, 22*, 251–362.

Harris, K. R., Graham, S., Mason, L. H., & Friedlander, B. (2008). *Powerful writing strategies for all students.* Baltimore, MD: Brookes.

Harrison. B. (2004). Writing across the curriculum: Teaching students to compose "exit tickets" as a formative assessment technique. Retrieved from http://writingfix .com/WAC/Exit_Tickets.htm

Hauth, C., Mastropieri, M., Scruggs, T., & Regan, K. (2013). Can students with emotional and/or behavioral disabilities improve on planning and writing in the content areas of civics and mathematics? *Behavioral Disorders, 38*(3), 154–170.

Haydon, T., Borders, C., Embury, D., & Clarke, L. (2009). Using effective instructional delivery as a class wide management tool. *Beyond Behavior, 18*(2), 12–17.

Hayling, C. C., Cook, C., Gresham, F. M., State, T., & Kern, L. (2008). An analysis of the status and stability of the behaviors of students with emotional and behavioral difficulties. *Journal of Behavioral Education, 17*, 24–42.

Herman, J. L. (1992). Complex PTSD: A syndrome in survivors of prolonged and repeated trauma. *Journal of Traumatic Stress, 5*(3), 377–391.

Herman, J. L., Perry, J. C., & van der Kolk, B. A. (1989). Childhood trauma in borderline personality disorder. *American Journal of Psychiatry, 146*(4), 490–495.

Hershfeldt, P. A., Rosenberg, M. S., & Bradshaw, C. P. (2010). Function-based thinking: A systematic way of thinking about function and its role in changing student behavior problems. *Beyond Behavior, 19*(3), 12–22.

Hodge, J., Riccomini, P., Bugord, R., & Herbst, M. (2006). A review of instructional interventions in mathematics for students with emotional and behavioral disorders. *Behavioral Disorders, 31*(3), 297–311.

Hoffler, T., Prechtl, H., & Nerdel, C. (2010). The influence of visual cognitive style when learning from instructional animations and static pictures. *Learning and Individual Differences, 20*, 479–483.

Hott, B., Jones, B., Rodriguez, J., Brigham, F., Martin, A., & Mirafuentes, M. (2019). Are rural students receiving FAPE? A descriptive review of IEPs for students with social, emotional, or behavioral needs. *Behavior Modification.* Advance online publication.

Howard-Jones, P. (2014). Neuroscience and education: Myths and messages. *Nature Reviews Neuroscience, 15,* 817–824.

Hunter, W., Elswick, S., & Casey, L. (2018). Efficient wraparound service model for students with emotional and behavioral disorders: A collaborative model for school social workers and teachers. *Children & Schools, 40*(1), 59–61.

Hurley, K., Trout, A., Griffith, A., Epstein, M., Thompson, R., Mason, W., . . . Daly, D. (2010). Creating and sustaining effective partnerships to advance research on youth with series emotional and behavioral disorders. *Journal of Disabilities Policy Studies, 21*(3), 141–151.

Idol, L. (2006). Toward inclusion of special education students in general education: A program evaluation of eight schools. *Remedial and Special Education, 27*(2), 77–94.

Individuals with Disabilities Education Improvement Act, 20 U.S.C. § 1400 (2004).

Ingram, G. P. D., & Bering, J. M. (2010). Children's tattling: The reporting of everyday norm violations in preschool settings. *Child Development, 81,* 945–957.

IRIS Center. (2017). High-quality mathematics instruction: What teachers should know. Retrieved from https://iris.peabody.vanderbilt.edu/module/math/

Jayanthi, M., Dimino, J., Gersten, R., Taylor, J., Haymond, K., Smolkowski, K., & Newman-Gonchar, R. (2018). The impact of teacher student groups in vocabulary teaching practice, teacher knowledge, and student vocabulary knowledge: A large-scale replication study. *Journal of Research on Educational Effectiveness, 11*(1), 83–108.

K12Reader. (n.d.). Retrieved from https://www.k12reader.com/worksheet/comic-str ip-templates-5-designs/

Kapuler, D. (2018). 30 Sites and apps for digital storytelling. Retrieved from https:/ /www.techlearning.com/tl-advisor-blog/30-sites-and-apps-for-digital-storytelling

Kauffman, J. (1993). How we might achieve the radical reform of special education. *Exceptional Children, 60*(1), 6–16.

Kauffman, J. (2003). Reflections on the field. *Behavioral Disorders, 28,* 205–208.

Kauffman, J. (2015). Opinion on recent developments and the future of special education. *Remedial and Special Education, 36,* 9–13.

Kauffman, J., & Badar, J. (2014). Instruction, not inclusion, should be the central issue in special education: An alternative view from the USA. *Journal of International Special Needs Education, 17*(1), 13–20.

Kauffman, J., & Badar, J. (2016). It's instruction over place—Not the other way around! *Phi Delta Kappan, 98*(4), 55–59.

Kauffman, J., & Hallahan, D. (1996). The illusion of full inclusion. *Behavioral Disorders, 21*(3), 255–256.

Kauffman, J., Landrum, T., Mock, D., Sayeksi, B., & Sayeski, K. (2005). Diverse knowledge and skills requires a diversity of instructional groups: A position statement. *Remedial and Special Education, 26*(1), 2–6.

Kauffman, J., Wiley, A., Travers, J., Badar, J., & Anastasiou, D. (2019). Endrew and FAPE: Concepts and implications for all students with disabilities. *Behavior Modification.* Advance online publication.

Kauffman, J. M., & Landrum, T. J. (2017). *Characteristics of emotional and behavioral disorders of children and youth* (11th ed.). Upper Saddle River, NJ: Pearson.

Kennedy, M. J., Hirsch, S. E., Rodgers, W. J., Bruce, A., & Lloyd, J. W. (2017). Supporting high school teachers' implementation of evidence-based classroom management practices. *Teaching and Teacher Education, 63*, 47–57.

Kennedy, M. J., Rodgers, W. J., Romig, J. E., Lloyd, J. W., & Brownell, M. T. (2017). The impact of a multimedia professional development package on inclusive science teachers' vocabulary instruction. *Journal of Teacher Education, 68*, 213–230.

Kersey, K. C., & Masterson, M. L. (2010). Is tattling a bad word? How to help children navigate the playground. *Childhood Education, 86*(4), 260–263.

Kilanowski-Press, L., Foote, C. J., & Rinaldo, V. J. (2010). Inclusion classrooms and teachers: A survey of current practices. *International Journal of Special Education, 25*(3), 43–56.

Kirschner, P. (2017). Stop propagating the learning styles myth. *Computers & Education, 106*, 166–171.

Klein, P. D., Haug, K. N., & Bildfell, A. (2018). Writing to learn. In *Best practices in writing instruction*. New York, NY: Guilford Press.

Knoll, A. R., Otani, H., Skeel, R. L., & Van Horn, K. R. (2017). Learning style, judgements of learning, and learning of verbal and visual information. *British Journal of Psychology, 108*(3), 544–563.

Koslowski, B. (1996). *Theory and evidence: The development of scientific reasoning.* Cambridge, MA: MIT Press.

Kourea, L., Gibson, L., & Werunga, R. (2018). Culturally responsive reading instruction for students with learning disabilities. *Intervention in School and Clinic, 53*(3), 153–162.

Kroeger, S. D., & Kouche, B. (2006). Using peer-assisted learning strategies to increase response to intervention in inclusive middle math settings. *Teaching Exceptional Children, 38*(5), 6–13.

Landrum, T., & Landrum, K. (2016). Learning styles, learning preferences, and student choice: Implications for teaching. In B. Cook, M. Tankersley, & T. Landrum (Eds.), *Advances in learning and behavioral disabilities: Instructional practices with and without empirical validity* (pp. 135–152). Bingley, UK: Emerald Publishing Limited.

Landrum, T., & McDuffie, K. (2010). Learning styles in the age of differentiated instruction. *Exceptionality, 18*(1), 6–17.

Landrum, T., & Sweigart, C. (2014). Simple, evidence-based interventions for classic problems of emotional and behavioral disorders. *Beyond Behavior, 23*(3), 3–9.

Lane, K. L. (2007). Identifying and supporting students at risk for emotional and behavioral disorders within multi-level models: Data driven approaches to conducting secondary interventions with an academic emphasis. *Education and Treatment of Children, 30*, 135–164.

Lee, D., Vostal, B., Lylo, B., & Hua, Y. (2011). Collecting behavioral data in general education settings: A primer for behavioral data collection. *Beyond Behavior, 20*(2), 22–31.

Lembke, E., Allen, A., Cohen, D., Hubbuch, C., Landon, D., Bess, J., & Bruns, H. (2017). Progress monitoring in social studies using vocabulary matching curriculum-based measurement. *Learning Disabilities Research & Practice, 32*(2), 112–120.

Lemons, C., Vaughn, S., Wexler, J., Kearns, D., & Sinclair, A. (2018). Envisioning an improved continuum of special education services for students with learning disabilities: Considering intervention intensity. *Learning Disability Research & Practice, 33*(3), 131–143.

Levy, S., & Chard, D. J. (2001). Research on reading instruction for students with emotional and behavioural disorders. *International Journal of Disability, Development and Education, 48*(4), 429–444.

Lloyd, B., Torelli, J., & Symons, F. (2016). Issues in integrating psychotropic and intensive behavioral interventions for students with emotional and behavioral challenges in schools. *Journal of Emotional and Behavioral Disorders, 24*(3), 148–158.

Lord, C., Ross, L., & Lepper, M. (1979). Biased assimilation and attitude polarization: The effects of prior theories on subsequently considered evidence. *Journal of Personality and Social Psychology, 37*(11), 2098–2109.

Losinski, M., Cuenca-Carlino, Y., Zablocki, M., & Teagarden, J. (2014). Examining the efficacy of self-regulated strategy development for students with emotional or behavioral disorders: A meta-analysis. *Behavioral Disorders, 40*, 52–67.

Losinski, M., Ennis, R. P., Sanders, S. A., & Wiseman, N. (2019). An investigation of SRSD to teach fractions to students with disabilities. *Exceptional Children, 85*(3), 291–308.

Luxenberg, T., Spinazzola, J., & van der Kolk, B. (2001). Complex trauma and the disorders of extreme stress (DESNOS) diagnosis, part one: Assessment. *Directions in Psychiatry, 11*, 373–393.

MacArthur, C. A. (1988). The impact of computers on the writing process. *Exceptional Children, 54*, 536–542.

MacArthur, C. A. (1996). Using technology to enhance the writing processes of students with learning disabilities. *Journal of Learning Disabilities, 29*, 344–354.

Macdonald, K., Germine, L., Anderson, A., Christodoulou, J., & McGrath, L. (2017). Dispelling the myth: Training in education or neuroscience decreases but does not eliminate beliefs in neuromyths. *Frontiers in Psychology, 8*(134), 1–16. Retrieved from https://www.frontiersin.org/articles/10.3389/fpsyg.2017.01314/full

Mackenzie, N. M. (2015). Interactive writing: A powerful teaching strategy. *Practically Primary, 20*, 36–39.

MacSuga-Gage, A., Ennis, R., & Hirsch, S. (2018). Understanding and trumping behavioral concerns in the classroom. *Preventing School Failure, 62*(4), 239–249.

Maggin, D., Wehby, J., Farmer, T., & Brooks, D. (2016). Intensive interventions for students with emotional and behavioral disorders: Issues, theory, & future directions. *Journal of Emotional and Behavioral Disorders, 24*, 138–147.

Maggin, D., Wehby, J., Moore-Partin, T., Robertson, R., & Oliver, R. (2009). Supervising paraeducators in classrooms for children with emotional and behavioral disorders. *Beyond Behavior, 18*(3), 2–9.

Maggin, D., Zurheide, J., Pickett, K., & Baillie, S. (2015). A systematic evidence review of the check-in/check-out program for reducing student challenging behavior. *Journal of Positive Behavior Interventions, 17*(4), 197–208.

Magiera, K., & Zigmond, N. (2005). Co-teaching in middle school classrooms under routine conditions: Does the instructional experience differ for students with disabilities in co-taught and solo-taught classes? *Learning Disabilities Research & Practice, 20*(2), 79–85.

Magrath, C. P., Ackerman, A., Branch, T., Clinton Bristow, J., Shade, L. B., & Elliott, J. (2003). The neglected "R": The need for a writing revolution. In *The national commission on writing.* New York, NY: College Entrance Examination Board.

Maheady, L., Sacca, M., & Harper, G. (1987). Classwide peer tutoring teams: The effects of peer-mediated instruction on the academic performance of secondary mainstreamed students. *The Journal of Special Education, 21*, 107–121.

Maheady, L., Sacca, M., & Harper, G. (1988). Classwide peer tutoring with mildly handicapped high school students. *Exceptional Children, 55*, 52–59.

Make Belief Comics. (n.d.). Retrieved from https://www.makebeliefscomix.com/

March, R., Horner, R. H., Lewis-Palmer, T., Brown, D., Todd, A., & Carr, E. (2000). *Functional assessment checklist for teachers and staff (FACTS).* Eugene, OR: Educational and Community Supports, University of Oregon.

Massa, L. J., & Mayer, R. E. (2006). Testing the ATI hypothesis: Should multimedia instruction accommodate verbalizer-visualizer cognitive style? *Learning and Individual Differences, 16*, 321–336.

Massachusetts Department of Elementary and Secondary Education. (2017). Professional development. Retrieved from http://www.doe.mass.edu/pd/

Massachusetts Department of Elementary and Secondary Education. (2018). *Handbook for candidate assessment of performance: For teacher candidates, supervising practitioners, and program supervisors.* Malden, MA: Authors. Retrieved from http://www.doe.mass.edu/edprep/cap/handbook/handbook.pdf

Mastropieri, M., Scruggs, T., Mantizicopoulos, P., Sturgeon, A., Goodwin, L., & Chung, S. (1998). A place where living things affect and depend on each other: Qualitative and quantitative outcomes associated with inclusive science education. *Science Education, 82*, 163–179.

Mastropieri, M., Scruggs, T., Norland, J., Berkeley, S., McDuffie, K., Tornquist, E., & Connors, N. (2006). Differentiated curriculum enhancement in inclusive middle school science: Effects on classroom and high stakes tests. *Journal of Special Education, 40*, 130–137.

Mastropieri, M. A., & Scruggs, T. E. (2014). Intensive instruction to improve writing for students with emotional and behavioral disorders. *Behavioral Disorders, 40*(1), 78–83.

McDuffie, K., Landrum, T., & Gelman, J. (2008). Co-teaching and students with emotional and behavioral disorders. *Beyond Behavior, 17*(2), 11–16.

McKenna, J. (2013). The disproportionate representation of African Americans in programs for students with emotional and behavioral disorders. *Preventing School Failure, 57*(4), 206–211.

McKenna, J., Adamson, R., & Solis, M. (2019a). Reading instruction for students with emotional disturbance: A mixed-methods investigation. *Behavior Modification*. Advance online publication.

McKenna, J., Adamson, R., & Solis, M. (2019b). *Reading instruction for students with emotional disturbance: A mixed methods study*. Paper presented at the American Education Research Association conference, Toronto, Canada.

McKenna, J., & Brigham, F. (2019). More than de minimis: FAPE in the post Endrew F. era. *Behavior Modification*. Advance online publication.

McKenna, J., Flower, A., & Adamson, R. (2016). A systematic review of function-based replacement behavior interventions for students with and at risk for emotional and behavioral disorders. *Behavior Modification*, *40*(5), 678–712.

McKenna, J., Flower, A., Falcomata, T., & Adamson, R. (2017). Function-based replacement behavior interventions for students with challenging behavior. *Behavioral Interventions*, *32*(4), 379–398.

McKenna, J., Garwood, J., & Parenti, M. (in press). Inclusive instruction for students with emotional/behavioral disorders: Service in the absence of intervention research. *Intervention in School and Clinic*.

McKenna, J., Kim, M., Shin, M., & Pfannenstiel, K. (2017). An evaluation of single-case reading intervention study quality for students with and at risk for emotional and behavioral disorders. *Behavior Modification*, *41*(6), 868–906.

McKenna, J., Newton, X., & Bergman, E. (2019a). Inclusive instruction for students receiving special education services for emotional disturbance: A survey development study. *Assessment for Effective Intervention*. Advance online publication.

McKenna, J., Newton, X., & Bergman, E. (2019b, April). *Inclusive instruction for students with emotional disturbance: A survey study*. Paper session presented at the annual meeting of the American Educational Research Association, Toronto, Canada.

McKenna, J., & Parenti, M. (2017). Fidelity assessment to improve teacher instruction and school decision making. *Journal of Applied School Psychology*, *33*(4), 331–346.

McKenna, J., Shin, M., & Ciullo, S. (2015). Evaluating reading and mathematics instruction for students with learning disabilities: A synthesis of observation research. *Learning Disability Quarterly*, *38*(4), 195–207.

McKenna, J., Shin, M., Solis, M., Mize, M., & Pfannenstiel, K. (2019). Effects of single-case reading interventions for students with and at-risk of emotional and behavioral disorders in grades K-12: A quantitative synthesis. *Psychology in the Schools*, *56*(4), 608–629.

McKenna, J., Solis, M., Brigham, F., & Adamson, R. (2019). The responsible inclusion of students receiving special education services for emotional disturbance: Unravelling the practice to research gap. *Behavior Modification*, *43*(4), 587–611.

McLeskey, J., Waldron, N., & Redd, L. (2014). A case study of a highly effective inclusive elementary school. *The Journal of Special Education*, *48*(1), 59–70.

McTighe, J., & Brown, J. (2005). Differentiated instruction and educational standards: Is détente possible? *Theory into Practice*, *44*, 234–244.

Miles, S. B., & Stipek, D. (2006). Contemporaneous and longitudinal associations between social behavior and literacy achievement in a sample of low-income elementary school children. *Child Development, 77*, 103–117.

Mitchell, B., Kern, L., & Conroy, M. (2018). Supporting students with emotional or behavioral disorders: State of the field. *Behavioral Disorders, 44*(2), 70–84.

Mitchell, B. S., Adamson, R., & McKenna, J. W. (2017). Curbing our enthusiasm: An analysis of the check-in/check-out literature using the council for exceptional children's evidence-based practice standards. *Behavior Modification, 41*(3), 343–367.

Morin, A. (2019, January). Writing types your child is expected to know. Retrieved from https://www.verywellfamily.com/four-types-of-writing-620805

Murawski, W., & Lochner, W. (2011). Observing co-teaching: What to ask for, look for, and listen for. *Intervention in School and Clinic, 46*, 174–183.

Nagy, W. E., & Townsend, D. (2012). Words as tools: Learning academic vocabulary as language acquisition. *Reading Research Quarterly, 47*, 91–108.

National Commission on Writing in America's Schools. (2006). *Writing and school reform*. New York: College Board.

National Council of Teachers of Mathematics. (2000). *Principles and standards for school mathematics*. Reston, VA: Author.

National Survey of Children's Health. (2011/2012). Data query from child and adolescent health measurement initiative, data resource center for child and adolescent health website. Retrieved June 20, 2019 from www.childhealthdata.org

Nelson, J. R., Benner, G. J., & Boharty, J. (2014). Addressing the academic problems and challenges of students with emotional and behavioral disorders. In H. M. Walker & F. M. Gresham (Eds.), *Handbook of evidence-based practices for emotional and behavioral disorders: Applications in schools* (pp. 363–377). New York, NY: Guilford Press.

Nelson, J. R., Benner, G., & Cheney, D. (2005). An investigation of the language skills of students with emotional disturbance served in public school settings. *The Journal of Special Education, 39*(2), 97–105.

Nelson, J. R., Benner, G., Lane, K., & Smith, B. (2004). Academic achievement of K-12 students with emotional and behavioral disorders. *Exceptional Children, 71*, 59–73.

Newcombe, N., & Stieff, M. (2012). Six myths about spatial thinking. *International Journal of Science Education, 34*(6), 955–971.

Newton, J., Todd, A., Algozzine, K., Horner, R., & Algozzine, B. (2009). *Team-initiated problem solving training manual*. Eugene: Educational and Community Supports, University of Oregon.

Newton, P. (2015). The learning styles myth is thriving in higher education. *Frontiers in Psychology, 6*(1908), 1–5.

Newton, P., & Miah, M. (2017). Evidence-based higher education: Is the learning styles 'myth' important? *Frontiers in Psychology, 8*(444), 1–9.

Niesyn, M. (2009). Strategies for success: Evidence-based instructional practices for students with emotional and behavioral disorders. *Preventing School Failure, 53*, 227–233.

Obiakor, F., Harris, M., Mutua, K., Rotatori, A., & Algozzine, B. (2012). Making inclusion work in general education classrooms. *Education and Treatment of Children, 35*(3), 477–490.

Organisation for Economic Co-operation, and Development. (2002). *Understanding the brain: Towards a new learning science.* Paris: OECD.

Pashler, H., McDaniel, M., Rohrer, D., & Bjork, R. (2009). Learning styles: Concepts and evidence. *Psychological Science in the Public Interest, 9*(3), 105–119.

Pasquinelli, E. (2012). Neuromyths: Why do they exist and persist? *Mind, Brain, and Education, 6*, 89–96.

Pelcovitz, D., van der Kolk, B., Roth, S., Mandel, F., Kaplan, S., & Resick, P. (1997). Development and validation of the structured interview for measurement of disorders of extreme stress. *Journal of Traumatic Stress, 10*, 3–16.

Perry, B. D., & Szalavitz, M. (2006). *The boy who was raised as a dog and other stories from a child psychiatrist's notebook.* New York, NY: Basic Books.

Peterson, L. D., Young, K. R., Salzberg, C. L., West, R. P., & Hill, M. (2006). Using self-management procedures to improve classroom social skills in multiple general education settings. *Education & Treatment of Children, 29*(1), 1–21.

Pierson, M. R., & Glaeser, B. C. (2005). Extension of research on social skills training using comic strip conversations to students without autism. *Education and Training in Developmental Disabilities, 40*, 279.

Powell-Smith, K., & Stewart, L. (1998). The use of curriculum-based measurement on the reintegration of students with mild disabilities. In M. R. Shinn (Ed.), *Advanced applications of curriculum-based measurement* (pp. 254–307). New York: Guilford Press.

Prater, M., Hogan, S., & Miller, S. (1992). Using self-monitoring to improve on task behavior and academic skills of an adolescent with mild handicaps across special and regular education settings. *Education and Treatment of Children, 15*, 43–55.

Prince, A., Yell, M., & Katsiyannis, A. (2018). *Endrew F. v. Douglas country school district* (2017): The U.S. Supreme Court and special education. *Intervention in School and Clinic, 53*(5), 321–324.

Public Agenda. (2004). *Teaching interrupted: Do discipline policies in today's public schools foster the common good?* New York: Author. Retrieved from http://www.publicagenda.org/files/teaching_interrupted.pdf

Rafferty, L. (2012). Self-monitoring during whole group reading instruction: Effects among students with emotional and behavioral disabilities during summer school intervention sessions. *Emotional and Behavioral Difficulties, 17*, 157–173.

Raines, T., Dever, B., Kamphaus, R., & Roach, A. (2012). Universal screening for behavioral and emotional risk: A promising method for reducing disproportionate placement in special education. *The Journal of Negro Education, 81*(3), 283–296.

Reed, D. K. (2008). A synthesis of morphology interventions and effects on reading outcomes for students in grades K-12. *Learning Disabilities Research & Practice, 23*, 36–49.

Reutebuch, C., Ciullo, S., & Vaughn, S. (2013). Using graphic organizers in secondary, inclusive content classes. In R. Boon & V. Spencer (Eds.), *Adolescent literacy: Strategies for content comprehension in inclusive classrooms* (pp. 65–77). Baltimore, MD: Paul H. Brookes Publishing Co.

Riccomini, P., Morano, S., & Hughes, C. (2017). Big ideas in special education. *Teaching Exceptional Children, 50*(1), 20–27.

Rice, K., & Groves, B. (2005). *Hope and healing: A caregiver's guide to helping young children affected by trauma.* Washington, D.C.: Zero to Three.

Rivard, L. O. P. (1994). A review of writing to learn in science: Implications for practice and research. *Journal of Research in Science Teaching, 31*, 969–983.

Roberts, G., Torgesen, J. K., Boardman, A., & Scammacca, N. (2008). Evidence-based strategies for reading instruction of older students with learning disabilities. *Learning Disabilities Research & Practice, 23*, 63–69.

Robinson, S. (2013). Disciplinary literacy. In R. Boon & V. Spencer (Eds.), *Adolescent literacy: Strategies for content comprehension in inclusive classrooms* (pp. 29–48). Baltimore, MD: Paul H. Brookes Publishing Co.

Rock, M. L., Gregg, M., Ellis, E., & Gable, R. A. (2008). REACH: A framework for differentiating classroom instruction. *Preventing School Failure: Alternative Education for Children and Youth, 52*(2), 31–47.

Rogowsky, B. A., Calhoun, B. M., & Tallal, P. (2015). Matching learning style to instructional method: Effects on comprehension. *Journal of Educational Psychology, 107*, 64–78.

Rohrer, D., & Pashler, H. (2012). Learning styles: Where's the evidence? *Medical Education, 46*, 34–35.

Roth, S., Newman, E., Pelcovitz, D., van der Kolk, B., & Mandel, F. S. (1997). Complex PTSD in victims exposed to sexual and physical abuse: Results from the DSM-IV field trial for posttraumatic stress disorder. *Journal of Traumatic Stress, 10*(4), 539–555.

Santangelo, T., Harris, K. R., & Graham, S. (2008). Using self-regulated strategy development to support students who have "trubol giting thangs into werds". *Remedial and Special Education, 29*(2), 78–89.

Schaaf, D. (2018). Assistive technology instruction in teacher professional development. *Journal of Special Education Technology, 33*(3), 171–181.

Schwartz, D. L., & Black, T. (1999). Inferences through imagined actions: Knowing by simulated doing. *Journal of Experimental Psychology: Learning, Memory, and Cognition, 25*, 116–136.

Scruggs, T. E., & Mastropieri, M. A. (1986). Academic characteristics of behaviorally disordered and learning disabled students. *Behavioral Disorders, 11*(3), 184–190.

Shaw, B., Wheatley, G., Kane, R., & Schaefer, M. (1980). *General math.* Boston, MA: Houghton Mifflin.

Sheridan, S., & Gutkin, T. B. (2000). The ecology of school psychology: Examining and changing our paradigm for the 21st century. *School Psychology Review, 29*, 485–502.

Shin, M., Lee, H., & McKenna, J. (2016). Special education and general education preservice teachers' co-teaching experiences: A comparative synthesis of qualitative research. *International Journal of Inclusive Education, 20*(1), 91–107.

Shonkoff, J. P., & Garner, A. (2012). The lifelong effects of early childhood adversity and toxic stress. *Pediatrics, 129*(1), e232–e246.

Siegel, D. J. (2003). An interpersonal neurobiology of psychotherapy: The developing mind and the resolution of trauma. In M. Solomon & D. J. Siegel (Eds.), *Healing trauma: Attachment, mind, body, and brain* (pp. 1–56). New York: W.W. Norton & Company.

Simonsen, B., Fairbanks, S., Briesch, A., Myers, D., & Sugai, G. (2008). Evidence-based practices in classroom management: Considerations for research to practice. *Education and Treatment of Children, 31*(3), 351–380.

Skiba, R. J. (2000). *Zero tolerance, zero evidence: An analysis of school disciplinary practice* (Policy Research Report #SERS2). Bloomington, IN: Indiana Education Policy Center. Retrieved from http://www.indiana.edu/~safeschl/ztze.pdf

Smith, B., & Sugai, G. (2000). A self-management functional assessment-based behavior support plan for a middle school student with EBD. *Journal of Positive Behavior Interventions, 2*, 208–217.

Smith, S., Poling, D., & Worth, M. (2018). Intensive intervention for students with emotional and behavioral disorders. *Learning Disabilities Research & Practice, 33*(3), 168–175.

Solis, M., Vaughn, S., Swanson, E., & Mcculley, L. (2012). Collaborative models of instruction: The empirical foundations of inclusion and co-teaching. *Psychology in the Schools, 49*(5), 498–510.

Souers, K., & Hall, P. (2016). *Fostering resilient learners: Strategies for creating a trauma sensitive classroom.* Alexandria, VA: ASCD.

Spinazzola, J., Ford, J. D., Zucker, M., van der Kolk, B. A., Silva, S., Smith, S. F., & Blaustein, M. (2005). Survey evaluates complex trauma exposure, outcome, and intervention among children and adolescents. *Psychiatric Annals, 35*(5), 433–439.

Spinelli, C. G. (2011). *Linking assessment to instructional strategies: A guide for teachers.* Boston, MA: Pearson.

Stahl, S. (1999). Different strokes for different folks? *American Educator, 29*(3), 1–5.

Stahl, S., & Fairbanks, M. (1986). The effects of vocabulary instruction: A model-based meta-analysis. *Review of Educational Research, 56*, 72–110.

Stieff, M. (2011). When is a molecule three-dimensional? A task-specific role for imagistic Reasoning in advanced chemistry. *Science Education, 95*(2), 310–336.

Stieff, M., & Raje, S. (2010). Expert algorithmic and imagistic problem solving strategies in advanced chemistry. *Spatial Cognition & Computation, 10*(1), 53–81.

Story Bird. (n.d.). Retrieved from https://storybird.com/

Sugai, G., George, H., & Putman, B. (2015). *Supporting and responding to behavior: Evidence-based classroom strategies for teachers.* Washington, DC: U.S. Office of Special Education Programs.

Sugai, G., Horner, R. H., Dunlap, G., Hieneman, M., Lewis, T. J., Nelson, C. M., . . . Turnbull, A. P. (2000). Applying positive behavior support and functional behavioral assessment in schools. *Journal of Positive Behavior Interventions, 2*(3), 131–143.

Sutherland, K. S., Lewis-Palmer, T., Stichter, J., & Morgan, P. L. (2008). Examining the influence of teacher behavior and classroom context on the behavioral and academic outcomes for students with emotional or behavioral disorders. *The Journal of Special Education, 41*, 223–233.

Swanson, E., Vaughn, S., & Wexler, J. (2017). Enhancing adolescents' comprehension of text by building vocabulary knowledge. *Teaching Exceptional Children, 50*(2), 84–94.

Texthelp. (2016). Read&Write [Mobile application software]. Retrieved from https://www.texthelp.com/en-gb/products/read-write/

Tillman, C. R., & Johnson, A. H. (2017). Current advances and future directions in behavior assessment. *Assessment for Effective Intervention, 42*(2), 77–80.

Time Warp Plus. (2006). Dallas, TX: Cambium Learning Group.

Tomlinson, C. A. (1999). Mapping a route toward differentiated instruction. *Educational Leadership, 59, 12–16*.

Tomlinson, C. A., Callahan, C. M., Tomchin, E. M., Eiss, N., Imbeau, M., & Landrum, M. (1997). Becoming architects of communities of learning: Addressing academic diversity in contemporary classrooms. *Exceptional Children, 63*(2), 269–282.

Torgesen, J., & Bryant, B. (1994). *Phonological awareness training for reading*. Austin, TX: ProEd.

United States Department of Education. (2008). The final report of the national mathematics advisory panel. Retrieved from https://www2.ed.gov/about/bdscomm/list/mathpanel/report/final-report.pdf

United States Department of Education. (2017). *Questions and answers (Q&A) on the U.S. Supreme Court case decision Endrew F. v. Douglas County School District re-1*. Washington, D.C.: Authors. Retrieved from https://sites.ed.gov/idea/files/qa-endrewcase-12-07-2017.pdf

United States Department of Education, Institute of Education Sciences, National Center for Education Evaluation and Regional Assistance, What Works Clearinghouse. (2017). *What works clearinghouse standards handbook version 4.0*. Washington, D.C.: Authors.

United States Department of Education, Office of Special Education and Rehabilitative Services, Office of Special Education Programs. (2017). 39th *Annual report to congress on the implementation of the individuals with disabilities education act, 2017*. Washington, D.C.: Authors.

United States Department of Education, Office of Special Education and Rehabilitative Services, Office of Special Education Programs. (2018). *40th Annual report to congress on the implementation of the individuals with disabilities act, 2018*. Washington, D.C. Retrieved from https://www2.ed.gov/about/reports/annual/osep/2018/parts-b-c/40th-arcfor-idea.pdf

van der Kolk, B. (2005). Disorders of extreme stress: The empirical foundation of a complex adaptation to trauma. *Journal of Traumatic Stress, 18*(5), 389–399.

van der Kolk, B. (2014). *The body keeps the score: Brain, mind, and body in the healing of trauma*. New York, NY: Penguin Books.

van Dijk, W., & Lane, H. (2018). The brain and the U.S. education system: Perception of neuromyths. *Exceptionality*. Advance online publication.

Van Loan, C., & Garwood, J. (2019). Facilitating high-quality relationships for students with emotional and behavioral disorders in crisis. *Intervention in School and Clinic.* Advance online publication.

Vaughn, S., Denton, C., & Fletcher, J. (2010). Why intensive interventions are necessary for students with severe reading difficulties. *Psychology in the Schools, 47*(5), 432–444.

Vaughn, S., Martinez, L. R., Linan-Thompson, S., Reutebuch, C. K., Carlson, C. D., & Francis, D. J. (2009). Enhancing social studies vocabulary and comprehension for seventh-grade English language learners: Findings from two experimental studies. *Journal of Research on Educational Effectiveness, 2*, 297–324.

von der Embse, N., Scott, E., & Kilgus, S. (2015). The sensitivity to change and concurrent validity of direct behavior rating single item scales for anxiety. *School Psychology Quarterly, 30*, 244–259.

Wagner, M., & Davis, M. (2006). How are we preparing students with emotional disturbances for the transition to young adulthood? Findings from the National Longitudinal Transition Study-2. *Journal of Emotional and Behavioral Disorders, 14*, 86–98.

Wehby, J., Lane, K., & Falk, K. (2005). An inclusive approach to improving early literacy skills of students with emotional and behavioral disorders. *Behavioral Disorders, 30*, 155–169.

Wehby, J. H., Symons, F. M., Canale, J., & Go, F. (1998). Teaching practices in classrooms for students with emotional and behavioral dis-orders: Discrepancies between recommendations and observations. *Behavioral Disorders, 24*, 52–57.

Weiss, M., & Lloyd, J. (2002). Congruence between roles and actions of secondary special educators in co-taught and special education settings. *The Journal of Special Education, 36*(2), 58–68.

Weiss, P., & Glaser, H. (2019). Instruction in co-teaching in the age of Endrew F. *Behavior Modification.* Advance online publication.

Werunga, R. N. (2018). *Effects of self-regulated strategy development on the writing skills and problem behaviors of students with emotional and behavioral disorders* (Doctoral dissertation). The University of North Carolina at Charlotte.

What Works Clearinghouse. (2012). Peer-assisted learning strategies. Retrieved from https://ies.ed.gov/ncee/wwc/Docs/InterventionReports/wwc_pals_060512.pdf

Williams, C., & Pilonieta, P. (2012). Using interactive writing instruction with kindergarten and first-grade English language learners. *Early Childhood Education Journal, 40*, 145–150.

Willingham, D. (2017). 3 Reasons most teachers still believe the learning styles myth. *Advancing Educational Excellence.* Retrieved from https://edxcellence.net/articles/3-reasons-most-teachers-still-believe-the-learning-styles-myth

Wood, S., Moxley, J., Tighe, E., & Wagner, R. (2018). Does use of text-to-speech and related read-aloud tools improve reading comprehension for students with reading disabilities? A meta-analysis. *Journal of Learning Disabilities, 51*(1), 73–84.

Yell, M. (2019). Endrew F. v. Douglas county school district (2017): Implications for educating students with emotional and behavioral disorders. *Behavioral Disorders, 45*(1), 53–62.

Yell, M., & Bateman, D. (2017). Endrew F. v. Douglas county school district (2017): FAPE and the U.S. Supreme Court. *Teaching Exceptional Children, 50*(1), 7–15.

ZimmerTwins. (n.d.). Retrieved from http://zimmertwins.com/splash

Zlotnick, C., Zakriski, A. L., Shea, M. T., Costello, E., Begin, A., Pearlstein, T., & Simpson, E. (1996). The long-term sequelae of sexual abuse: Support for a complex posttraumatic stress disorder. *Journal of Traumatic Stress, 9*(2), 195–205.

Index

absenteeism, 64
academic and behavioral support, 10, 13, 30, 47
academic engagement, 36, 145
academic failure, 93
academic intervention, 10, 84, 157
academic performance, 11, 17, 19–21, 24, 27, 30, 42, 50, 74, 121, 134, 139, 142–43, 146, 150, 157, 163
academic progress, 14, 27, 30, 71, 84, 144
academic supports, 41
accommodations, 22, 25, 29, 47, 77, 83–84, 86, 91, 112, 114, 116, 148, 157, 169, 172, 178
accuracy, 19, 85, 88, 142
achievement, 8, 17–19, 21–23, 25, 27, 29, 45, 50, 66, 74, 110, 115, 134, 137, 148, 155, 159, 167, 181–82
active supervision, 37, 78, 94, 115
ADAPT, 85
adaptations, 28, 85, 116, 147, 182
adult attention, 101, 112–13
adverse, 2, 6–9, 17, 83, 86–87, 92, 117, 119, 135, 139, 152, 154
adverse childhood experiences (ACEs), 119
advocacy, 74, 109, 132, 151, 173, 176
aggression, 109, 175

alternative, 9–10, 35, 54, 61, 102, 120–22, 125, 160
alternative placements, 10
alternative teaching, 160
amendments, 15
analyze, 20, 30, 76–77, 79, 85, 110, 114–15, 145
anchor texts, 56
annual review, 8, 15
antecedent, 83, 95, 112–16
anxiety, 51, 90, 109–11, 157, 158, 164, 173
assessment, 6, 8, 10, 14, 26, 54, 57, 60, 63, 69–70, 74–79, 81, 84, 89, 113–14, 133–35, 137, 140–44, 149–50, 156–57, 159, 162–64, 173–74, 179
assistive technology (AT), 77, 83–84, 89
attendance, 64, 119, 158, 164
attention, 6, 28, 34, 45, 57, 60, 80, 86, 91, 94, 98–99, 101, 110–13, 126, 129, 131, 168, 178
attention deficit hyperactive disorder (ADHD), 6
avoidance, 41, 56, 94

background knowledge, 33, 35, 36, 39, 43, 46, 64, 77
baseline, 76, 79, 173

behavioral assessment, 6, 114
behavioral difficulties, 12, 33, 90, 91,
    151, 152
behavioral supports, 3, 8, 41, 75, 115
behavior contracts, 99, 100, 107
behavior intervention plan (BIP), 6
behavior progress monitoring, 75
behavior specific praise, 37
best practices, 18, 137
board certified behavior analysts
    (BCBAs), 171, 177
brain, 45, 60, 89, 115, 117–19, 125,
    127, 131–33, 135

case manager, 159, 182
challenges, 2–4, 13–14, 27, 30, 46,
    49–50, 63, 90, 97, 119–20, 126, 141,
    153–55, 170–71, 183
checklist, 65–66, 87, 114, 156,
    171
classroom norms, 114
classwide peer tutoring, 21, 22, 24
coaching, 13, 68, 75, 162
cognitive psychology, 74
collaboration, 3, 13, 27–30, 44–46, 56,
    148, 151–65
collaborative planning, 28
college and career readiness standards,
    17, 142
communication, 49, 98, 109–12, 116,
    123–24, 128, 151–53, 159, 163–64,
    168, 182
comorbid, 151
competency, 28, 45, 48, 73, 87, 157
competing pathway, 94, 110–14
complex systems, 144
components, 41, 45–47, 57, 69, 76, 94,
    97, 98–99
comprehension, 32–33, 86–87, 149,
    162
comprehensive system, 94
computer-based, 86–90, 144
concept maps, 47
conditions, 3, 77, 96, 99–100, 109–10,
    112, 114, 135, 156, 183

confirmation bias, 136
consequence, 49, 54, 96, 98, 102,
    112–16, 122
consultation, 22, 24–25, 28, 55, 158,
    162, 164, 170–71
content acquisition, 41–43, 45, 47, 73
context, 12, 31–33, 35–36, 39, 46, 52,
    58, 64, 76, 86, 94, 109, 111, 114–16,
    131, 146, 155–57, 168–69
contingencies, 9, 13–14, 37, 56, 78, 84,
    114, 154, 178, 181
continuum of placement, 3, 10, 28–29
cope, 121, 171
co-planning, 28
co-teaching, 13, 75, 78, 159–62
criteria, 18, 21, 95, 97, 99–100, 137,
    145–47, 149
cultural beliefs, 114
culturally appropriate, 155
culturally responsive, 156
current levels, 9, 14, 73, 83, 91, 116,
    139, 157
curriculum, 1, 3, 6, 11, 17, 25, 32, 34,
    38, 42, 47–48, 51, 52, 53–54, 58, 61,
    67–69, 71, 73–77, 79, 94, 140,
    142–43, 161, 168, 171–75
curriculum based measurement, 71, 142,
    143, 149
curriculum standard, 142, 168
CUT, 65

daily progress reports (DPR), 94–107
data, 3–4, 8, 10, 14, 20, 24, 30, 63, 70–
    71, 74, 76, 78–79, 96–99, 114, 116,
    139, 143–49, 157, 167, 170, 174, 182
data collection, 96, 97, 143–48
de minimis, 6–7, 18
dedicated classrooms, 3, 10, 20, 169,
    182
dedicated settings, 10
deficits, 12–13, 17, 63, 83, 86, 90–91,
    157, 168–69, 175, 177, 180
definitions, 31, 33–35, 38, 55, 132
depression/depressive, 2, 164
descriptive writing, 52, 55

device, 46, 84, 92, 145, 150
diagnostic, 70
differential reinforcement, 75
differentiated instruction, 10, 22, 23, 25, 43, 73–80, 85, 116, 128, 164, 169–71, 178
digital, 59–61, 86, 89
digital text, 86, 89
direct behavior ratings, 144, 145, 150
direct observation, 144–46
disruptive behavior, 64, 77, 145, 150, 164
dreams, 11

ecological factors, 114
EDIT, 65–66
educational placement, 3, 8
educational settings, 1, 10, 17, 29, 140
effectiveness, 3, 8, 10–11, 13, 18, 30–31, 38, 75, 77, 84, 87, 90, 114, 135, 137, 142, 153, 160–61
effective support, 13, 41
empirical, 18, 29, 133–35
engagement, 12, 35–36, 39, 42, 58, 59, 68, 77–78, 83, 87, 92, 162, 167, 171–73, 178
environment, 1, 5, 13, 20, 42, 47–48, 53, 61, 73–76, 78, 80–81, 83, 94–95, 97, 100, 109–16, 120, 125, 129, 132, 145, 148, 156–57, 160, 163, 168–69, 172, 174–79, 181
equal/equality, 21, 122–23, 128, 135, 153, 155, 160, 182
escape, 110–11, 118, 123, 128, 157, 163, 173
essential elements, 52
essential practices, 115
executive functioning, 43, 118
exit ticket, 52, 53, 70
expectations, 7–8, 12, 19, 39, 47, 51, 54, 63, 76, 80, 94, 95, 98–100, 115, 121, 126–27, 129, 147, 156, 158–59, 163–64, 168, 170–74, 177–79
explicit feedback, 80, 94, 116
explicit instruction, 26, 28, 31–39, 46, 56, 80, 84, 87, 88, 90, 116, 136

expository writing, 53, 55
Every Student Succeeds Act (ESSA), 18
evidence-based practice (EBP), 18–19, 64, 136, 161

feedback, 4, 13, 28, 50, 56–58, 67–70, 78, 80, 94, 97–100, 115–16, 140, 150, 153, 161, 181, 183
feelings, 2, 75, 109, 124, 128, 162, 174, 177, 179
fidelity of implementation, 14
FILMS, 65
flash cards, 21, 150
fluency, 23, 26, 45–46, 85–88, 146, 149, 173
formative, 57, 140–41, 143
framework, 18, 46, 48, 75–76, 78, 81, 85, 91, 113, 115, 132, 140, 172
free appropriate public education (FAPE), 1, 5–15, 18, 19, 30, 126, 152, 157, 176
frequency, 14, 95–96, 144, 146, 159, 178
functional behavior assessment and interventions, 8, 93, 94, 99, 101, 109–16, 123, 124, 128, 156, 165, 168
function based thinking, 109–16

general education classroom, 1–3, 5, 9–13, 17–21, 24–25, 30–31, 51, 73–75, 77, 83–84, 86–87, 93, 126, 132, 142, 151, 157, 174, 182
general educators, 29, 161, 171
generalize/generalization, 35, 38, 42, 46, 69, 97, 174–75
goal acquisition, 148
goals, 3, 4, 6–9, 11, 15, 18–20, 27, 41, 43, 45, 47, 48, 73, 75, 76, 95, 97, 100, 110, 119, 125, 140, 141, 145–48, 157, 158, 162, 163, 167, 170, 171, 173, 181, 182
gold standard, 135
grade level, 7, 18, 29, 31, 32, 41, 56, 67–70,, 76, 142, 148, 157, 168, 171, 172, 174–77, 179

grading, 57–58, 127
graphic organizers, 36, 41–44, 46–48,
    52, 56, 86, 88–90
guided practice, 39, 44–46, 50, 56,
    65–66, 68–70, 80, 87–88, 90

handwriting, 50, 58, 87, 91
hypothesis, 114

IEP teams, 4, 7–8, 10–11, 14–15, 27,
    41, 84, 182
inclusion, 3, 25, 28–29, 35, 41, 48, 50,
    115, 143, 167, 178
inclusive instruction, 1–4, 10–13,
    18–19, 20, 27–30, 61, 73–76, 83, 85,
    87, 89, 91, 109, 111, 113, 115, 117,
    139–40, 142–43, 151–55, 157, 159,
    161–63, 165, 181–83
independent practice, 39, 46, 50, 51, 53,
    54, 56, 65–66, 69–70, 78, 80, 87, 116
Individualized Education Program
    (IEP), 4, 6–12, 14, 15, 18, 20, 27, 41,
    46, 47, 84, 112, 139–41, 145, 146,
    148, 151, 154–62, 164, 167, 168,
    178, 181–83
Individuals with Disabilities Education
    Improvement Act (IDEIA), 2, 5, 18
instructional decisions, 18, 137, 159
instructional methods, 2, 3, 13, 38, 74,
    78, 80, 85, 114, 132–37, 140
instructional time, 12, 38, 110, 136–37,
    140–41, 147
instructional tools, 76, 114
insufficient progress, 8, 14
intensity, 119, 122
intensive, 10, 13, 30, 71, 84, 99, 115,
    143, 149, 160–61, 164
intensive intervention, 10, 13, 30, 71,
    84, 87, 99, 115, 143, 149, 160, 161,
    164
interest inventories, 156
interests, 7, 11, 28, 73, 78, 157–58, 172,
    182
interventions, 6, 8, 10, 13, 17–30, 50,
    64, 67–68, 70–71, 76, 84, 93, 97–99,

101, 114–16, 123, 126, 128, 143,
    145, 148–49, 157, 159–65, 168, 174,
    178–79
interview, 70, 156
isolate, 99, 116, 147, 168, 175, 178, 180

jargon, 155

law, 3, 11, 18
learning difficulties, 29, 80, 85, 135,
    152
learning disabilities (LD), 21
learning environment, 114
learning styles, 131–38
least restrictive environment (LRE), 1,
    5, 8–10, 20, 29, 73, 83
limbic system, 118
literacy, 29, 49, 57, 89, 168, 171–78

mastery, 26, 73, 146, 168–69
measure of performance, 98
memory, 118, 173, 177
mental health, 117–29, 139, 159, 164
mindset, 148, 170, 176, 180
mini lesson, 58
misdirective, 32
misbehavior, 98, 125
mnemonic devices, 46, 64–66, 75–81
modalities, 135
modeling, 1, 13, 24, 36, 37, 39, 44–47,
    50, 51, 56, 66–70, 78, 80, 87, 88,
    116, 141, 159–61, 171, 172
modifications, 10, 12, 83, 84, 86,
    91, 112, 116, 146, 147, 157,
    171, 180
mood, 2, 118
morpheme, 37–38
mozart effect, 133
multidisciplinary, 27, 30, 165
multitiered systems of supports, 10, 13,
    20, 27–30, 99, 114, 115, 157

narrative writing, 53, 55
National Center on Intensive
    Intervention, 30, 71

Nations Report Card, 10
needs, 1–3, 5–6, 9–10, 13–15, 17, 30,
   42–44, 46, 48, 57–58, 61, 64, 66, 67,
   75–78, 84, 93–94, 97–98, 109–12,
   114–17, 119, 120–22, 124, 127–29,
   131–32, 134, 143, 151–53, 162, 165,
   175, 181
negative pathway, 111–12
neuromyths, 131–37
non-examples, 26, 35–36, 100

objective data, 3
objectives, 7, 9, 145–47, 168, 170
obtain, 6, 9, 25, 95, 96, 110–13, 123–28,
   140, 142, 151, 154, 169
off task, 12, 37, 39, 77, 95–96
operational definition, 7
operationalization, 11
opportunities to respond/opportunity to
   respond (OTR), 142
oppositional, 119
organization, 43–47, 57, 127, 143,
   145–49
Other health impairment (OHI), 27
outcome, 27, 42–43, 49–51, 55, 61, 98,
   116, 125, 142, 148, 152, 175

PALS, 67–68, 71
parallel teaching, 160
paraprofessionals/paraeducators, 21, 28,
   144, 145, 161–62
parents/guardians, 2–4, 6–9, 11, 13–14,
   30, 53, 91, 120, 129, 133, 139, 140,
   148, 152–58, 167, 174, 175, 182–83
peer tutoring/peer mediated instruction,
   21–25, 39, 56, 67–68, 77, 79, 85–86,
   95, 101, 115, 141
perception, 22–23, 25, 90, 127, 139, 175
performance feedback, 13, 161, 181
persuasive/opinion writing, 53–55
phonics, 136, 172
placement, 1, 3, 5, 8–12, 28–30, 83,
   93–95, 110–11, 114, 116, 126, 146,
   156–57, 173, 179, 182
planned breaks, 12

planned ignoring, 113
policymakers, 4, 120, 129
positive behavior, 8, 12, 39, 61, 73, 84,
   91, 95, 101, 110–14, 157, 160–61,
   163–64, 174
Positive behavior interventions and
   supports (PBIS), 28, 115
positive outcomes, 1, 51
positive reinforcement, 12
practitioners, 2–4, 11, 18, 19, 21, 39,
   139, 152, 155, 181, 182
precorrection, 94
prediction, 86, 88, 89, 94, 96, 110, 112,
   114, 120, 125, 135, 157, 175
preference assessment, 75
prefrontal cortex, 118
prerequisite skills, 2, 11–13, 25, 28, 29,
   64, 69, 80, 83, 85, 91, 93, 131, 157,
   175
preschool, 54
presentation, 77, 78, 80, 99, 141
probes, 144, 146
problem behavior, 50, 54, 83, 93, 95,
   96, 99, 109–16, 145, 156, 157, 159,
   163
professional development, 3, 13–14,
   75–76, 129, 131, 137, 160, 181
professional expertise, 7, 10, 18, 19, 27
professional judgment, 4, 19, 32
proficiency, 2, 11, 41, 63, 76, 83, 95,
   99, 142
progress monitoring, 4, 8, 14, 25, 27,
   30, 70–71, 139–44, 149, 182
psychiatrists, 124
public education, 1, 5, 7, 9, 11, 13, 15,
   18, 83, 126, 152, 176, 181

REACH, 75, 76, 79
readiness, 39, 64, 120, 142, 167–80
recommended practices, 50, 75, 114
reflection, 58, 141
regression, 6
reinforcement, 12, 37, 39, 46, 75, 80,
   91, 93, 96, 98–100, 160, 167
reinforcers, 75

related services, 155, 162
relationships, 2, 11, 12, 86, 98, 99, 119,
    121, 122, 124, 128, 152
remediation, 77, 113, 143, 159
replacement behaviors, 94, 95, 111, 114,
    146, 156
research-based, 3, 8, 13, 18, 30, 38, 71,
    75–79, 134, 136–38, 149, 157, 163,
    174, 181, 182
research design, 18, 21, 135
resource room, 20, 21, 23, 24, 26, 28,
    29
response cards, 66, 67, 70, 71
response to intervention (RTI), 115
responsibility, 57, 90, 118, 120, 121,
    127, 144, 147, 160, 161, 177
rules, 98, 109, 115

scapegoating, 152, 182
schedule, 33, 97, 98, 145–47, 154, 161,
    171, 178, 181
school administrator, 28, 153
school psychologist, 18, 162, 164
scribe, 58, 141
seatwork, 55, 64, 96, 112, 113, 116,
    156
segregated, 1
self-assess, 26
self-care, 126, 127, 129
self-determined, 74, 158
self-monitor, 23, 26, 46, 65, 66, 98, 144,
    145
self-regulated strategy development
    (SRSD), 46, 56, 57, 64–66, 71
self-regulation, 46, 56, 78, 167
signal, 14
skill development, 18, 29, 83, 88
socialize, 1
special education services, 2, 5, 7, 9, 10,
    17, 20, 24–26, 73, 83, 93, 95, 111,
    151, 181
special education teachers, 27, 29, 75,
    78, 133, 145, 151, 162
specialized school, 20
specialized services, 5, 7, 9, 11

speech and language impairment (SLI),
    27
self-contained, 20, 27, 29
self-fulfilling prophecy, 170
self-image, 56
service delivery, 30, 152, 164
small group, 22, 26, 27, 36, 37, 39, 54,
    66, 80, 85, 122, 143, 157, 160, 173
social workers, 18, 162, 163, 171
stakeholders, 1, 2, 148, 149, 152
strengths, 3, 11, 12, 14, 15, 25, 28, 46,
    70, 74–76, 153, 156, 157, 162, 163,
    181
stress, 11, 90, 109–11, 117–19, 122,
    124–26, 128, 154, 157, 164
structural analysis, 75
student interests, 7, 11, 28, 73, 78, 157,
    158, 172, 182
students with disabilities, 1–3, 5, 7,
    9–10, 17–18, 20, 22–25, 27, 29–30,
    50, 63–65, 67–68, 83–85, 131, 140,
    151, 161
substantially separate school, 9
success, 3–4, 11, 13–14, 29–34, 39,
    41–51, 54, 57, 61, 68, 71, 73, 75, 80,
    86–87, 91, 93–95, 97–99, 112, 114–
    16, 119–22, 126, 146–49, 152–58,
    161–63, 167–70, 172–80, 182, 183
summarize, 42, 52, 89
summative, 140, 142
supplementary intervention, 13, 157
Supreme Court, 5–9, 17–18, 153

tangible outcomes, 11
teams, 4, 7, 8, 10–12, 14–15, 17, 21–22,
    24–25, 27, 30, 41, 84, 87, 93, 145,
    155–56, 160–61, 164–65, 170, 177,
    182
technology, 44, 58–59, 77–78, 83–85,
    89–92, 141, 173
therapeutic, 169–71, 176, 178–79
think aloud, 69–70
tiered systems, 10, 13, 27–30, 114
tier 2 interventions, 20, 30
tier 2 vocabulary, 32

tier 3, 20, 30, 32
tier 3 vocabulary, 32
token economies, 37, 75, 91
transition, 2, 7, 80, 101, 156, 171, 173, 182
trauma, 117–25, 127–29
trauma sensitive, 120, 124, 125
treatment, 122, 141, 159
trend lines, 147
triggers, 61, 129
tutors, 24–25

underperformance, 2

variability, 75

Venn diagram, 43, 47
vision statement, 11, 20, 154–55, 158, 181–82
visual, 26, 34–35, 43–45, 47, 53, 56, 97–98, 132, 135, 171
vocabulary, 31–50, 69, 86–89, 142, 149, 155

What Works Clearinghouse (WWC), 19, 21, 24, 26–27, 68, 138
whole group, 26, 39, 54, 66, 78, 80
workload, 27–28, 159–60
written representation, 34

zones of regulation, 75

About the Authors

John William McKenna is an associate professor of Moderate Disabilities and an affiliate of the Center for Autism Research and Education (CARE) at the University of Massachusetts Lowell. Prior to earning his PhD at the University of Texas at Austin, he served as a child behavior specialist, home-based family worker, parent/guardian trainer, case manager, and special education teacher in a variety of different settings ranging from residential treatment centers to public school settings. His research interests include evidence-based practices for students with emotional and behavioral disorders, responsible inclusion, and methods for improving student access to research-based instruction. Dr. McKenna's work has been widely published, including in *Exceptional Children, Behavior Modification, Beyond Behavior,* and *Intervention in School and Clinic.* He serves on a variety of editorial boards and provides consultation services to districts both locally and nationally. He currently teaches master's level courses in special education methods for general education teachers and doctoral-level courses in Improvement Science.

**Reesha Adamson** is an associate professor at Missouri State University in Springfield, Missouri. Reesha is an academic adviser for special education graduate students and teaches both in the undergraduate and graduate programs. Previously Reesha worked as a special education teacher in a K-5 classroom for students with emotional and behavioral disorders, as an educational provider within a juvenile justice center and as a districtwide behavior specialist. She has also worked as the project coordinator in Missouri for the Center for Adolescent Research in Schools (*CARS*), an IES-funded, national randomized control trial examining the efficacy of a multi-prong intervention within high schools on lessening risks associated with challenging behavior, both externalizing and internalizing, among youth with disabilities.

Reesha specializes in working with school districts, preservice teachers, and current practitioners to implement evidence-based practices for students with and at-risk for emotional and behavioral disorders. She is familiar with all educational levels of instruction and across a variety of educational settings. She has presented numerous times at the local, state, national, and international levels, and some of her work can be found published in leading journals within the field of special education.

About the Contributors

Eliza Bobek is a clinical assistant professor in the College of Education at UMass Lowell and the director of the Undergraduate Program in Elementary and Special Education. Eliza holds a BA in Neuroscience from Barnard College, Columbia University, an MA in Elementary Education from Brooklyn College, City University of New York, and a PhD in Cognitive Science in Education from Teachers College, Columbia University. Eliza has synthesized research and practice in the field of education in numerous settings from elementary education to adult learners, and has published and presented in the field of learning sciences.

Maria Kolbe is an inclusion facilitator currently teaching within the Newton Public Schools system in Newton, Massachusetts. She is a doctoral student in the Educational Leadership Program at the University of Massachusetts Lowell.

Dr. Jessica Nelson is an assistant professor at Missouri State University in Springfield, Missouri. Dr. Nelson is an academic adviser for special education graduate students within the teacher preparation program and teaches undergraduate and graduate classes. With over fifteen years of experience in the field, Nelson has worked with hundreds of students with behavioral challenges and grades ranging from kindergarten through eighth grade.

Dr. Felicity Post is an assistant professor of Special Education at Peru State College in Peru, Nebraska. She teaches both undergraduate and graduate courses in the areas of trauma, social emotional learning, behavior management, and special education law. Before becoming a professor, Dr. Post was an elementary resource teacher for eleven years in the Manhattan-Ogden School District in Manhattan, Kansas.

Dr. Robai Werunga is an assistant professor of Special Education in the Department of Curriculum and Instruction in the College of Education, University of Massachusetts, Lowell. Her research focus is in early academic and behavioral interventions through multitiered systems of support (MTSS). Dr. Werunga's target population is students with or at-risk for Emotional/Behavioral Disorders (EBD) and/or Learning Disabilities with a focus on culturally and linguistically diverse (CLD) learners.

CPSIA information can be obtained
at www.ICGtesting.com
Printed in the USA
LVHW051721120621
689903LV00008B/867